Automated Library Serials: An Introduction

Automated Library Serials: An Introduction

Aditya Rajput

RANDOM

RANDOM PUBLICATIONS

NEW DELHI (INDIA)

Automated Library Serials: An Introduction

ISBN 978-93-5111-848-0

Published in 2016 in India by

RANDOM PUBLICATIONS

4376-A/4B, Gali Murari Lal, Ansari Road
New Delhi-110 002
Phone : +9111-43580356, 011-23289044, 011-43142548
e-mail: sales@randompublications.com,
info@randompublications.com, randomexports@gmail.com

Type Setting by : Friends Media, Delhi-110089
Printed at : Mehra Printers, Delhi-110 092

Preface

Automation of the library helps take some of the workload off of librarians and other staff members in the areas of acquisitions, cataloging and circulation, which in turn allows them to better serve their patrons. This extra time can lead to more programs being facilitated in the library and make library staff available to answer reference questions and help people who having trouble researching or finding the right information. Automated cataloging standards, such as MARC (Machine Readable Cataloging), allow for quicker cataloging of library items. Not only does this allow the librarian more time to dedicate to improving customer service, but it also makes the sharing of materials from location to location much easier and much more affordable. Not only does automation of library materials make it easier to find books, buy it also makes it easier to access journals and some books online from a home computer or elsewhere. The automation of library collections also allows the library to be more flexible when it comes to any increases in demand.

Automation of the library allows for an improvement in the variety, amount and quality of materials that are available in the library's collection. It can also help make weeding out old, outdated and irrelevant books and materials from the collection, which helps keep the library's collection more streamlined and easier to find the right item.

Automation is also a way of preparing the collection to become sustainable with the ever-increasing shift to a technology-based society, in terms of information dissemination, paired with the ever-decreasing amount of funding for libraries. Automation will help libraries who begin to struggle and are forced to lay off staff. Switching to an automated system allows libraries to add on features when they become available in the future, in stead of having to do a complete overhaul of their collections and cataloging methods. Libraries are using technology in general, and computers in particular, to automate a wide range of administrative, public, and technical services tasks. This book is designed as an overview of major facets of automation activity and the book examines the current state of computer applications in areas of library work.

Libraries have used technology in general, and computers in particular, to automate a wide range of administrative, public, and technical services tasks. Designed as an overview of major facets of automation activity, this books examinations the current state of computer applications in areas of library work. The discussion briefly indicates the motives for automation and describes current dominant approaches, citing examples of representative products and services.

Library automation refers to the use of computers to serve the needs of library users. The operations of a library get a quantum jump with the introductions of computers. The computers help to provide fast and reliable access to the resources available in the library as well as elsewhere. The application of computers in the library operations avoids repetitive jobs and saves lot of labour, time, speeds up operations, increases use of library resources. Computers are not only used as a tool for processing the data, but also for data storage and accessing.

Automation should always be used as a means to achieve overall better patron service. Careful planning for technology will assure that your automation project is sustainable, i.e., enhances the organization's ability to meet its service mission without disrupting the organizational stability of the institution.

– ***Author***

Contents

1

Introduction to Serials Cataloging

If you are a new cataloger or a cataloger who hasn't cataloged serials before, cataloging a serial for the first time may seem daunting. How do you catalog from multiple issues? What happens when you don't have the first issue? How do you indicate that something has changed? How much data should be included and at what level will the record be created? Furthermore, working with serials often extends beyond cataloging. Many serials catalogers are becoming increasingly involved in serial holdings, publication pattern creation, and other aspects of serials control. This module will take a broad look at serials, discussing what makes them unique, what kind of challenges they pose to the cataloger, and what is involved in cataloging them.

THE SIGNIFICANCE OF SERIAL PUBLICATIONS

Serials are an essential and integral component of every major research library collection because the information they contain reflects the most current developments in all fields of activity. The basic nature of the serials publishing process insures that their "sequential products" are distributed in a timely fashion; timeliness is fundamental to their relevance. It logically follows that efficient processing of these materials is key to providing the necessary timely access to them.

Cataloging rules set only three basic criteria for a serial publication: 1) it is issued in discrete parts; 2) generally, each part carries a number or date that uniquely identifies it; 3) the publication has no predetermined conclusion (see Module 2).

Within these basic requirements one finds material that differs as widely as one can imagine. Many government documents are issued serially and contain unique information that only such an agency could develop (e.g., CIA reports). On the other extreme one finds more ephemeral material that is generated by individuals with desktop publishing capabilities (e.g., family-specific genealogical information). From annual reports to car repair manuals, the serials cataloger typically handles a great variety of material that presents numerous challenges and also leads to an exposure to a wide body of knowledge.

Recent history only reinforces the significance of serial publications. The price explosion of scholarly journals in the 1980s forced libraries to reevaluate their collections and to economize. The public outcry that followed reductions in serials' subscriptions only underscored the basic value of the literature. Some libraries were compelled to cooperate more with other libraries in their region, to identify their singular and collective strengths, and to focus their acquisitions policies accordingly.

During recent years we have seen several new technologies dramatically affect the serials publishing industry. Various types of electronic publications and formats have presented new challenges to serials cataloging. The same technologies offer new capabilities to researchers that were barely imagined years ago. Some serial titles are now available exclusively online or in CD-ROM and these serials often defy our understanding of the basic characteristics of serials. As publishers continue to use emerging technologies we find our field of librarianship confronted with providing the best and most timely access to these materials.

THE NATURE OF SERIALS

CHARACTERISTICS OF SERIALS

- Serials *are* different! They don't always look or behave like other types of publications. Here are some of the characteristics of serials.
- Serials are extremely diverse, including scholarly journals, popular magazines and newspapers, newsletters, annual and statistical reports, directories and yearbooks, and monographic series.
- Serials are issued on a continuing basis, often with a regular frequency (e.g., annual, monthly, etc.).
- Many serials do not have a title page. Instead, the title is found on the cover or at the beginning of the text. This is particularly the case with periodicals (magazines, journals, etc.), newsletters, and newspapers.
- Most serials have numbering — numbers or dates or combinations of both that distinguish the individual issues. The only category of serial that does not routinely bear numbering is unnumbered monographic series.
- Serials do not usually have personal authors. Most persons associated with serials are editors or compilers. Serials are more often the work of one or more corporate bodies that have "issued" the serial.
- Serial titles are often given in more than one place in the issue and sometimes in different forms.
- Serials are often related to other serials (or monographs or integrating resources) — as earlier or later titles, companions, sections, language editions, translations, etc.

- Serials may have supplements, indexes, reprints, or special issues or may, themselves, be a supplement, index, reprint, or special issue.
- Because serials are issued continuously, the information presented on them may change. Such changes may be in the title, issuing body, form of numbering, frequency, size and physical appearance, or just about anywhere else!
- How cataloging a serial differs from cataloging a multipart item or an integrating resource
- Serials, incomplete multipart items, and integrating resources are all issued over time and, thus, exhibit seriality. However, cataloging practices differ. In the case of multipart items, the distinguishing factor is the fact that multipart items are finite and serials are continuing. In the case of integrating resources, it is the mode of issuance that is the distinguishing factor.

Successive Entry Cataloging

A new serial record is created each time a major change occurs according to *AACR2* 21.2C1 and 21.3B1a. This cataloging convention is called " successive entry cataloging." (See Module 16 for a complete list of potential major changes.) Each successive entry record contains information relevant only to the span of issues covered by that record. The relationship of successive entry records is shown through linking entry fields (Module 14). The record for the "dead" serial is "closed off"—i.e., data elements are added or changed in the record to show that the title is no longer current (see *CCM* 21.3).

Multipart items that are not complete as first issued are also successively-issued and changes in title or entry may also occur. However, because multiparts are finite, a single record is made, rather than successive entry records, and changes to later parts are given in notes. Multiparts are cataloged according to "earliest entry" conventions. (*AACR2* 21.2A1 and 21.3A2)

For integrating resources, because there is only one chief source at any one time, a single record is made and most changes (FN1) are reflected in notes (field 247 , 500 , 550 , etc.). This convention is known as latest entry cataloging and was also applied to serials prior to the adoption of *AACR2* in 1981.

Description Based on the First or Earliest Issue

Serials consist of a succession of issues, but the basic description of the serial is created from one issue. The primary difference between *AACR2* and earlier rules is that under *AACR2* the description is based on the first or the earliest available issue (FN2). Every *AACR2* serial record must indicate the issue upon which the description is based, either in area 3 (field 362 , 1st indicator=0) or in a note. Once a serial is described from the first issue, the " body of the entry" (FN3) is not changed (except when adding successive numbering schemes, variations in physical description, or closing off the record for a "dead" title). An indication of changes appearing on later issues, that do not require a new record, is given in the notes, as appropriate. Serials described from issues other than the first, however, may be "backed up" when the first issue is available. As mentioned above, generally multipart items are also described from the first issue with most later changes described in notes.

Integrating resources are described from the latest *iteration*. The word iteration is used because there are no separate issues. An integrating resource is described based on the information that is current at the time of cataloging. If this information changes on subsequent iterations, the description is changed and earlier information is given in notes.

Numbering

In citing the issue upon which the description is based, the cataloger also describes the numbering system used by the serial. Numbering is a collective term that may consist of numerical (or alphabetical) designations (volumes, numbers, etc.), chronological designations (dates), or a combination of the two. Numbering is important to serials because it provides the only means for distinguishing the individual issues of the serial.

Multipart items may or may not be numbered. Integrating resources do not use numbering in the same way that serials do. While updates to a loose-leaf publication or database may be numbered or bear revision dates, this numbering refers only to the update and not the publication as a whole. Thus, while the numbered update of a loose-leaf might be checked in according to that numbering, it is not reflected in the bibliographic record.

Uniform titles (created according to **AACR2** *and* **LCRI** *25.5B)*

Because so many serials are entered under title according to *AACR2*, and because serials are frequently listed in other files, such as check-in files, it is important to be able to distinguish one serial from another. *AACR2* 25.5B and the accompanying *LCRI* (25.5B) provide guidance for creating uniform titles to distinguish different serials with the same title. The uniform title consists of the title proper and a qualifier (see Module 5). In determining whether there is a conflict, catalogers consider all other serials but not monographs or integrating resources.

Analyzed multipart items are assigned uniform titles according to LCRI 25.5B because they are treated similarly to series; unanalyzed multiparts are not given uniform titles according to the LCRI.

Linking entry fields

Serials are often part of "family" relationships. They may have parents (earlier titles), children (later titles), siblings (other editions, splits, etc.), and cousins (other related works). *AACR2* specifies that these relationships be mentioned in notes. The MARC 21-defined linking entry fields (760-787) may provide such notes, when desired, as well as linking the related records in a database (see Module 14).

Linking entry fields are defined for monographs as well as serials, but have not been used on monograph records as extensively as with serials.

Because there is a single record for the entire multipart, there is no need to link to earlier or later titles. Links to other physical formats may be provided, however.

Much of the same can be said for integrating resources, because a single record is involved. However, there are cases where links are appropriate and Chapter 12 rules for linking notes apply also to integrating resources.

The cataloging record must represent the entire serial

In general, information contained in serial records must be broad enough to pertain to the span of issues covered by each successive entry record or a subset of those issues as noted by date spans. This is perhaps the most difficult concept for an experienced monograph cataloger to grasp. Information that is specific to a single issue is usually omitted because it does not relate to the serial as a whole.

For example, dates and numbers that represent the issue are dropped from the title statement, titles specific to one issue are omitted, and so forth. When information is given that relates to certain issues but not all, dates are given to indicate the span of issues to which the information pertains. Such dates are most often given with notes.

Because multipart items are finite, more detail can be provided in the record, such as a complete contents note.

Integrating resource records are very similar to serials in that they too must cover the entire resource. It may be the case that earlier information has completely disappeared from an online integrating resource and catalogers must use judgment in determining what to retain in notes.

Serial vs. monograph cataloging: economy and access

Module 2 discusses the criteria that are used to determine whether a publication is cataloged as a serial, a monograph, or an integrating resource. While the distinction between a serial and an integrating resource is based on the manner in which it is issued and is usually clear, the distinction between monographs and serials is based on whether or not the resource will continue over time, and this is often not clear at all! Frequently the cataloger is left to decide the most appropriate treatment. The following considerations of economy and access are presented for situations in which a publication could be cataloged as either.

Economy

When a title is cataloged as a serial, all issues are represented by one record—at least until the title changes. If successive issues are received, they can be checked-in and added to the shelf without further cataloging. Other types of records (e.g., check-in records) are also created. If nothing else is received (i.e., the publication is really a monograph), nothing need be changed. Just think of it as a "dead" serial!

When a publication is cataloged as a monograph, however, and turns out to be a serial, the monograph records have to be canceled and the publication recataloged as a serial. On the other hand, treatment as a monograph is preferable when it appears that each issue will have a different title. If separate records are going to have to be made for each issue due to constant title changes, it is more economical to catalog as a monograph because the records do not have to be linked nor do check-in records or union list records need to be created.

Access

If serials are classed by a library, treatment as a serial enables the shelving together of all issues, regardless of title changes. Usually the title will also be accessible in sources other than the catalog, such as union lists, check-in files, and so forth. The cataloging record, however, will be less complete than individual monograph records would be, since one entry must serve for all issues. If there is important information that is specific to each issue, treatment as a monograph may be preferable. This is often the case for monographic series whose individual titles may require separate subject headings and classification numbers to provide the appropriate level of access.

2

Implementation of Automated Library Management System

LIBRARY AUTOMATED IN DEVELOPING COUNTRIES

When Information Development was launched in 1984, library automated was, looked at from today's perspective, very much in its infancy. The largest libraries in the world such as the Library of Congress and the British Library had sizeable databases of catalogue records.

University library catalogues were available on-line within their institutional four walls and library circulation was also automated, but data was generally confined to the institution that held it since, there was no network resembling the internet. In 1983 the JANET network had begun to connect the universities in the United Kingdom, and some catalogues were beginning to be available online from other institutions.

The most common way of accessing remote data if there was a possibility at all was by dial-up modem using ordinary phone lines and a modem or an acoustic coupler in which the phone handset was pushed into a rubber holder to ensure no extraneous noise seeped into the phone line when it was transferring electronic signals between computers. Businesses including libraries were also connected by dedicated phone lines to locations where their computers were located when they were remote. But most automated was firmly confined to the institution where it was based. Twenty five years ago was also the beginning of the period when computers were being introduced as desk top computers, with IBM PCs and subsequently IBM PC lookalikes. Personal computers were about to make a huge impact on automated in libraries as no longer was it necessary to have a dedicated air-conditioned room to house computers.

In the early days cataloguers had to have terminals on their desks to enable access to the catalogue but eventually all staff had PCs for general administration so no longer was it was the responsibility of the library budget to purchase desk-top computers. Modems were in fact used to access remotely catalogues for bibliographical purposes, to search databases like Medline. It was already possible to dial up databases such as the British Library's BLAISE database or the US National Library of Medicine's Medline. But these facilities required good phone lines and were not available outside Western Europe and the United States.

There was no such thing as 'full text' then. Computers did not have the capacity to store so much data and data stored was often coded to ensure that it did not take up more space than was necessary. 25 years ago, while most libraries in industrialised countries had not only computerised their catalogues but also computerised their circulation, in developing countries there was very little library automated outside that organised by the United Nations agencies such as FAO's AGRIS and IAEA's INIS and these were very much in their infancy or in their planning stages.

To return to the situation in industrialised countries. In the early 1990's catalogues began to be accessible on the internet but were not web-based and required the catalogue software to be run interactively across the Internet using various different protocols. By the end of the decade, true web-based catalogues using the power of hypertext were available. Libraries began to include in their catalogues digital resources internally held and externally held (predominantly external). MARC formats thenceforward incorporated a field 856 used to link to an external resource by means of a URL (the internet address).

Users of the catalogue could click on a link and go straight to a digital resource that could be anywhere in the world. Subscriptions were possible to electronic journals but they were often not available in developing countries or if they were available the bandwidth of tehinternet in those countries was not enough to enable the materials to be read. Digital library software became available and UNESCO encouraged its implementation in developing countries by making Greenstone available free-of-charge, a digital library software package developed at Waikatu in New Zealand. Links could be made from a library catalogue to material in such a digital library. Material available on the internet which might not be easily accessible in institutions in developing countries with low bandwidth could be downloaded or sent on CD-ROM to the digital libraries and hosted locally.

The Soros Foundation set up eIFL (Electronic Information for Libraries) with the aim of creating national purchasing consortia. They have since, become involved in supporting other activities such as promoting library automated systems, mindful of the fact that without a catalogue of print and digital materials the library user cannot easily find out what is accessible. eIFL supported the European Union funded project to implement NewGenLib, a system under development in India, in Aleppo and Al Baath university libraries in Syria alongside providing them with licences at a reasonable price to access electronic resources.

INASP, the International Network for the Availability of Scientific Publications, was set up by the International Council of Scientific Unions (ICSU) in 1992. Aware of the need to establish good catalogues in order to access scientific litreature, they have also participated in some library automated projects. The Andrew W. Mellon Foundation, well known for philanthropic projects in developing countries, is also supporting the development of a new library automated system at Duke University, the Open Library Environment (OLE). Although there is no participation from developing countries at this stage it is likely that any open source package developed would be supported with necessary tailoring in line with the needs of developing countries wherever they might be different.

The main feature in the last 25 years then has been in the expansion of computers into every aspect of libraries. Possibly the biggest change has been the development of digital libraries, acquiring, transforming or accessing data in digital format. In developing countries this methods of digitisation has taken place to a certain extent.

TRENDS IN THE INDUSTRIALISED WORLD

Library systems in developing countries have obviously developed alongside systems in the industrialised world. First we should look at systems for large institutions. The majority of library systems have been developed in the United States. Many commercially available integrated library systems were developed by universities for their own use and later made available to a wider audience. Dynix was one such, developed for a university library and later sold around the world to universities, public libraries and special libraries. Other systems were based from the outset on cooperatives, such as TALIS which originated as BLS, the system of BLCMP (Birmingham Libraries Cooperative Management Project) which was a cooperative set up with government funding in the 1960s.

This project was one of two established from the beginning by OSTI, the UK Office of Scientific and Technological Information, to support cooperative cataloguing. They had less incentive to expand outside their country of origin as it was their aim to serve a cooperative all of whose members were equal. In 1967, the Ohio Colleges Library Centre was established to bring library automated to Ohio academic institutions by sharing costs. OCLC as it is now has developed from being a cooperative between libraries in Ohio to being an international cooperative, and at one time promoted a library management system.

Then they ceased to support it returning eventually to the market by acquiring OLIB, an Oracle based library system. Its vision is to connect libraries of the world. Originally, as with BLCMP, it was a shared cataloguing system receiving records from participating libraries and adding them to a database which in turn could be used by member libraries to populate their own catalogues. Records were transferred between computers initially by sending large magnetic tapes, a thing of the past, from the Centre to the remote libraries. Later they were transferred by telephone lines and subsequently the transfer was done by a client computer, a PC in a remote institution, accessing the Centre's servers by the Internet. Jumping to the present, OCLC have established Worldcat which could act as a large union catalogue for the world if every library in the world added its holdings.

This concept is called Cloud Computing, on the basis that the computer is somewhere remote and no one knows or cares where exactly it is! To return to library systems established in individual institutions, VTLS (Virginia Tech Library System), another large library automated system, always had an interest in working with developing countries and have a large number of installations in the Third World after having expanded into Eastern Europe as well. Another popular system, Aleph, is based in Jerusalem surrounded by a number of developing countries some of which have considered installation though by far the largest share of the market is in Europe.

As for cooperatives like OCLC, there has existed for many years in former Yugoslavia a miniature version of OCLC, COBISS (Co-operative Online Bibliographic System and Service), which since, the break-up of Yugoslavia has expanded to include Albania and Bulgaria on the same basis as other ex-Yugoslav states.

They act as a cooperative cataloguing agency but they also keep data on research projects. This institution would be a good model for other regions to adopt. Now and again a commercial library system has been licenced to a developing country institution which has subsequently found it difficult to pay the maintenance fees. Maintenance in any case is often more expensive in a developing country because of economies of scale and distance from the supplier. Additionally there may be problems caused by shortages of foreign exchange.

Now the internet reaches much of the world, distance is not so important. But there have been many instances of institutions retaining a package but not paying maintenance fees and therefore not updating it. Marshall Breeding keeps records of as many library automated packages and the sites where they are used as he can find the information. He publishes the results each year in Library Journal. The latest was published on the web in January 2009. He reviews the market as well as providing statistics about library automated suppliers.

This is a useful guide to make comparisons with developing countries. Only the distinction between the US and the rest of the world. However he also includes a general review and this year he reported that the use of Open Source packages is increasing mainly bring provided by third parties. For example, a company called Equinox provides support for the Open Source package Evergreen.

PACKAGES WHICH HAVE HAD AN IMPACT IN DEVELOPING COUNTRIES

Large libraries in developing countries had always had a certain amount of access to library automated systems. For example, the National Library of Venezuela had a system found in many US academic libraries called NOTIS. However this library's catalogue is still not available on the web. A number of countries in the former Soviet Union use IRBIS, the CDS/ISIS clone developed by the Russian National Library for Science and Technology. But ordinary libraries, public and academic, in developing countries have always lacked a wealth of possibilities for library automated. Hardware used to be expensive, and relatively speaking is still expensive for developing countries. Other problems raised by writers on the subject range from the power supply to the problems of training staff. Another issue not often raised is the need for collaboration both within and between institutions to get library automated project off the ground and then maintain it.

This is a much more complex activity than a pre-automated situation where there is a library card catalogue maintained by cataloguers and used manually by staff and library patrons. Smaller systems than the ones developed for universities or networks have been developed which could be regarded as being similar sized to CDS/ISIS, for instance Inmagic and Tinlib. Some of these were not very easy to use and were not well maintained. Others were adopted by consortia or organisations in the industrialised world with branches in developing countries such as the British Council.

The main problem in developing countries has been support because of their remoteness and so those packages offering less support would be more attractive as they would be less expensive overall. This may well change in the future with the increase in the power of the internet and the next 25 years will surely see a difference in the availability of and the charges for support.

CDS/ISIS

CDS/ISIS has undoubtedly had a huge influence on library automated in developing countries. This author reviewed the package onits twentieth anniversary. Time and again, libraries have begun automated. There is even a reference to a library which began with Tinlib and has migrated to CDS/ISIS. Since, CDS/ISIS is well mentioned in the litreature, concerning library automated in developing countries, it will not be covered here.

However the most interesting feature which has become available over the last five years in CDS/ISIS is a Z39.50 import facility which is available as part of IsisMARC, and which enables MARC records from external sources to be downloaded into a CDS/ISIS database compatible with the version of MARC of the records. CDS/ISIS is not essentially a library management system, rather a database management system aimed at bibliographic records which by their very nature are variable length (with for example book titles being of indeterminate length) rather than fixed length which is the case for most data processing systems.

Because it is attractive to small institutions with little funding and because of its parentage (UNESCO), it has attracted a certain kind of institution, for example those in the development community. UNESCO developed a DOS version in 1985 and a Windows version which was available for many years as a beta test version but was eventually released around 1998.

However libraries were already requiring to place their catalogues on the web and a number of organisations began to develop compatible web-based systems which could be used by institutions which were developing databases for in-house use on Windows or DOS versions of CDS/ISIS. The main developer of the official version was BIREME with WWWISIS but already others were available such as Webisis. CDS/ISIS is no longer being developed by UNESCO but BIREME in cooperation with UNESCO is leading the development of ABCD on an Open Source basis.

Tinlib

Tinlib was a package which was used extensively in British Council libraries. In Ilorin Nigeria it was used from 1996 as reported by Adewoye. The library had by 2001 almost replaced its card catalogue by the OPAC. The chapter was optimistic about the future and reporting on the use of other electronic resources. However e-mail and the internet were not then available. However, TINLIB had its problems. It was not an easy system to use and contracts for it dwindled outside developing countries and it ceased to be supported. Adeyoyin describes in 2004 how the Development Policy Centre Library in Ibadan migrated their catalogue from Tinlib to CDS/ISIS.

DEVELOPING COUNTRY SCENARIOS

It is of course a fallacy to make assumptions that all developing countries will have approached and will approach library automated in the same way. The wealth of the country the distribution of that wealth and the culture of the residents will make a difference.

Nigeria and other African Countries

Nigeria has oil money and had automated early, being one of the first users of CDS/ISIS for mainframe computers. Already in1989 Eyitayo could write a paper on the attitude of automated library system vendors to investing in Nigeria. Many respondents hoped to open an office and increase their marketing. Enakrire describes a few instances in Africa where automated has been implemented, indicating that, except for branches of international organisations, it depends on the generosity of donors. In Makerere University in Uganda, the library has benefited from donor funding through the African Virtual University Library Initiative of the World Bank to equip the library with computers and installed Internet connectivity. Other university libraries are developing their information service as they are also benefiting from the Programme for the Enhancement of Research of (PERI) under the sponsorship of the International Network for the Availability of Scientific Publications (INASP).

Through PERI, donors have paid subscriptions on behalf of libraries in Africa to access web-based journals. The University of Ibadan had a long history of automated, having begun in 1979. Georgina D. Ekpenyong wrote in 1997 about the history so far. The University of Ibadan Library was already seen as a leader in Nigeria. At that time they used CD-Rom extensively to provide bibliographic data.

They took training seriously but did not yet have an OPAC. In 2008, the John D. and Catherine T. MacArthur Foundation in Chicago awarded grants totalling US $7.1 million to expand academic and research programme and strengthen staff development at two Nigerian universities as part of the Foundation's efforts to improve higher education in Africa. The result is that they signed up to VTLS, Virginia Tech Library System, a commercially available package developed originally as Virginia Tech's own system.

Thailand

In Thailand there were efforts in the 1990s to computerise the libraries with foreign-based systems being purchased. Thammasat University library had Dynix, supported from Ameritech's Australia office, and planned to move to Ameritech's new system Horizon. In 1997 the university library sent three cataloguers to Middlesex University to learn to use Horizon. Since, then they have implemented Horizon and exchange of experience took place between Middlesex University and Thammasat University until the Systems librarian at Thammasat moved to a different post around 2006. Many universities in Thailand are able to purchase these systems often through local distributors of international or American packages. Early on though, CDS/ISIS was used and at Thammasat University they used it for databases of journal articles.

OPTIONS FOR DEVELOPING COUNTRIES

Developing countries depend on developments in the industrialised world but they do not necessarily benefit from the same options as the industrialised world can use. Moreover, some of the options may be much more attractive in developing countries or at least may seem to be so.

Developing a Library System

One solution for organisations in developing countries which might have problems with paying organisations in foreign currency but which have good local technical staff is to develop their own software system. One interesting example of this is the University of Colombo in Sri Lanka. They had begun to automate in 1991 by using CDS/ISIS and then later adopted CDS/ISIS for Windows when it became available. In 2002, Seneviratne and Amaraweera reported in Information Development that in Sri Lanka there was discussion on developing a library automated system to bridge the gap between CDS/ISIS and what commercial software was able to provide, such as Alice for Windows (UK commercial) and LibSys (Indian).

In 1997 the National Agency for Research Energy, Science and Agriculture (NARESA) now the National Science Foundation, used the CDS/ISIS DOS version to handler acquisitions, cataloguing, serials management, Current Awareness Services as well as cataloguing and indexing; this package called PURNA was then used in 34 special and academic libraries. AGRIS using CDS/ISIS was widely influencing libraries in the agricultural sector and the Windows version was then used in the National Library of Sri Lanka for its union catalogue.

Now they are using Genisis, a package to make it easy to implement BIREME's WWWISIS on the web, development of which was undertaken in France by Pierre Chabet but for which a manual was written in Sri Lanka (partially a translation from the documentation in French) by Ms. Deepali Talagala Director/Information of the Sri Lanka Scientific and Technical Information Centre based at the National Science Foundation in Colombo Seneviratne and Amaraweera discussed in their paper the features a system would need and the platforms, hardware and operating system, most used and as a result decided to make a prototype using MS Access on Windows. Development took two phases.

Firstly a web-based interface to physically dispersed databases with a user-friendly front-end reported by Kumara et al in 1998, and a library automated system described in a BSc dissertation by DMS Dilrukshi, 1999 NetLib—a library management system through the Internet. In 2002 a prototype had been developed and the system was due to be maintained by the Computing Service Centre of the University of Colombo. Unfortunately there is a high overhead in developing and maintaining systems especially for a small client base.

In the UK all university libraries have commercial systems. Newcastle, used to have their own system in the 1980s but only Lancaster remained, eventually contracting with Ex Libris to take Aleph in 2001. By 2008 both the University of Colombo and the National Library of Sri Lanka had signed up to Softlink Europe's Alice system, a system used by the British Council worldwide (for example in Oman, Jordan and Sudan: the catalogue of the British Council in Sudan is available on the internet) and so has proven maintenance in developing countries. So developing one's own system is not to be recommended: Eyitayo noted that despite the availability of numerous off-the-shelf systems, most libraries in Nigeria that have attempted automated have chosen to commission expensive and time-consuming in-house projects, most of which have suffered severe set-backs and in most cases are not adequate for library work and often lack the capability for sharing information and interconnection with other systems.

Open Source

In the context of moving towards commercially supported systems, it is interesting to see that CDS/ISIS was attractive to libraries in developing countries. It was available without charge and so there was no danger of not being able to pay for it. Of course it was supported by an organisation with as much prestige though not so much turnover as many industrial companies. It also operated on a legal footing. Institutions had to sign a licence agreement to use the software. No doubt many institutions obtained the software illegally but the software was protected in law by the licence agreement. UNESCO were more concerned with illegal copies being made and sold for illegal profit than with institutions using the software without being officially licenced since, the spirit of the software following the ethos of the developer Giampaolo Delbigio was that it should enable institutions to participate in worldwide record sharing at many different levels.

Nevertheless there was established a network of distributors which is still in place. Some acted merely as local distributors sending out the software on diskettes by post and thereby easing the burden of the hard-pressed office in UNESCO dealing with this. Other distributors were able to provide support usually of a limited nature though sometimes of a more extensive nature akin to the commercial support that is found in the large-scale library automated systems. The shareware movement was in place when CDS/ISIS was released in 1985.

In 1984, Andrew Fluegleman programmed a communications software package, PC-Talk and Jim Knopf a file management application called PC-File a year before the IBM PC was released and called it Freeware. The developers wanted to avoid commercial distribution networks and distribute the software over the now seemingly primitive and slow dial up systems whereby PC users could transfer programmes by dialling up a central computer using a modem and phone lines. The idea was that users would download the software, test it and if they liked it make a small contribution to the developer to support further development. Knopf established the term freeware as his own and no one else could use it.

There were other microcomputers around at the time, most notably the Apple Macintosh and others which are only part of history such as the BBC Microcomputer, though none ever reached the level of popularity that the IBM PC with the Microsoft Windows operating system has now reached. Incidentally Fluegleman distributed his software with the source code which led to many other developers producing their own versions and PC-Talk was improved and sold on by other developers such that Fluegleman lost control of it. Knopf however established a multi-million dollar company on the basis of PC-File.

In 1983 Bob Wallace created PC-Write which became a well used word processor and was used extensively in developing countries. Because the word freeware was reserved he called it shareware. The concept was pretty much the same. Over the years, freeware and shareware became less used as concepts probably because the most used programmes for business purposes were monopolised by Microsoft with the operating system and Microsoft Office applications. Shareware was in a sense reborn with the open source movement. It is difficult to see any difference between Open Source and shareware but the Open Source Movement has been supported from the outset by large foundations such as the Soros Foundation which founded the Open Society Initiative.

In English 'Open Source' means freely available source software which developers can use to advance the software in question. In all these cases, software developed is free though usually developers ask for a voluntary contribution. They cannot be sold on. Open Source does not necessarily mean free-of-charge but there is an implication that the availability of the source code will enable organisations to acquire and develop it for free. CDS/ISIS was no shareware or open source but many of the features of open source and shareware were responsible for the popularity of CDS/ISIS.

For example, Open Source has the possibility for users with access to programming skills to make their own developments. CDS/ISIS has a feature of being able to write programme exits which enable further development. Unlike open source the source code was not made widely available but UNESCO did make it available to BIREME in Brazil where further developments have taken place. Moreover, in the Soviet Union the Russian National Library for Science and Technology developed with permission from UNESCO IRBIS, a functionally equivalent package copied from the DOS version of ISIS.

The Open Source movement gained much greater political credibility than the earlier movements did and UNESCO came under pressure to support the movement. They now have on their web site a Free and Open Source software portal. Because of UNESCO's lead in this concept, CDS/ISIS came under pressure to be declared open source in the early 2000s. But the source code is still not available.

This author believes it would lead to many different versions of the software that could generate records in databases that were no longer compatible with each other. Moreover, Open Source is seen by some as the solution to some of the problems facing the library software industry. Is Open Source all it promises to be? Over the last few years there has been a spate of mergers in the library systems industry led by the equity market resulting in a trend to discontinue the development if not the support of library systems when a company has acquired more than one such package. This severely inconveniences the using institutions which have to migrate from one system to another. Would open source be a protection against this? Open Source has become so much a fashionable option for library software that the International Federation of Library Associations and Institutions held a meeting in Senegal prior to the annual conference's meeting in Durban South Africa.

The proceedings are illustrative of the views on Open Source. The argument in Savard's introduction goes that Open Source may help to smooth out the inequalities between industrialised and developing countries. The connection with commerce is weaker than with commercial software but it is not non-existent. In industrialised countries libraries often use third-party services to support Open Source. This means the connection with the commercial world strengthens. There is no way put from paying for support. The question is who pays and there is not much difference between paying a developer or a third party.

In the conclusion of these proceedings, Diop feels there are clearly economic advantages to adopting an open source software solution but agrees that mastering open source software can take a lot of time and effort because library and information professionals are often isolated. User communities need to be built up to provide mutual help. However it remains to be seen what will be the impact of open source on library automated, particularly integrated library systems in the industrialised world. A pessimistic outcome might be that the institutions using such software feel no differently being supported by the commercial open source support companies than by the current range of commercial companies who promote systems they themselves own.

THE CURRENT SITUATION AND FUTURE PROSPECTS

Making predictions is a very hazardous occupation in anything to do with computers since, the future only tends to bring surprises. Developments in many developing countries are not as advanced as might be expected and in some places there is still a problem with electric supply: Adebibo reporting on usage of catalogues by students at the University of Ilorin in Nigeria stated: "Most respondents claimed to know how to use the card catalogues and OPAC but only a few use them. The possible reason for this low level use of the OPAC is power outages, which have become the rule in Nigeria rather than an exception. Overall, as the power of the internet increases, particularly its bandwidth and its reliability, library automated in developing countries will have the same capabilities as the industrialised world, but not the finance to support it.

In developed countries it is felt by some that the future of library automated lies in open source (outside the control of commercial suppliers) or 'Cloud Computing' (very much controlled by commercial suppliers who provide software on their own hardware and the clients access the data via the Internet). However if solutions to library automated are hosted services in the industrialised world, the suppliers of the service would be able to charge developing countries as little as they wish on the basis that every amount, however little, is profit. This has happened with hosted electronic journals where deals have been made by publishers to cover entire countries which are less than the licence fee required for a university in the west. As suggested, see if this happens. As with e-journals, it needs a champion like eIFL to promote to the suppliers the benefits of their working with developing institutions in what may be perceived as an altruistic way.

CIRCULATION CONTROL

Library interest in automated circulation control is, in large part, based on a long-standing awareness of the problems inherent in manual circulation systems. These problems include labour-intensive and time-consuming record keeping work routines, inaccuracy, high personnel turnover, an inability to generate statistics about circulation activity, and the lack of an interface between circulation files and other library files which contain much the same bibliographic data. Circulation control is one of the most widely automated library operations, and it is often the first and simplest activity to be automated in a given library, possibly because circulation control systems bear an obvious resemblance to inventory management, retail charge card operations, and other transaction processing activities which have been successfully automated in general business applications.

While specific circulation policies and procedures may be subject to considerable local variation, the major component of circulation control-the check-out/check-in procedure—is typically performed in a straight forward manner that is easily understood by computer application developers and systems analysts lacking formal library training. As library users, many data processing professionals have experienced the circulation activity firsthand and are at least broadly familiar with its purpose and nature. Because the bibliographic data required for automated circulation control are often less extensive and complex than those required to computerise such activities as cataloguing and acquisitions, data conversion costs, software development time, and storage requirements may be substantially reduced. Perhaps more than any other library activity, the historical development of automated circulation control has reflected changes in state- of-the-art data processing technology.

Through the mid-1970s, most automated circulation control systems were custom-developed for a single library or library system. As early as the 1930s and extending into the 1960s, a number of libraries used keypunched cards in combination with sorters, collators, and other unit record equipment as an alternative to manual record keeping. Tabulating keypunched cards with information about books, borrowers, and due dates could be sorted to select overdue items or to identify all books on loan to a given person. Such 'precomputer' data processing systems, several of which were developed for academic libraries by methods and procedures analysts and operations research specialists, were typically based on inventory control models used in business.

With the introduction of computers for business applications in the mid-1960s, a number of libraries developed computerised circulation control systems based on batch processing techniques. Such systems were usually implemented on a computer located in a data processing centre operated by a university, municipality, corporation, or government agency with which the library was affiliated. In the typical installation, keypunch or key-to-tape devices were used to convert information about individual circulation transactions to computer-processible form.

The resulting data were then hatched for processing at predetermined intervals, a computer writing individual borrower numbers into item records contained in a master circulation file maintained on magnetic tape and printing a list of all items in circulation for library reference. While some of these batch-processing circulation control systems remain in use, they are now mainly of interest for their limitations and impact on the design of subsequent systems. As a particular disadvantage, the printed lists produced by batch-processing systems necessarily reflect the status of a library's circulating collection at the time when the last batch of transaction records was processed. Part of the information contained in such lists is necessarily invalidated by circulation transactions occurring after that time. By the mid-l970s, library automated specialists had begun to concentrate on the development of online, real-time circulation control systems which process circulation transactions as they occur. Because pertinent data files are updated immediately, such real-time systems accurately reflect the status of a library's circulating collection. Printed lists are replaced by online terminal enquiries to determine the circulation status of specific items.

While real-time circulation control systems have been custom- developed for individual libraries, a number of vendors offer generalised, preformulated approaches to the computerisation of circulation control that eliminate the need for customised system development and speed the implementation process.

Such preformulated approaches, currently the dominant method of automating circulation control, can be divided into two related groups:

- Prewritten circulation control software intended for execution on a computer system operated by or for a given library; and
- Turnkey systems, consisting of preconfigured combinations of hardware and software marketed as self-contained products.

Introduced in the early 1970s, the earliest prewritten circulation control software packages and turnkey circulation systems were single-purpose products designed specifically and exclusively for library circulation activities. While such single-purpose systems remain available, library administrators, systems analysts, automated planners, and pro- duct developers are increasingly emphasising integrated, multifunctional turnkey systems and software packages which combine circulation control with other capabilities.

In addition to circulation control, the most complete integrated system implementations include interrelated application modules for cataloguing, online catalogue access by library users and/or staff, acquisitions, and serials control, a community bulletin board system, and electronic message transmission. In some cases, circulation is a standard integrated system component which may be implemented alone or in conjunction with other functions; in others, circulation control is an optional application module which must be purchased separately. Whether designed as single-purpose products or as integrated system components, prewritten circulation software packages and turnkey systems can be implemented far more quickly than customised circulation control systems which may require months or perhaps years to develop. Speed of implementation is an especially important consideration in applications where automated of the circulation activity will result in a cost reduction.

Similarly, prewritten software packages and turnkey systems minimize or eliminate requirements for local software expertise. Libraries acquiring such products usually do not need to hire programmers. In fact, customer programming is specifically prohibited by most vendors. Because the system design is predetermined, user training is limited to operational considerations. As a distinctive advantage of turnkey implementations, procurement-related tasks are greatly simplified by the availability of a preconfigured combination of hardware and software components that are specifically designed to work together. With a single source for central processing equipment and peripheral devices, the necessity of dealing with multiple hardware vendors is eliminated, as are potential problems of equipment compatibility.

While prewritten circulation control software packages are available for computers of all types and sizes, medium-sized and larger public and academic libraries have typically relied on mainframe—and minicomputer-based products. Examples for IBM mainframes include the NOTIS software package, originally developed by Northwestern University for its own use; IBM's own DOBIULIBIS programme; and the TECHLIB/STATS implementation of the BASIS software package which is marketed by the Information Dimensions subsidiary of Battelle.

Originally developed by libraries in the Minnesota State University system, the PALS software package is marketed by Unisys for use with its own mainframe computers, while the LIAS system, developed by Pennsylvania State University, operates on Honeywell computers. Examples of circulation software packages for popular minicomputer systems include Comstow's Bibliotech system for Digital Equipment's VAX product line; the Georgetown Library Information System (LIS) for Digital's PDP-11 Series models; the Washington

University BACS system for Data General and other minicomputers which run under the MIIS operating environment; and the VTLS and Index systems for the Hewlett-Packard HP-3000 product line. Minicomputer- based turnkey circulation control systems are available from CLSI, Geac, Data Research Associates (DRA), Dynix, OCLC, Universal Library Systems, and other vendors.

Reasonably priced and designed for readily available hardware configurations, microcomputer-based circulation control programmes have proven particularly popular with small public, school, and special libraries. Vendors include Follett, Gaylord, Easy Data, Data Trek, Aball Software, Nichols Advanced Technologies, Scribe Software, Winnebago Software, and Richmond Software.

While the earliest circulation control programmes and turnkey systems forced libraries to accept predetermined loan periods, borrower categories, and other operating parameters, most newer products flexibly support a varied range of library requirements.

Unlike earlier systems which contained rigidly coded procedures to control charging, discharging, and related activities, all newer products are parameterised, *i.e.*, they allow libraries to specify the conditions under which items will be circulated, file enquiries made, and printed output produced. Rather than being written into programmes, particular operating parameters are selected by libraries from a range of possibilities. The resulting flexibility broadens the range of applications which a given system can address and is particularly important in installations where a single prewritten software package or turnkey system will be shared by many libraries.

LIBRARY AUTOMATED IN ACADEMIC LIBRARIES

The history of library automated is sufficiently old now. It started in early fifties in the Untied States of America. The landmark was the initiation of MARC project by the Library of Congress. During 1960s some experiments were carried out in India in this field but very sparingly. During late seventies there were some achievements like production of National Union Catalogue of Scientific Serials by INSDOC, production of Union Catalogue of DRDO libraries of Western Region by the Institute of Armament Technology at Pune. Then came eighties and the whole focus of the librarians shifted towards library automated.

A number of seminars were organised on the library automated and still being done so. We graduated from simple library operations to specialised functions including networking. Now we talk about digital libraries and e-journals. We have come a long way. But we are a country where bullock cart and cars are seen on the same road so blocking the fast moving traffic and those bullock carts restrict the speed of the cars to its own speed. To overcome this problem there are only two ways. First, replace the bullock cart with a car, and second, bypass the bullock cart and leave it behind. The state of library automated in our university libraries is more or less the same. We have the libraries like IIT libraries which are highly automated and also totally manual libraries which are really restricting the speed of academic and research in the country.

FACTORS RESPONSIBLE FOR AUTOMATED IN ACADEMIC LIBRARIES

There are several reasons which can be cited for this difference.
Some of them are:

- Attitude and awareness of the management
- Attitude and awareness of the Users specially faculty
- Resources available
- Non-availability of suitable software
- Level and skill of staff
- Geographical locations.

Attitude and Initiative of the Management

Attitude and initiative on the part of the management has played major role in library automated in Indian University Libraries. The management here includes both the university management and the librarian as a secretary of the management whose task is to carry out the decisions taken by the executive bodies of the university, such as Syndicate, Executive Council, etc. If the Librarian had the initiative then he was able to convince the authorities about this emergent need.

In some of the cases, the initiative also came from top and the Librarian was forced (or bypassed) to do it. But the best blend was when the initiative of both the Librarian and University Authorities was synergised. If there was no initiative on both the ends than there was no progress.

Attitude and Initiative of the Uses

A library may be as smart as its readers. If the readers are smart and well aware they may force the authorities to work towards library automated. If the readers are knowledgeable about the development being taking place in the information technology, they have influenced the use of computers in library to a great extent. This is more true about faculty as they are the people who participate in decision making process. The good examples are the libraries of IITs and other higher engineering educational institutions.

Resources Available

The third important factor is the resources available with the university libraries. The resources include both financial as well as human resources. In most of the universities, the librarians are given funds only for books and journals. Some libraries do not want to or are not allowed the funds received for books and journals to be used for any other purpose, even though the University Grants Commission (UGC) guidelines permit the use of a certain percentage towards such activities (In VIII Plan it was 15 per cent and in IX plan 10 per cent).

Most of the libraries depend on the funds provided by the UGC under Inflibnet project. The distribution of the money under this project was not done logically. Big and small libraries were equated at par and as a result while some libraries remained fund starved some were not able to use the funds. Before distributing funds to libraries there should have been a survey of the requirement and certain guidelines laid down. Besides this there are no other financial resources available with the university libraries.

In order to save the university libraries from going further down UGC must do something in this direction. Another very serious problem, may be more serious than the financial one, is the lack of trained manpower.

Many of our library science schools have not based their curricula on the automated requirement of the university libraries. Some of them are even teaching today what was designed thirty or forty years back although that has become totally outdated. Not many library schools produce a candidate who can straight away go the Automated Department of a University Library and can independently work without any further training. The bifurcation of the library science schools from libraries are perhaps the one of the main important reasons for that.

As a result our profession became the only profession where practice went far ahead of the teaching. In the country people are talking about digital libraries and web-OPACs and we are teaching fundamental of computers in our library schools. This is the only profession where getting a professional degree does not require any professional training. Can you imagine a doctor without hospital training or an engineer without a training in Industry.

Non-availability of Suitable Software

Non-availability of suitable software has also played an important role. Though there are a number of software available for library management but most of them are non- standard. The main reason behind is that most of the software have been developed without the help of a qualified librarian. As a result there were a stream of non-standard software. Some of these softwares have been developed by big corporations like CMC but have not been proved very successful. The software developed by institutions (for example DESIDOC, INSDOC, etc.,) could not be successful as they were lacking in marketing and after sales service. The librarian is confused as he is not in a position to decide what to select.

Level of Skill of Library Staff

The level of skill of library staff also played a very important role. In our country there are no standard for level of subordinate staff to be recruited in academic libraries. There educational and professional qualification vary from state to state. In some of the cases the library assistants are recruited with 12th pass and a six months certificate in library science while in Central institutions like IITs and Central Universities it is minimum graduation and degree in library science.

The institutions having better stuff went far ahead (though there are exceptions to that). The better qualified staff was better oriented towards progressive thinking which could move the things fast. This point emphasises the requirement of a uniform qualification policy for the recruitment of staff in academic institutions.

Geographical Location

Geographical location of an institution also played a very important role. The institutions near to a metro city were benefited by the availability of the resources. They were having better approach to hardware and software market and also the manpower for data entry. They were having approach to better training facilities. Hyderabad is a good example which can be cited.

PRESENT STATUS OF LIBRARY AUTOMATED IN UNIVERSITY LIBRARIES

The real boost in library automated came from the establishment of the INFLIBNET Centre. Before Inflibnet scattered efforts were being made in academic libraries specially in the institutions of special characters like IITs, IIMs, etc. INFLIBNET proved a real catalyst. Inflibnet started with scratch. At that time there were no financial assistance available to the University Libraries for automated. For the first time it was established that automated was the need of hour. The finances were allocated for the first time. The standards were established about the data capturing. The format was finalised and the Karvan started. As one estimate at present about 120 university libraries have been using computers in their activities. Some of the University libraries are even establishing digital libraries not only of already available digital resources but are digitising their own litreature. About 50 university libraries have their web pages.

AREAS WHERE COMPUTERS ARE BEING USED

The following are the areas where computer are being used at present:

- Online public access catalogue
- Circulation
- Acquisition

- Serial control
- Intranet
- Internet
- CD-ROM services

Online Public Access Catalogue (OPACs)

The problem being faced by the users in locating the document was the first to be targeted in the library automated. As a result the work first started in this direction. There was one more reason for this and that was the availability of CDS/ ISIS software which had the facility of catalogue only. It was in contrast of the special libraries where the work first started on providing information services like CD-ROM search. Even today this area of automated has more activity than any other area. It has now graduated to Web-OPAC (web based online public access catalogues) where university libraries have made their databases available on their web sites. This has eliminated the need of installation of search software on the user's terminal. One potential which remains unutilised is the use of search data for research purpose as the search history can provide very useful tools for the librarians to formulate their collection development plans.

Circulation

Circulation is one of the main activities of a university library or any library per say. In university libraries, however, the number of books issued and retuned are more than in special libraries. Therefore, the next area which was taken up was the circulation. In some of the libraries the number of books issued/ returned may be more than one thousand per day. We at IIT Roorkee (formerly University of Roorkee) has experience of issuing 1500 books in six working hours. Sometimes there used to be a queue of more than 100 students, since, the free hours for all students used to be the same, before automated circulation started.

Use of barcodes had made the life very simple due to added accuracy and speed. Besides speeding up the issue/return, printing reports, sending reminders also become very easy. Circulation data also provides a very important insight into the book use pattern. Librarians should try to use this data for research and development purpose.

Acquisition

Use of computers in acquisition remains a low priority area. Not many libraries are using computers in acquisition. On reason may be the continuously reducing budget for purchase of books. But this area needs to be strengthened. Computerisation at the stage can help not only in order processing but also can be a very effective tool in budget control. You can allocate funds to different departments based on a set formula, can send department heads about non-availability of funds, can control over ordering and also utilise the data entered at this stage for technical processing and OPAC.

Serial Control

Idiosyncracies involved in serial control affects the use of computers in serial control and hence, the area is not very well represented at automated scenario. One more reason is the unsuitability of serial control modules available in most of the library Management Softwares. The procedures developed by these softwares are so cumbersome that sometimes it looks easier to use normal method rather than automated. However, this area provides very good stage for use of computers as it can help tracking the missing issues very efficiently and provide the current awareness services and even the SDI services besides budget control.

Intranet

Making the information available on intranet is also growing popularity as it eliminates the need of installing the software on the users' terminals. Users can access the catalogue through intranet or they can find the status of the books issued to them through web access. CD-ROM resources and other digital resources can be accessed on intranet. The beauty is that one need not be conversant with the software as the web links are available through the web page. Growing installation of campus wide networks is also playing a positive role in this direction.

Internet

Use of Internet for academic purposes is also increasing day by day. More and more libraries are putting their resources on Internet. Internet is the medium both to access and disseminate information. Internet has emerged as a very big virtual library which has information on practically every subject and in every media may it be text, audio or video. Libraries should use this facility to the best of their capability. They should provide links to similar type of libraries through web pages. One very good use can be designing of e-gates where user can have access to the electronic resources through a common user interface.

Digital Libraries

Digital library has recently become the buzzword for librarians. In the last year most of the seminars and the conferences had 'digital libraries' as their theme. Digital libraries can be of two types, *i.e.*, digital libraries of the digital text available in the market such as e-journals, CD-ROM databases, e-books, software, etc., or it can be developed from the printed text available in the library. If a library takes a decision to develop a digital library of its collection specially theses, dissertations and old journals, it can solve the problem of space and preservation both. But the decision about creating such decision is taken to be very carefully as it will prove a very costly venture both in terms of money and manpower.

PROSPECTS

Having talked about the problems and areas of applications let us talk about future prospects. I can definitely say that the things are changing for the good. Now University authorities are realising that there is no way to escape library automated. They are finding various ways to finance their library automated projects.

Librarians are also realising that they can not remain indifferent to the change, otherwise they will be labelled outdated. One area of concern is the library science graduates being produced by our library schools It is surprising that UGC is giving responsibility of refresher courses of library science to the library science school and not to the libraries who are established themselves as advanced libraries and uses the technology far ahead than the library science schools. Existing staff is getting rid of the fear of computerisation. They are coming forward to learn and make themselves suitable to face the challenges of the new millennium. Standardisation is increasing and the better softwares are available.

AUTOMATED CATALOGUING

Descriptive cataloguing is an intellectual activity requiring considerable decision-making and one that is time-consuming. As a result, many libraries experience cataloguing backlogs which impede the flow of materials into circulating and reference collections thereby preventing library catalogues from representing those collections fully and accurately.

Recognising that the cost of descriptive cataloguing can approach or even exceed the value of certain materials, many libraries do not catalogue paperbound books, low-cost government publications, or other relatively inexpensive items.

In some research libraries, materials of presumably limited interest may be placed in off-site storage facilities with only an abbreviated catalogue record created. In most libraries, conventional descriptive cataloguing is not even considered for individual titles in large microform sets, even though such materials may significantly augment a library's resources in particular subject areas, and the failure to catalogue them impairs their utility. To simplify decision-making, to save time, and to reduce costs associated with descriptive cataloguing, libraries have historically relied on cataloguing copy, *i.e.*, descriptive cataloguing information prepared by other libraries, especially the Library of Congress.

The automated of descriptive cataloguing depends on the availability of such cataloguing copy in computer-processible form. In the late 1960s, the Library of Congress developed the MARC format for the communication of bibliographic data on magnetic tape and began distributing machine- readable cataloguing copy through its MARC Distribution Service. Since, the late 1960s, MARC formats have been developed for various types of library materials, and the scope of the MARC programme-once limited to English-language monographs—has broadened steadily and significantly. The LC MARC database-the accumulation of Library of Congress cataloguing data in machine-readable form-now contains more than 2.5 million records, most of them catalogued since, the inception of the MARC programme.

Although MARC tapes can be purchased from the Library of Congress for input to local computer systems, most libraries obtain access to MARC data through products and services developed by publishers, computer system developers, time-sharing services, and other intermediaries. Among the earliest of these MARC-derivative products were computer-generated micro publications such as MARCFICHE, produced by MARC Applied Research, and Books in English produced by the British Library. Created by Computer-output Microfilm (COM) technology, both products provided more timely and varied access to LC cataloguing data than could be obtained through the conventionally printed National Union Catalogue, which was itself discontinued in favour of a COM implementation in the early 1980s.As an equally timely and flexible alternative, several search services, including DIALOG and WILSONLINE, offer online access to the LCMARC database.

A growing number of vendors supply the MARC database on CD-ROM disks or digital optical videodiscs accompanied by software which supports the retrieval of specific cataloguing records and the printing of card sets. Examples include the BIBLIOFILE system from the Library Corporation in Washington, D.C., the LASERSEARCH system from General Pesearch Corporation, and the MINI MARC II system from Library Systems and Services Incorporated. Although these products and services are important, most libraries obtain access to machine-readable cataloguing records through one of the bibliographic utilities-organisations which maintain large databases of cataloguing records and offer online access and other services to subscribing libraries.

Examples include the Online Union Catalogue implemented by the Online Computer Library Centre (OCLC), the Research Libraries Information Network (RLIN) operated by the Research Libraries Group, the cataloguing support service operated by the Western Library Network (WLN), the Cataloguing Support System (CATSS) offered by Utlas International, the LIONS system operated by the New York Public Library, the AGILE II service offered by Auto- Graphics Incorporated, and Brodart's Interactive Access

System (IAS). While they differ in database size and composition, the number and nature of their subscribers, and the specific capabilities they support, these bibliographic utilities each maintain a database of MARC records obtained from the Library of Congress and other sources, supplemented by original MARC-format cataloguing contributed by subscribing libraries. Working at local terminals, participating libraries can retrieve cataloguing copy, modify it to meet local requirements, and order printed card sets, machine-readable cataloguing records on magnetic tape, and other bibliographic products.

Local workstations are also used to input original cataloguing records for use by other subscribers. Supporting thousands of online terminals accessing millions of machine-readable records, the bibliographic utilities are among the world's largest and most intensively utilised computer-based information services.

PLANNING FOR LIBRARY AUTOMATED

Library Automated refers to the use of computers to serve the needs of library users.

The operations of a library get a quantum jump with the introductions of computers. The computers help to provide fast and reliable access to the resources available in the library as well as elsewhere. The application of computers in the library operations avoids repetitive jobs and saves lot of labour, time, speeds up operations, increases use of library resources. Computers are not only used as a tool for processing the data, but also for data storage and accessing.

Planning for an automated system, no matter how big or small, should be part of an overall long-range plan for the library. Automated should always be used as a means to achieve overall better patron service. Careful planning for technology will assure that your automated project is 'sustainable', *i.e.*, enhances the organisation's ability to meet its service mission without disrupting the organisational stability of the institution.

The present scenario of library worldwide is:

- Vastly expanded storage of indexes, statistical data bases, and document databases within the library.
- Full-text storage of documents, complete with full-text keyword searching and on-demand printing.
- Access by users to library databases from home or office, with direct downloading of information and text on demand.
- The ability to access remote databases across the country and the world, and to download information and text on demand.
- Storage of pictorial and graphic material.
- Availability of 'intelligent systems' providing transparent, one-step searching and access to various library in-house and remote databases.

These capabilities and far more have become reality. Accordingly, today's integrated system must not only provide access to the traditional cataloguing, circulation, public catalogue (OPAC) and acquisitions modules, but must be capable of connecting through the local system into the systems of other vendors, remote bibliographic databases, CD-ROM drives on a local area network (LAN), and the Internet.

Users are expecting that their library systems be capable of, among other things:

- Providing seamless integration between system gateway and OPAC modules.
- Providing access for external users on the Internet to the library's OPAC.
- Monitoring the usage of remote databases that have been accessed through the gateway.
- Accessing the Internet using a variety of graphical interfaces.

Essentially, what this means is that libraries must plan to use a local library system as a vehicle for achieving access to resources outside that system. Stimulated by the Internet, which has created universal connectivity to information resources heretofore unknown and/or inaccessible, and by Z39.50 interoperability standards and 'gateways,' users of individual local systems are expecting to access the resources of other systems—anywhere and anytime. Moreover, the traditional definition of 'publishing' has been stretched by the creation and instant availability of informational home pages and Web sites worldwide.

Given such increased complexities and heightened levels of expectation, libraries must learn all the more how to plan for the introduction of automated in an organised and systematic fashion. There is little mystery involved here: It is entirely a matter of building upon what you already know about your library, using tools that are readily at hand and, most importantly of all, involving the people—staff and users—who must live with the consequences of any automated decisions.

WHAT IS LIBRARY AUTOMATED

Traditional library work consisting of acquisitions, technical processing, serials control, circulation and reference services all entail time consuming manual work. Though these activities are essential to proper functioning of a library, they consume professional staff time that might otherwise go towards user services and library development.

Library computerisation is now gaining importance necessitating the establishment of profession-wide standards. Comprehensive studies of library computer systems world over include discussions of machine-managed acquisitions, cataloguing, serials control, circulation and bibliographic service modules. The litreature in this area highlights major aspects of computer's role in the library environment. Similar to several aspects of library management, the demand for more and faster information services and the decline in library resources are compelling librarians to appreciate the role of computers within their operations.

In general, librarians are looking to maximize the benefits of automated by spreading computer use to as many aspects of library activities as possible by taking advantage of developments in computer hardware and software and telecommunications.

NEED FOR LIBRARY AUTOMATED

Even though this question seems to be very fundamental it is essential to emphasise this aspect, as the library automated is yet to take off in majority of the Indian libraries. Secondly, while justifying need for library automated more than cost-effectiveness the benefits derived by the library users become the major consideration. To appreciate the advantages it becomes necessary to highlight the different levels of library automated.

Following are considered as important factors for Library Automated:

- Information explosion.
- Increase in the collection of libraries.
- Inability of users to explore the unlimited litreature and information of their interest.
- Advances in the computer and communication technology.
- Wastage of user/ staff time in locating the information.
- Provide wide access to resources within the libraries and elsewhere.
- Better access.
- Quality in service.
- Cooperative efforts (Resource Sharing).

Out of all libraries an academic library has a difficult task of defining its mission and operating objectives. The automated programme will have to mange a wide range of litreature associated with numerous departments and educational programmes of the academic institution. Furthermore, in an academic library the collections will be diverse unlike a special research library where the collection is relatively homogeneous.

The user group will also range widely, including faculty, staff, students, scholars, administrators and the general public. The position of an academic library funded largely by the government further complicates the process of identifying and prioritising objectives.

As difficult as the task might at first appear, it is nevertheless essential to the process of establishing automated systems of any type. In addition the overall health of ones library operation will benefit from a modicum of intellectual rigour in this area.

AREAS OF LIBRARY AUTOMATED

As a first step in a planning process, it is desirable to formulate a model for computerisation listing all itemised and prioritised information systems being maintained on a manual basis by the library. For this exercise it is necessary to break down these procedures into their constituent parts. When further subdividing these activities, each item is to be considered of its functional elements. The systems and subsystems listed below are only indicative and may vary with differing library system environments.

These are:

- Acquisitions:
  - — Selection
  - — Ordering
  - — Claiming/cancellation
  - — Receiving/invoice processing
  - — Extended procurements
  - — Gift tracking
  - — Fund Control
  - — Maintains information about all library related funds
  - — Ability to group funds (nesting)
  - — Track fund allocations and adjustments
  - — Fund encumbrance
  - — Fund expenditure
  - — Cash Balance
  - — Free Balance
  - — Automatic updating of fiscal information through recording of specific transactions
  - — Track year-to-date expenditures
  - — Create Purchase Orders
- Technical Services:
  - — Books
  - — Serials
  - — Special Collections
- Cataloguing:
  - — Books
  - — Serials
  - — Special Collections
- Circulation:
  - — Charge/Renewal
  - — Discharge
  - — Loan Periods
  - — Processing schedules
  - — Holds

  - Messages
  - Blocks
  - Notices
  - Transaction Recording Devices for off-line processing
  - Member control
  - Inventory control
- Serials Control:
  - Receipt (check-in)
  - Claiming
  - Bindery control
  - Replacements
  - Monographic serials
  - Invoice processing
- Reference Services:
  - Desk services
- User tools
- Bibliographic utilisation
- Reprography
- Inter-library communications
- General Administration
- Grants Administratiuon
- Library Publications
- Bindery
- Periodical Citation Searching
- OPAC
- Bibliographic Database

PLANNING OF LIBRARY AUTOMATED

Planning for library automated has been defined as planning for 'integrated systems' that computerise an array of traditional library functions using a common database. While this is still generally true, rapid technological change is forcing a re-examination of what it means to 'automate the library.' As physical, spatial and temporal barriers to acquiring information are crumbling, libraries must plan for a broader and more comprehensive approach to providing automated services.

DEVELOPING A LIBRARY 'PROFILE'

One of the most important planning tools involves collecting basic statistical information on the library and its operations. You will find that the same basic data will be needed again and again—whether for vendors from whom you are requesting cost estimates, or for other libraries with whom you may be seeking to cooperate in implementing automated.

The following are examples of commonly needed data:

- Number of titles and volumes in the collection, current and projected.
- Number of borrowers, current and projected.
- Number of materials circulated, current and projected.
- Number of new materials acquired, current and projected.
- Interlibrary loans, lent to and borrowed from other libraries.
- Description of any cooperative arrangements involving the library.
- Library address and hours of operation.

In addition, it is important to take stock of any existing automated in the library by compiling the following data:

- Percentage of collection that has catalogue records in machine-readable form.
- Description of collection without machine-readable records, by category, (, monographs, audiovisuals).
- Description of currently-automated library functions (if any).
- Estimates of the location and number of workstations (to show where you intend to have equipment in any future system).
- Specifications for any existing equipment to be re-used with any future system (if any).

At the same time that this data is being assembled, it is important to assess user needs and set service priorities. This can be accomplished by undertaking a focused, strategic planning process designed to involve the library's 'stakeholders.'

DEVELOPING A STRATEGIC PLAN

A library planning to automate should undertake a process by which representative staff and users can identify service needs and objectives. The purpose of such an effort is to allow participants to articulate their interests and concerns, share perspectives and learn about possibilities in a collaborative setting. Group interaction is an important contributing factor in the success of the goal, which is to develop and sustain library automated in the years ahead.

Here are the basic steps involved in this process:

- Plan on a two-day, intensive planning effort.
- Ask participants to identify strengths, weaknesses, opportunities and threats in the library's environment (known as 'SWOT' factors in strategic planning) that are characteristic of or that confront the library.
- Group these factors into critical issue areas that are likely to have an impact on the libraries' future in developing and sustaining automated.
- *Ask participants to identify ideas and perceptions in relation to the question*: "How do you see the library providing user-friendly, cost-effective automated services in five years?

- Through a method of your own devising, ask participants to prioritise all of the ideas that come out of the above two 'brainstorming' exercises.
- Ask participants to shape these priorities into the draft of a strategic 'vision' for automated development consisting of a statement of purpose, goals and objectives for the library.

SETTING SERVICE PRIORITIES

Your strategic vision must now provide the framework or context for the next step in the automated process, which is to determine which library functions should be automated and in what order of priority. For example, processes that are repetitive, occupy large amounts of staff time, require retrieving information from large, unwieldy files, or are high-profile functions of the library (such as the public catalogue) are prime candidates for automated. Determining the functions that you wish to automate and their priorities relative to each other is important for all sorts of reasons.

If needs and priorities are clear, functions can be automated in phases, allowing for more effective use of frequently scarce funding. Moreover, it is a way to develop credibility with funding agencies and be able to take advantage of 'sudden' funding opportunities. Finally, evaluations of systems and options will be easier and more productive if you are able to match your highest functional priorities against the corresponding modules available in the marketplace.

A WORD ABOUT COSTS

Speaking of funding, planners need to be aware that there are certain cost elements involved in the installation and operation of any automated system.

These may be summarised as follows:

- Planning and consulting costs include direct, out-of-pocket costs, (*e.g.*, hiring a consultant) and indirect costs, (*e.g.*, training staff) associated with getting started.
- Purchase of the system includes the cost of acquiring the initial system hardware and software, as well as the cost of preparing a site for the computer system.
- Telecommunication costs are those fees paid to telephone companies for connecting remote terminals or workstations to a central computer system.
- Conversion costs are those associated with the creation of machine-readable bibliographic and, for circulation systems, patron, records.
- On-Going Operating costs include:
  — Maintenance fees
  — Utility costs

  - — Bar code labels
  - — Miscellaneous supply costs
  - — Telecommunications costs
  - — Salaries and benefits (if extra staff are hired).
- Additions to the existing system may be required to maintain performance specifications, to accommodate new users, or to allow for additional automated functions.

SYSTEM SPECIFICATIONS

At some point, you will need to re-formulate your functional priorities into 'functional specifications,' which may be defined as what you want an automated system to do for you, including things that your current manual system cannot do. 'Technical specifications' must also be established. These include standards that must be adhered to, system performance, operation, and maintenance, as well as infrastructure requirements, such as stable sources of electricity and telecommunications, and sufficient bandwidth. Developing clear and accurate functional and technical specifications that are specific to your library is one of the most important, if not THE most important, activity that you will engage in as you plan for your automated system.

These specifications will carry you through the entire procurement process, and will ensure that the system which most closely matches them will be the most useful and the most responsive to your needs.

DEVELOPING A FORMAL SPECIFICATIONS DOCUMENT

It is very difficult to compare systems sensibly and pragmatically solely by randomly looking at systems, talking to sales representatives, reading litreature or comparing broad cost quotations. For this reason, libraries use a formal document—often known as a 'Request for Proposal,' or RFP—that organises and standardises the information provided to and requested from the various system vendors. Utilising an RFP to solicit written responses from vendors makes it possible for you to systematically compare functionality, cost, maintenance, support, and all the other issues that are involved in system procurements. The process can save you money and will result in a wiser decision.

An RFP document should include these essential elements, among others:

- Background information on the library.
- A description of how the proposals should be arranged and submitted.
- Instructions on receiving vendor business and financial information.
- Criteria the library will use to evaluate vendor proposals.
- Questions regarding vendor training and documentation.
- Your functional and technical specifications.

Also, vendors should be asked to describe:

- How they will create bibliographic, item and borrower databases.
- Their system maintenance programmes and services.
- Their site preparation requirements.
- Their delivery and installation methodologies.
- Their system performance guarantees.
- Their pricing and cost strategies, in detail.

EVALUATING VENDOR PROPOSALS

Upon the receipt of vendor proposals, it will be time to begin the process of system evaluation and selection.

This process involves a number of key steps:

- If possible, form a project team of persons to assist with the evaluations and the selection who have some knowledge of automated or who work in the area(s) being automated. People involved in the strategic planning process would be a good choice.
- Try to weed out proposals that are 'fatally flawed,' *e.g.*, where the vendor fails to reply to any of the functional specifications or the system is missing a module for a high-priority function.
- Begin in-depth reading of the 'surviving' proposals, carefully noting both deviations from the requirements as defined by the RFP and any aspect that is handled unusually well. Make a list of any parts of the response that are not clear and require further clarification.
- Schedule system demonstrations. They are an important component of the evaluation process. Allow the vendors to show off the vendor's system in the most attractive light; however, be prepared with a list of what you want to see along with questions you would like answered. Use the same list with each vendor. This permits more effective cross-comparisons.
- Consider using computerised spreadsheet software in order to compare and evaluate vendor cost proposals. Costs may not be what they seem at first glance.
- Contact some of each vendor's current clients—sites of the same library type, and of similar size, where the hardware and software modules that have been proposed to you are currently in use.
- Assign point values to the criteria listed in the RFP and assign scores to the different proposals. The system with the highest score becomes the number one finalist, the system with the second highest score number two and so on. To maintain a negotiating edge, it is better to cut to two vendors rather than one. If that is impossible, maintain the illusion anyway. Remember: The selection process is not over until the contract is signed. Until that point,

never let any vendors know that they have been eliminated, including those with fatal flaws.

PUTTING SYSTEMS INTO PLACE

After the system selection process is complete, there are several important steps which must occur. You and your vendor will have to negotiate and sign a contract. You will want to test the system and make sure it suits your needs. You will want to make provisions for system maintenance. Finally, you will want to train both your staff and your users as much as possible to prepare them for when the system is up and running.

With regard to training, the following must be considered: In thinking of automated planning, there is often a tendency to focus on the hardware and software aspects of planning, and to ignore the human aspects of automated—training and public relations. Without these, however, even the most carefully designed system may not be accepted by library staff or library users. To assure the success of your hard planning work, a training and public relations plan should be part of any automated project.

Fortunately, training can begin long before the system is installed. By involving staff at all levels in the analysis of operations, the identification of needs, the setting of priorities, the development of specifications, and the evaluation of systems, staff will gain much of the knowledge they need as the planning progresses. User acceptance and enthusiasm for your new automated system is certainly an important ingredient in a successful planning effort. If you are implementing a public access catalogue, it is probably the most important measure of success.

Public relations can allow you to accomplish three things:

- Make users aware of your new system and services;
- Motivate them to use the system; and
- Train them in using the new system and services effectively.

RETROSPECTIVE CONVERSION

In the rush to acquire hardware and software, librarians often forget that their most valuable product is the library's database. The creation of a high-quality machine-readable database provides the cornerstone upon which all present and future automated efforts rest.

Vendors will come and go, hardware will become obsolete, software will be replaced, but a well-constructed, well-maintained database, with its accompanying local holdings, will be the library's transportable and viable link from system to system. Moreover, as library users begin to access not only their local system but systems in other libraries as well, the quality of respective databases will influence both the outcome of search strategies and the availability of materials.

Database readiness has several important facets:

- Catalogue records must be carefully converted from manual to machine-readable formats.
- Collections must be prepared for conversion through effective and ongoing weeding and inventory programmes.
- Once converted, collections must be properly maintained as titles are added, withdrawn, transferred and recataloged.
- Standards—for bibliographic, item and patron records as well—must be adhered to. In particular, adherence to well-established and accepted standards of description for bibliographic information in a machine-readable database is critical because: without standards, files cannot easily be transferred from one automated system to another.
- It is essential for libraries wishing to participate in resource sharing arrangements with other libraries, who will require such adherence as a condition of participation.

SERIALSCONTROL

Current serials automated activities are directed towards two types of tasks-the bibliographic control of serial publications and the management of serials collections in individual libraries. The task of bibliographic control is the establishment of definitive bibliographic information about serial publications.

Among automated approaches to this task, R.R. Bowker offers machine-readable versions of its various printed guides to serial publications including Ulrich's International Periodicals Directory.

The International Serials Data System (ISDS) and the International Centre for the Registration of Serials are charged with responsibility for the establishment and maintenance of a comprehensive machine-readable registry of bibliographic information about serials published through out the world. In the United States, the Library of Congress has developed a MARC format for serial publications and participates in the CONSER programme which creates and maintains a high-quality machine-readable database of cataloguing records. The CONSER data-base is maintained by OCLC, and CONSER records are disseminated through the MARC distribution service.

To manage local collections, a number of libraries and several vendors have developed systems which automate one or more aspects of serials processing, including union list production, ordering, check-in, claiming, and the routing of received issues to designated persons. Computer-based production of union lists of serials is routinely sup- ported by data management software or word processing systems. Such lists may be printed on paper or microfiche. The last option is especially useful for very long lists that will be mailed or otherwise distributed to multiple locations. As an example, microfiche is the output medium for the California Union List of Periodicals (CULP) which contains information for over 63,000 periodicals held by 700 California libraries.

The CULP database is also accessible online through BRS. As with conventional book acquisitions, computers can be used to minimize the labour-intensive sorting, filing, and other paper-handling work routines associated with manual serials processing. A number of libraries developed customised serials control systems during the 1960s and 1970s. The PHILSOM system, developed by the Washington University School of Medicine Library, is perhaps the most famous example. As an alternative to the time and expense associated with customised system development, libraries can obtain access to serials control capabilities on a time-sharing basis through subscription ser- vice companies. Examples of such time-shared serials control services include F.W. Faxon's LYNX system and the EBSCONET system offered by EBSCO Subscription Services.

Several companies and other organisations have developed pre- written software and turnkey systems designed specifically for serials control. The INNOVACQ Acquisitions and Serials Control System, for example, offers a comprehensive range of serials ordering, check-in, and claiming capabilities. It can download records from bibliographic utilities and transfer serials records to a local circulation control or public access catalogue system. Among microcomputer-based products, OCLC's SC350 Serials Control System can retrieve bibliographic information, local data, and publishers' addresses from the OCLC online union catalogue.

It facilitates the check-in of received issues, produces claims and claim cancellations, maintains binding instructions, and prints bindery slips. It can also transmit serials records to OCLC's union list component. As an alternative to single-purpose implementations, several integrated library systems support serials control modules, and others have announced such capabilities for future implementation.

COMPUTER-PRODUCED CATALOGUES

The automated of descriptive cataloguing addresses only one part of the cataloguing activity. In addition to using computers to facilitate access to cataloguing copy, libraries are interested in computer-based solutions to the much discussed problems of card catalogues. The most frequently cited of such problems include substantial space consumption; the purchase of expensive cabinets and supporting furniture; labour-intensive and time-consuming catalogue maintenance routines which are intensified by changes in cataloguing rules affecting the choice and form of entries; and limited convenience and retrieval capabilities.

These problems can be minimized or eliminated by the replacement of card catalogues with computer-based book-form or online catalogues. Broadly defined, a book-form catalogue contains successive bibliographic records listed in a page format on paper or microforms. Among the earliest applications of library automated, computer preparation of book-form catalogues can lower production time and costs while eliminating the labour-intensive file maintenance routines associated with card catalogues.

As an alternative to computer printed or typeset catalogues, computer-output microfilm catalogues have been widely implemented by libraries and library systems since, the early 1970s.

A number of service bureaus, book jobbers, bibliographic utilities, and other vendors have developed software to produce COM catalogues from library-supplied data, thereby eliminating the need for in-house COM recorders and customised programming catalogues.

Broadly defined, an online catalogue is an organised, machine-readable accumulation of bibliographic records which are maintained on disks or other direct-access computer storage media for retrieval by library users and staff members working at inter- active terminals or appropriately configured microcomputer workstations.

In addition to saving space and automating file maintenance, online catalogues permit remote access by authorised persons equipped with compatible terminals, and they can support information retrieval operations—such as keyword searching of titles and series names—which are not conveniently possible with card or book-form catalogues.

Online catalogues may be custom-developed for specific library installations or purchased as prewritten software packages or turnkey systems. Examples of custom-developed online catalogues include the Library of Congress Computerised Catalogue, the MELVYL system at the University of California, the LIAS system at Pennsylvania State University, the Library Computer System (LCS) at Ohio State University, and the Dartmouth College Online Catalogue.

Prewritten software packages suitable for online catalogue implementations include BRS/SEARCH from BRS Information Technologies, a powerful information retrieval programme that is available in mainframe, minicomputer, and microcomputer versions; INMAGIC, a versatile data management programme for dominated by integrated library systems which combine database management and catalogue access capabilities with circulation control, acquisitions, serials control, and other operations.

Such systems may be implemented as complete turnkey configurations of hardware and software or as prewritten software packages designed to operate on a library owned mainframe, minicomputer, or microcomputer. Vendors include CLSI, Geac, Notis, Dynix, OCLC, Virginia Tech, Data Research Associates, Carlyle, Comstow Information Systems, Universal Library Systems, Sobeco, Sigma Data/Centel, George- town Medical Library, Washington

University, IBM, Inlex, Sirsi, Utlas, Innovative Interfaces, Eyring Research Institute, Easy Data, Data Trek, and Unisys. Among the newest and most widely publicised approaches to online catalogue implementation, a growing number of vendors offer public access catalogue systems which employ CD-ROM storage technology.

Examples include the IMPACT system from Auto-Graphics, LASERGUIDE from General Research, THE INTELLIGENT CATALOGUE from the Library Corporation, and the LEPAC system from Brodart.

In such implementations, the library provides a machine- readable version of its catalogue, typically consisting of MARC format records on magnetic tapes obtained from bibliographic utilities or other sources, to a CD-ROM system vendor who indexes and otherwise prepares it for conversion to one or more CD-ROM disks.

The disks themselves are created by a mastering process in special manufacturing facilities, and the library receives a specified number of disk copies plus menu-driven software designed for public catalogue access at microcomputer-based workstations. Updated by periodic replacement in the manner of book-form catalogues, such CD-ROM catalogues are increasingly mentioned as an alternative to computer output microfilm for union catalogues and similar implementations.

AUTOMATED REFERENCE SERVICE

Since, the late 1960s, many publishers of printed bibliographies, indexing and abstracting journals, and other reference works have offered machine-readable versions of their products for use in computer assisted reference applications. Initially intended for government, corporate, and academic libraries supporting research in scientific and technical disciplines, such machine-readable reference sources have become widely available in business, the social sciences, and the humanities. In addition to databases which correspond to printed publications, a growing number of reference sources have been developed specifically for use in computer-based systems and have no printed counterparts.

While the earliest machine-readable databases were bibliographic in character, non-bibliographic numeric and directory-type databases are increasingly commonplace. During the late 1960s and early 1970s, a number of libraries purchased machine-readable bibliographic and non-bibliographic databases for processing on in-house computers using custom-developed information retrieval software. Most libraries, however, lacked access to the hardware and software resources required to implement such systems.

Through the early 1970s,the needs of such libraries were addressed by fee-based search services operated by the producers of machine-readable databases or other organisations such as large research libraries. Such services, which operated in the offline, batch processing mode, were replaced in the mid-1970s by services offering online database searching on a time sharing basis to libraries equipped with conventional terminals.

Now widely utilised by libraries of all types and sizes, online search services can be divided into two broad groups:

- Multidisciplinary services—including DIALOG, BRS, ORBIT, WILSONLINE, DATA- STAR, and ESA-IRS-that provide database coverage of a varied range of subjects for a broad clientele; and
- Specialised services-such as the NLM SEARCH SERVICE, STN INTERNATIONAL, LEXIS, and WESTLAW-that provide online access to one or more databases relevant to a single subject discipline, profession, or activity, such as medicine, law, or engineering.

Various types of specialised search services provide online access to databases containing a specific type of information such as news. Examples include the NEXIS, VUITEXT, DATA TIMES, and NEWSNET search services. While they differ in the number and type of databases offered and in the specific retrieval capabilities supported, multidisciplinary and specialised search services share a common operating methodology: they purchase or otherwise obtain bibliographic and non-bibliographic data-bases in machine-readable form from their producers, convert the dataases to a form required for storage on their computers, and allow libraries or other subscribers to perform various retrieval operations on such data using prewritten data-base management software. The software features a non-procedural query language which permits a user at an online terminal to initiate litreature searches or other information retrieval operations by entering specified commands.

While their query languages are relatively easy to learn, online search services are more often providing menu-driven interfaces for novice users. Some services also offer private file capabilities which allow libraries to establish their own databases.

As a recently implemented supplement or alternative to online search services, an increasing number of bibliographic and non-bibliographic databases are available on CD-ROM disks. Accompanied by information retrieval software, such CD-ROM reference products permit database searching at local microcomputer workstations (over 100 titles were available at the time of this writing).

Offered on a subscription basis, they can prove less expensive than online searching for databases that are accessed frequently, although infrequent updating, slow response time for complex searches, and other performance limitations may make them unsuitable for some applications.

As a hybrid implementation with potentially attractive cost/performance characteristics, several vendors combine CD-ROM searching of back file data with online access to the most current information.

ACQUISITIONS

More informed decision-making through improved statistical analysis and reporting of procurement activity is the most frequently cited motive for automating acquisitions operations.

Since, the 1960s, automated acquisitions systems have been implemented in at least four different ways: as a custom-developed programme designed to operate on a computer owned by a library or its parent organisation; as an acquisitions-specific prewritten software package or turnkey system; as an application module supported by a multifunctional integrated library system; or as a time-sharing service offered by a bibliographic utility or a book jobber.

Each method has advantages and limitations. Customised acquisitions systems, an implementation option in any automated application, can be developed to a particular library's specifications but are expensive and time-consuming to create.

Prewritten acquisitions-specific software, and the acquisitions application modules supported by integrated library systems, can minimize the worst implementation problems associated with customised software development, but a library must have access to required hardware and system software components. Turnkey systems, consisting of preconfigured combinations of hardware and software, are available as both acquisitions—specific products and as integrated systems.

In the latter group, the integration of acquisitions with cataloguing and circulation in a single system offers several advantages, including the ability to establish a preliminary bibliographic record at the time an item is ordered. All of the foregoing approaches require a substantial capital investment which can be minimized if automated acquisitions capabilities are obtained on a time-sharing basis through a bibliographic utility or bookseller.

Because charges are incurred as the acquisitions facility is used, this approach is especially attractive to libraries with modest annual volumes of acquisitions activity.

Use of a bibliographic utility for acquisitions offers other advantages as well. Its database can be used for bibliographic verification, and data can be transferred from cataloguing records to facilitate order preparation. In addition, the use of a single system for acquisitions and cataloguing simplifies staff training requirements, while the immediate online availability of information about the holdings of other libraries supports cooperative collection development. Acquisitions systems offered by booksellers typically feature online access to inventory data with electronic ordering capabilities.

CONCLUSION

Since, the 1960s, libraries have used technology in general, and computers in particular, to automate a wide range of administrative, public, and technical services tasks. Designed as an overview of major facets of automated activity, this chapter surveys the current state of computer applications in six areas of library work: circulation control, descriptive cataloguing, catalogue maintenance and production, reference service, acquisitions, and serials control. For each area, the discussion briefly indicates the motives for automated and describes current dominant approaches, citing examples of representative products and services.

3

Changing Management Techniques as Libraries Automated

INTRODUCTION

The participant oriented change strategy provides the best overall approach to managing library automated and migration projects. Of the strategies which have been outlined, it offers the highest degree of employee communication and participation. These are the same areas that caused the most problems if they were inadequate. One of the chief advantages of this strategy is that it involves the users of the system at the earliest possible stage of the project. That is during the teleological process of identifying reasons for the project and setting goals or criteria for a new system. Involving the employees at this stage reduces the need for normative attitude-adjusting sessions latter in the process.

This is not to say that managers who adopt this strategy can just ignore employee attitudes later on. Change will still be stressful, and people may still resist it at various points. But, management will not have to invest as much effort in convincing staff that the new system is better if the staff were involved in selecting it. The rational-empirical strategies of employee training programmes will still have a role to play, as the process moves on. As was demonstrated in the failed attempt at implementing the CASE system, this strategy is not sufficient by itself. But users must learn how a new system works if they are to use it at all. Within the overall context of participant oriented strategy, other employees provide much of that training. With their hands-on experience, employee led training can be more effective than vendor supplied 'canned presentations'.

This also promotes an atmosphere in which employees will be comfortable sharing their learning experiences, tricks and shortcuts following implementation. The other two strategies, phased implementation and power-coercive can not be recommended across the board. The power-coercive strategy is divisive, and is likely make the change harder instead of easier.

This strategy aggravates fears about job security, which is one of the sources of change anxiety. While a degree of control needs to be maintained, a threatening approach is not desirable as a general strategy.

The strategy of phased implementation will be helpful for some situations, but not for all. For libraries currently using manual systems or automated systems that are not integrated, this method may help to ease the transition. For libraries that already have a well-integrated system, it could create even more chaos. Within the context of participant-oriented change, the choice of whether to include it rests with the employees who actually work with the system.

MANAGEMENT FUNCTIONS

The traditional roles of management are planning, organisation, coordination and control. These can be applied to these change strategies.

RATIONAL-EMPIRICAL

The rational-empirical strategy is primarily concerned with dispensing information, presuming that the plans for change have already been made. It involves the organising function of management, in the sense that the managers determine what information needs to be given to which employees in order to implement the changes. It also involves the control function, in that the management is seeking to influence behaviour through the information it dispenses.

NORMATIVE-EDUCATIONAL

The normative-education strategy is concerned with influencing attitudes and behaviour. As such, it involves the control function of management, but in an indirect manner. That is, rather than controlling behaviour directly, the management attempts to instill attitudes which are likely to result in the desired behaviour. Like the rational-empirical strategy, it also involves the coordinating function, as managers decide who should be involved in which programmes.

POWER-COERCIVE

The power-coercive strategy concerns the management role of control in a straight- forward fashion. It is mainly concerned with seeing to it that the change decisions are carried out as directed. To ensure this, it dispenses rewards or penalties to individuals or groups depending or whether they have implemented the changes. In the extreme, employees who fail to change are fired.

PHASED IMPLEMENTATION

Phased implementation involves both the planning and coordinating functions to a large degree. Planning includes determining the order in which to implement the modules and setting timetables for each phase. Coordination includes meshing together the efforts of different groups associated with each phase, and ensuring that each module is integrated with the previous ones when it is brought into production. As more modules are brought into the 'live' mode, coordination becomes essential in order to see that the different areas function smoothly.

PARTICIPANT-ORIENTED CHANGE

Participant oriented change involves the coordinating function of management. Since, much of the planning and decision making is delegated downward to the staff, management must integrate these plans and decisions. This is particularly important when implementing an integrated library system, as the activities of staff in one area will have more impact on other areas than they are accustomed to.

The actual delegation of these responsibilities to employees involves the organising function. Determining how and to whom these responsibilities are delegated is in important part of the change process.

This may involve organising employees into self-managed teams, work groups, or interdepartmental task forces. How these groups are organised, the amount of authority they have, and how they will interact with each other are crucial decisions.

CHANGE ISSUES IN THE PUBLIC AND PRIVATE SECTORS

While the specific issue of library automated is located principally in the public sector, the processes and challenges of change are common to both areas.

HUMAN FACTORS IN LIBRARY AUTOMATED

Librarians, staff and patrons must make a number of adjustments as a result of any library automated project, whether it is an original implementation or a migration. One key area is the relationship between people and technology. People have to change the way they behave and think to work effectively in an automated environment. They skim through cards to find a catalogue record in a manual system. To find a catalogue record in an automated system they use computer commands.

In a migration scenario, this might be a change from typing keyboard commands to choosing buttons or menu items on a graphical interface. For long-term employees, this requires yet a third 'mental map.' These demands for change easily lead to stress reactions of fear or anger, especially when they are large-scale or frequent. Smith mentions several sources for these emotions, such as loss of control, worries about identity and security in the workplace, and breakdowns in interpersonal relationships. It is no wonder that people often resist change. However, Smith cautions against regarding human responses solely as a barrier to change. For leaders who pay attention to social issues, these responses provide valuable feedback and help to implement a more successful system.

HISTORICAL PERSPECTIVE

The early history of library automated can be divided into three phases, the Developmental Phase, the Operational Phase, and the Integrative Phase. The development phase was the period of early experimentation up to the early seventies. During this period a small number of institutions engaged in automated projects. While management hoped that systems could be transferred from one institution to another, this was not the case with these early efforts. Libraries did not have similar computer operating systems, they did not have standardised procedures, and they could not agree on outputs.

However, the development of the MARC record was a significant development that allowed libraries to communicate bibliographic records in a standard format. The operational phase, in the mid-to-late seventies, saw the expansion of automated in a wider variety of libraries. Vendor-supplied systems, shared computer resources, and networking made this possible. Since, libraries were no longer forced to develop their own systems from scratch, it was an easier and less expensive task.

During this phase most library automated projects still focussed on discrete tasks, such as check-in or circulation. Operational areas were not integrated, and the overall workflow stayed basically the same, "it has been utterly possible to use the automated system as inefficiently and ineffectively and with as little knowledge of what is going on as with the manual system". Montague proposed that the next phase would be an integrative phase, in which the automated systems would cut across operational lines, actually change the way libraries do business, and improve service.

There were a number of obstacles during these stages of library automated:

- Lack of direction and oversight from library managers to systems staff;
- Lack of technical training for library managers;
- Failure to develop long-range plans;
- Lack of up and down communication between managers and staff;
- Lack of staff input;
- Lack of staff training;
- Lack of feedback mechanisms.

Overall, it appears that the several problems, training, oversight, input, feedback, all involved a general lack of communication.

MIGRATION—SECOND GENERATION SYSTEMS

Since, many libraries, including Notre Dame, have or plan to migrate to second generation library systems, it is important to consider whether the obstacles are the same. One view is that they are not the same. Migrations are said to be easier than initial implementations. Although there may be some staff apprehensions, staff morale is reported to improve.

A significant advantage is that second-time buyers have a better understanding of what they want in a system, and focus more on quality and customer support, instead of low bids. There is one potential source of resistance, which is never present in an initial automated project, that is a hostile 'soon-to-be former vendor.' Another important distinction is whether the library is migrating after successful implementation of a system which simply no longer meets their needs, or whether the library is desperately seeking a new system after a failed effort.

The reaction of librarians to this viewpoint is to be mixed. Some libraries have reported a very similar degree of 'techno stress' during migration projects, with similar emotional responses. Staff are required to change procedures, and in many cases the new procedures are not clear-cut—of course, the procedures in the 'old' system were not clear-cut in the beginning either. On the other hand, the majority of directors in a survey of 33 libraries that had undergone system migrations felt that 'promoting' the system change to the staff was unnecessary.

This seems to be primarily due to staff frustration with the old systems, providing a clear motivation for change.

The worse the original system, the less staff resistance there was to migration. However, there were still some symptoms of technostress. Many found the vendors training programmes to be inadequate, consisting of 'canned' presentations were did not apply to local needs. Due to 'rush jobs,' the staff at many libraries did not have adequate time to become familiar with the new system before it was made available to the public. In one particularly egregious case, the staff and patrons were given access to the system at the same time. The staff 'hated this.' A two-month lead-time between staff and public access gave optimum results.

PRIVATE SECTOR EXPERIENCES

While library automated, *per se*, is not a major issue in the for-profit world, automated in general definitely is. As such, experiences in the private sector provide helpful comparisons. One very familiar theme from corporate settings in the need to consult with users prior to any sort of migration or automated project.

This is true even with systems that are not central to the users' jobs. Gaudin relates several stories of companies that tried to implement new systems without consulting users. One case involved replacing a mainframe e-mail system with a desktop system. After the company spent $3 million, the employees rejected it because it was not fast or stable enough.

In another case, FedEx introduced a scheduling system without consulting their own employees. This became one of the issues in a potential strike against the company. One manager pointed out the importance of remembering that 'users might like their old systems'. This is an important lesson for library managers to remember in a migration, especially when the original system was basically successful.

Even a failed system may have features the employees liked. Another illustration is provided by Norman's study of a failed automated effort. An attempt to introduce the CASE system in a management information firm provides valuable lessons for both sectors.

The goal of the CASE project was to establish a 2-1 ratio of CASE workstation usage among the MIS staff and achieve a 10 to 15 per cent increase in productivity. The project is considered to be a failure, because people are not using it. The company has lost business to competitors who do use the system. Norman identifies a number of factors in the CASE implementation, which contributed to its failure. From the beginning, the decision to implement CASE was made by a small high-level committee, without involving staff. There was a successful pilot project, following which the company attempted to expand the system.

Their main methodology was a staff-training programme. Management assumed that if they provided training, the programmers would use the system. While the training was described as 'adequate,' it was informational only, and there was no effort made to change attitudes. The most critical barrier identified in the study was the high learning curve for using CASE. Management did not make any effort to reduce this learning curve. Instead, each work group that attempted to use the system had to learn it on their own. There was no sharing of tricks or shortcuts, or any help given by those who had already started using the product to new users. Interdepartmental friction and a rigid chain-of-command that stifled communication between units prevented this type of cooperation.

A related factor was the lack of any visible benefits or rewards for using CASE. Instead rewards were based on completing projects under-time and under-budget. Since, CASE is intended to increase productivity, it might seem that this would reward its use. But "this means that the rewards are indirect and totally dependent upon the successful use of the tool". In conjunction with the high learning curve, this becomes a negative incentive – the system is likely to slow production in the short-term, until the learning curve is past. If the programmer fails to learn it quickly, rewards are lost rather than gained.

THEORIES AND STRATEGIES FOR CHANGE

In discussing theories of organisational change, many theorists divide changes into different types. Before delving too deeply into specific strategies for change, I would like to examine the relationship between library automated projects and descriptive theories.

CONTINUITY

In the Age of Unreason, Handy tells us that "Change is not what it used to be". He distinguishes continuous and discontinuous change. Continuous change is gradual and predictable, with one situation leading into the next. This is relatively comfortable for most people. But he asserts that the changes in the workplace now are discontinuous. That is, changes are abrupt and unpredictable, and hence, far less comfortable. Handy frequently links discontinuous change to technology.

As such, it is easy to reach the conclusion that a library automated project is a discontinuous change. People who worked with paper switch to online systems, and their jobs are altered or even eliminated. But we should not be too quick to classify it this way. Particularly in the early automated projects, automated tasks were substituted for manual tasks on a one-to-one basis. Because of this, there was no drastic change in the overall workflow; even when specific tasks were drastically altered. It could be argued that automated has had a more significant impact since, that time, as library systems have become integrated.

CALM AND TURBULENT WATERS

Robbins focuses on the frequency of change. He uses two metaphors, 'calm waters' and 'whitewater rapids.' In the calm-waters scenario, change is the exception. Most of the time is spent in a state of equilibrium, until some crisis forces a change. After the change is past, the organisation regains a new state of equilibrium. In the white-water scenario, change is continuous, though in a different sense than Handy uses the word.

There is no state of equilibrium; instead one period of change is followed directly by another. It is very tempting to identify library automated projects with the 'calm water' metaphor. In fact, Saunders uses a very similar model in her article on library system migration. First various forces bring about a need for change, which requires unfreesing process. This is followed by a period of instability.

When this is over, the library establishes a new state of equilibrium, as new patterns and procedures are frozen into place. Because automated efforts are not made frequently, this model appears to be a good match.

In an original automated project, the library has been using a manual system as long as it has been in existence. Once the project has been completed, the library will continue to use the new system indefinitely. Even in a migration project, the library may have been using its old system for many years, and certainly would hope the new system would be long-lived. One potential problem with this model is that it ignores the wider picture of overall changes. At the same time as a library is contemplating an integrated library system, the staff may be dealing with new online indexes, electronic journals, e-mail systems, computer operating systems, and even a building renovation. Taken in this larger context, the white water metaphor seems more appropriate to the library environment. It is often not just the project at hand that causes problems for staff and users, but the 'unrelenting demand' of changes in many areas. Another issue is the continuing change following the implementation of an automated system due to new releases and upgrades to the system.

Even after a new system is fully implemented, it may not be as 'calm' as the old manual system. One significant problem with the white-water model as a model for change is that it suggests a reactive style of management with unplanned changes.

But most library automated and migration projects are planned, as are many of the other changes affecting the library staff. This model seems most apt for dealing with the external changes impacting an organisation.

THE FOUR MOTORS OF CHANGE

Van de Ven and Poole give a more fully fleshed taxonomy of change. They identify two crosscutting distinctions, the level and the mode of change. The level of change is whether the change involves single or multiple entities. The mode of change is either prescribed or emergent. A priori changes are planned, predictable or follow set rules or patterns. Emergent change is discontinuous and unpredictable.

This combination yields four 'motors of change:'

- Life-cycle (single entity, prescribed);
- Teleological (single entity, emergent);
- Dialectical (multiple entities, emergent); and
- Evolutionary (multiple entities, prescribed).

While these motors can be separated in theory, most real-life changes involve interaction between them. The four motors model provides a more complete description of organisational change, and avoids over simplification problems. If we examine library automated projects in this e-context of the four motors of change that Van de Ven describes, as suggested, find rather complex interactions.

The teleological theory, which is characterised by planning and goal setting, provides the closest description of the first stage in an automated project. Libraries may have a variety of motivations for undertaking an automated or migration project.

In the case of migration, this might include negative factors, like dissatisfaction with the current vendor, as well as positive ones, like a desire to expand capabilities. These motivations provide the Aristotelian final cause for the project. Most libraries engage in goal setting activities, such as compiling lists of desired features. This stage may be described as teleological in Van de Ven's scheme because it primarily involves one entity and the process is emergent. At the beginning of this stage, it is not clear where it will finish. Although the process is planned the goals are identified during the process, and may provide a dramatic break with the existing manual or automated system.

The dialectical motor may be present to a lessor extant, as different stakeholders interact with each other, and occasionally present conflicting goals. This teleological description fits most, but not all migration projects. For 79 per cent of cases in a migration survey, the projects were planned. But in some cases, the libraries did not have time to develop plans due to legal or financial problems. In those cases, the teleological motor would only apply in a trivial sense, if at all.

Those cases are obviously not ideal scenarios. Towards the end of the selection process, the library must compare its goals and desires to the actual systems available. At this point, the process could be described as dialectical, involving the library and the vendors who would like to supply the system. Vendors and librarians both regard this process as different for migration projects compared to first-time automated efforts.

In a first-time automated, libraries tend to rely on numerical evaluation of vendors' proposals and claims. In migration projects, libraries find site visits to be the most effective way to evaluate quality and hands-on work issues. At some point either during the final selection process or shortly after a vendor is chosen, the process shifts to a life-cycle model. The life-cycle motor is also primarily concerned with the library as a single entity. At this point, the plan, which was developed in earlier stages, becomes the guide for the process.

The library engages is a series of steps that were laid out in the plan, possibly on a strict timeschedule. This includes all of the steps technically necessary to implement the system as well as steps to prepare the users. This process is imminent in, or prescribed by the plan, and is much more predictable than the earlier stages. The library may have even planned for contingencies. Once the actual conversion in done, and the new system is live, the process become somewhat less predictable. Procedures that worked on paper or in test may fail under the pressure of real-life use.

While none of the motors seem to be completely dominant at this point, the evolutionary theory is closest. Procedures that work 'survive' while others are discarded. The changes may still be described as imminent, however, because they are constrained by the system. The others motors continue to play some role, as plans are made and carried out, and different stakeholders disagree on various issues. The dialectical motor may become dominant from time-to-time as the vendor announces new releases, or the library recommends enhancements for the system. At these times the possibilities for change are less constrained, and the results become more emergent.

STRATEGIES

The authors who describe actual automated projects also list key lessons and make recommendations. There are a number of general, and some very specific, suggestions along with a couple of common threads. One of the common threads is communication. Whether it is between management and employees, between systems and users, or between the employees at large, it seems that more communication is always better. A related thread is the need to involve the users in the process as early as possible. Several of the authors suggested that users should be involved at the very beginning, during the selection process. Montage, Norman, Gaudin, Hallmark and Smith all cite lack of user involvement in the selection or planning stage as an obstacle to successful implementation. Since, these two threads stand out, we may conclude that if any overall strategy is too be effective, it must include a high level of communication and user participation.

STRATEGIES FROM THE CASE IMPLEMENTATION

Norman described three change strategies in his evaluation of the CASE implementation. These strategies could be used independently or in conjunction with each other.

Rational-empirical

This strategy focuses on training and information. It is presumed that teaching people to use the system and providing a rational explanation of why it is better will lead them to use it. This strategy could easily be applied to a library automated or migration project, as many of the authors indicated the importance of training programmes.

Normative-educational

This strategy focuses on group strategies for promoting acceptance of the new systems and providing motivation to use it. First, identify the attitudes that create resistance, and then develop programmes to change them. This is similar to developing training sessions in the rational-empirical strategy. The difference is that the sessions are intended to develop positive attitudes instead imparting information.

Power-coercive

In this strategy individuals are induced to use the new system by the threat of loosing their job or other benefits. This can be a fairly direct approach to implement change, but it also runs a high risk creating bad feelings, job dissatisfaction, and tension between management and employees. Threats, whether explicit or implicit, will also add to the fear and anxiety already identified as an obstacle to change. A variation of this strategy can be applied in a positive way by offering employees incentives for change. While this is can be regarded as a power-exercise it is less confrontational. In the CASE implementation, the main strategy that was applied was the rational-empirical strategy.

The normative-educational strategy was largely ignored, and the power-coercive strategy was inconsistently applied. Management made statements that employees were required to use the system, but did not follow-up when it was not used. Management also did not provide any direct positive incentives. This strategy may also be applied to library systems in the sense that when the old system is shut-off, employees will not be able to perform their duties without using the new system.

PHASED IMPLEMENTATION

Saunders recommends a strategy of phased implementation. The idea of this strategy is to minimize the impact of the new system has on staff by introducing modules in a gradual fashion. For example, a library might implement cataloguing or acquisitions functions first, and circulation latter. This strategy has some advantages. Successful implementation of one module should increase staff willingness to use another. Also, management can deal with the staff in smaller groups, concentrating on the area currently being automated, instead of dealing with all areas at once. The chief drawback of this strategy is found when the current system is already well integrated.

In this case, phased implementation may mean that user's are initially presented with a system that has fewer features than their previous system. There may also be technical difficulties that preclude phased implementation, as the two systems are not likely to communicate with each other well, if at all. Where it is usable, this strategy should also be combined with other strategies. Saunders specifically emphasises the importance of training and communication issues.

PARTICIPANT-ORIENTED CHANGE

Zeffane advocates the strategy of participant-oriented change, which is based on the premise that change works best when comes from the bottom up rather than from the top down. One reason for this premise is that if the employees introduce change, then they will not have an authority figure to rebel against. It is also based on the idea that collegial affiliation is a positive motivation for change. That is, employees will be more motivated to help with a changes initiated by someone at, or close to, their level. To use participant oriented change, management needs to shift the responsibility for change away from themselves and towards the employees.

This strategy goes beyond considering the users' needs, or soliciting input, to actually delegating authority to the participants. This strategy takes advantage of the fact that the employees who are closest to the hands-on work have the most detailed knowledge about it. This also frees the upper management from concentrating on this level of detail, and to concentrate on overall strategic planning. This strategy may not be effective in all types of organisations.

There are some essential elements for participative strategies to work. First, the employees given responsibilities for change must be well informed. Second, the employees must understand and agree with the mission of the organisation. Unless these requirements are met, management cannot expect that the decisions will be beneficial to the organisation. The third requirement is that this style of change must be supported by the organisation culture. The management must be comfortable with this type of delegation.

4

Serials Cataloguing

A library catalogue (or library catalogue) is a register of all bibliographic items found in a library or group of libraries, such as a network of libraries at several locations.

A bibliographic item can be any information entity (*e.g.*, books, computer files, graphics, realia, cartographic materials, etc.) that is considered library material (*e.g.*, a single novel in an anthology), or a group of library materials (*e.g.*, a trilogy), or linked from the catalogue (*e.g.*, a webpage) as far as it is relevant to the catalogue and to the users (patrons) of the library.

The card catalogue was a familiar sight to library users for generations, but it has been effectively replaced by the online public access catalogue (OPAC). Some still refer to the online catalogue as a "card catalogue". Some libraries with OPAC access still have card catalogues on site, but these are now strictly a secondary resource and are seldom updated.

Many of the libraries that have retained their physical card catalogue post a sign advising the last year that the card catalogue was updated. Some libraries have eliminated their card catalogue in favour of the OPAC for the purpose of saving space for other use, such as additional shelving.

GOAL

Charles Ammi Cutter made the first explicit statement regarding the objectives of a bibliographic system in his *Rules for a Printed Dictionary Catalogue* in 1876.

Those objectives were:

- To enable a person to find a book of which either (Identifying objective)
  - The author
  - The title
  - The subject
  - The category
- To show what the library has (Collocating objective)
  - By a given author

  - On a given subject
  - In a given kind of literature
- To assist in the choice of a book (Evaluating objective)
  - As to its edition (bibliographically)
  - As to its character (literary or topical)

These objectives can still be recognized in more modern definitions formulated throughout the 20th century. 1960/61 Cutter's objectives were revised by Lubetzky and the Conference on Cataloguing Principles (CCP) in Paris. The latest attempt to describe a library catalogue's goals and functions was made in 1998 with Functional Requirements for Bibliographic Records (FRBR) which defines four user tasks: find, identify, select, and obtain.

TYPES

Traditionally, there are the following types of catalogue:

- *Author Catalogue:* A formal catalogue, sorted alphabe-tically according to the authors' or editors' names of the entries.
- *Title Catalogue:* A formal catalogue, sorted alphabe-tically according to the title of the entries.
- *Dictionary Catalogue*: A catalogue in which all entries (author, title, subject, series) are interfiled in a single alphabetical order. This was the primary form of card catalogue in North American libraries just prior to the introduction of the computer-based catalogue.
- *Keyword Catalogue:* A subject catalogue, sorted alphabetically according to some system of keywords.
- *Mixed Alphabetic Catalogue Forms:* Sometimes, one finds a mixed author/title, or an author/title/keyword catalogue.
- *Systematic Catalogue:* A subject catalogue, sorted according to some systematic subdivision of subjects. Also called a *Classified* catalogue.
- *Shelf List Catalogue:* A formal catalogue with entries sorted in the same order as bibliographic items are shelved. This catalogue may also serve as the primary inventory for the library.

HISTORY

Library catalogues originated as manuscript lists, arranged by format (folio, quarto, etc.) or in a rough alphabetical arrangement by author. Printed catalogues, sometimes called *dictionary catalogues*, began to be published in the early modern period and enabled scholars outside a library to gain an idea of its contents. Copies of these in the library itself would sometimes be interleaved with blank leaves on which additions could be recorded, or bound as *guardbooks* in which slips of paper were bound in for new entries.

Slips could also be kept loose in cardboard or tin boxes, stored on shelves. The first card catalogues appeared in the late 19th century after the standardization of the 5 in. x 3 in. card for personal filing systems, enabling much more flexibility, and towards the end of the 20th century the Online public access catalogue was developed.

These gradually became more common as some libraries progressively abandoned such other catalogue formats as paper slips (either loose or in sheaf catalogue form), and guardbooks. The beginning of the Library of Congress's catalogue card service in 1911 led to the use of these cards in the majority of American libraries. An equivalent scheme in the United Kingdom was operated by the British National Bibliography from 1956 and was subscribed to by many public and other libraries.

- *C. 245 BC:* Callimachus is considered the first bibliographer and is the one that organized the library by authors and subjects. The *Pinakes* was the first ever library catalogue. Variations on this system were used in libraries until the late 1800s when Melvil Dewey developed the Dewey Decimal Classification in 1876, which is still in use today.
- *C. 800:* Library catalogues are introduced in the House of Wisdom and other medieval Islamic libraries where books are organized into specific genres and categories.
- *1595: Nomenclator* of Leiden University Library appears, the first printed catalogue of an institutional library.
- *1674:* Thomas Hyde's catalogue for the Bodleian Library.
- *1791:* The French Cataloguing Code of 1791

More about the early history of library catalogues has been collected in 1956 by Strout.

SORTING

In a title catalogue, one can distinguish two sort orders:

1. In the *grammatical* sort order (used mainly in older catalogues), the most important word of the title is the first sort term. The importance of a word is measured by grammatical rules. for example, the first noun may be defined to be the most important word.
2. In the *mechanical* sort order, the first word of the title is the first sort term. Most new catalogues use this scheme, but still include a trace of the grammatical sort order: they neglect an article (The, A, etc.) at the beginning of the title.

The grammatical sort order has the advantage that often, the most important word of the title is also a good keyword, and it is the word most users remember first when their memory is incomplete.

However, it has the disadvantage that many elaborate grammatical rules are needed, so that only expert users may be able to search the catalogue without help from a librarian.

In some catalogues, person's names are standardized, i. e., the name of the person is always sorted in a standard form, even if it appears differently in the library material. This standardization is achieved by a process called authority control. An advantage of the authority control is that it is easier to answer question (which works of some author does the library have?). On the other hand, it may be more difficult to answer question (does the library have some specific material?) if the material spells the author in a peculiar variant. For the cataloguer, it may incur (too) much work to check whether *Smith, J.* is *Smith, John* or *Smith, Jack*.

For some works, even the title can be standardized. The technical term for this is *uniform title*. For example, translations and re-editions are sometimes sorted under their original title. In many catalogues, parts of the Bible are sorted under the standard name of the book(s) they contain. The plays of William Shake-speare are another frequently cited example of the role played by a *uniform title* in the library catalogue. Many complica-tions about alphabetic sorting of entries arise.

Some examples:

- Some languages know sorting conventions that differ from the language of the catalogue. For example, some Dutch catalogues sort *IJ* as *Y*. Should an English catalogue follow this suit? And should a Dutch catalogue sort non-Dutch words the same way?
- *Some Titles Contain Numbers, For Example 2001:* A Space Odyssey. Should they be sorted as numbers, or spelled out as *Two thousand and one*?
- *De Balzac, Honouré* or *Balzac, Honouré de*? *Ortega y Gasset, José* or *Gasset, José Ortega y*?

In a subject catalogue, one has to decide on which classification system to use. The cataloguer will select appropriate subject headings for the bibliographic item and a unique classification number (sometimes known as a "call number") which is used not only for identification but also for the purposes of shelving, placing items with similar subjects near one another, which aids in browsing by library users, who are thus often able to take advantage of serendipity in their search process.

ONLINE CATALOGUES

Online cataloguing has greatly enhanced the usability of catalogues, thanks to the rise of MAchine Readable Cataloguing = MARC standards in the 1960s. Rules governing the creation of catalogue MARC records include not only formal cataloguing rules like AACR2 but also special rules specific to MARC, available from the Library of Congress and also OCLC. MARC was originally used to automate the creation of physical catalogue cards. Now the MARC computer files are accessed directly in the search process.

OPACs have enhanced usability over traditional card formats because:

- The online catalogue does not need to be sorted statically. The user can choose author, title, keyword, or systematic order dynamically.
- Most online catalogues offer a search facility for any word of the title. The goal of the grammatic word order (provide an entry on the word that most users would look for) is reached even better.
- Many online catalogues allow links between several variants of an author name. So, authors can be found both under the original and the standardised name (if entered properly by the cataloguer).
- The elimination of paper cards has made the information more accessible to many people with disabilities, such as the visually impaired, wheelchair users, and those who suffer from mold allergies.

WHAT IS WRONG WITH THE LIBRARY CATALOGUE

Problems for the online library catalogue did not begin with the advent, quick development or broad adoption of the web. For more than 20 years, the library catalogue has been criticised for its difficult use and poor functionality. Despite a number of studies and papers suggesting ideas for improving library catalogues, changes have been slow and many of the ideas have not been implemented.

Most of the changes have been made on surface rather than in the core functionality, leaving library catalogues hard to use. Studies show that besides falling behind the trends on the web, the most problematic area is the catalogue's interface, lacking in functionality, intuitivity, and content.

Traditional library catalogues are poorly designed for the tasks of finding, discovering and selecting resources available in libraries. They are best at locating and obtaining known items, so the user must know precisely what he/she wants. But this emphasis on know-item searching does not follow the actual user behaviour and mental models in information retrieval.

Information retrieval process often begins with only a vague idea, which is then gradually formulated sufficiently to begin searching. Besides that, query formulation is difficult as the user needs to have the conceptual knowledge of how the terms can be combined and is required to use the terms that match those in the catalogue.

Boolean logic in query formulation is hard for the user to comprehend and research shows that there is in fact only minimal usage of Boolean operators. Due to the common use of the web, users are accustomed to naturallanguage searching and simply type multiple search terms (keywords) on a single line without connecting them with Boolean operators. They also build queries using only terms they have in mind, without consulting the controlled vocabulary the library uses, all leading to poor results.

That is why many think that a better alternative to query formulation would be searching by browsing, recognition and discovery. Browsing is recognized as a natural and effective way of searching that requires less effort and knowledge. It is also easier for the user to recognize than recall information.

As Bates points out "information seeking is, after all, about finding out things that one does not know before the search begins". These are all reasons for turning the traditional paradigm "query-first-then browse" upside down, making the exploration and discovery by browsing the primary search interface, supported by secondary query method.

The second problematic area in library catalogues is the results list and navigation between results. Queries often return hundreds or thousands of hits, but users are willing to look at only a very limited number. Web search engines have therefore developed very sophisticated systems for relevance ranking of results.

Accustomed to get the most relevant results first, users are confused when in library catalogues irrelevant records appear before items they were looking for. With a large number of search results it is also very time-consuming to look at every hit in order to decide whether it is relevant or not. To enable easier and faster selection, result clustering and faceted navigation should be applied to quickly narrow and filter the results to a manageable number.

One possibility for meaningful clustering of results is also the use of Functional Requirements for Bibliographic Records (FRBR). The third most frequent reproach against the library catalogue is the lack of information presented to the user. Most records in the library catalogue display only basic textual bibliographic data.

To improve the user experience, the library catalogue needs to be enriched with cover art images, tables of contents, summaries, reviews, excerpts, popularity ranks, recommen-dation lists and features such as "find similar" or "users who borrowed this book also borrowed...". These are all things already available on some other web destinations, especially online bookshops. They offer users all this additional information in order to promote their collection and to help users choose the items they need.

PURPOSE OF CATALOGUING LIBRARY MATERIALS

Library collections house a wide variety of materials on many different topics and in many different formats. The challenge in making these things available for the use of library patrons is letting those patrons know what is in the library collection. This is the reason for having a library catalogue, and for taking the time to correctly catalogue library materials.

The library catalogue might be compared to the index for a book. The index provides the reader with a way to find information in the book without having to read every page. The index tells the reader the page on which the information about a specific subject can be found. The library catalogue does the same thing. It tells the library user exactly where materials meeting their specific needs can be found, with the call number of the book corresponding to the page number in an index. The information contained in the cataloguing record provides the many access points needed by the patron looking for information in the library. Traditionally, the library card catalogue provided access by the author's name, the title of an item, and the subject(s) covered in the item.

Other points of access were additional authors, names of series, illustrators, and sometimes the titles of contents. Computer catalogs can, in theory, provide access to any part of the information contained in the record for an item in the library. The development of MARC (Machine Readable Cataloguing) in the 1960's made it possible to encode all areas of a cataloguing record to be searchable. In MARC cataloguing, each piece of information in a catalogue record is given a numerical code, or field, and sometimes an alphabetical or numerical sub field. This coding makes it possible for a computer programme to be written that looks for particular numbered fields when a particular type of search, such as a subject or title, is requested.

Because all of the information in the cataloguing record is encoded, searches could optionally be done by ISBN number, by series, by publisher, by date or by any of the pieces of information stored in the cataloguing record. MARC has set the standard for all computer catalogs used in libraries today, and if the records contained in the catalogue comply with MARC requirements, the only controls on areas to be searched are the limits of the particular cataloguing programme.

When library materials are catalogued in a careful and complete manner, access is provided for the library patrons and staff to all sources of information on a particular topic, by a particular author, or in a particular format, that the library possesses. The better the access, the more use the collection receives, and the more satisfied the patron is in his or her search for information in the library.

TECHNICAL PROCESSING SERVICES

AACR2 defines a catalogue as:

- A list of library materials contained in a collection, a library, or group of libraries, organized according to some definite plan.

Obviously, cataloguing, or bibliographic control, is the process of preparing such a list. The catalogue consists of a description of each item, which is retrievable by several of its important characteristics used as headings, or access points: the author, title or subject matter. In a manual system, there are several copies of each description which are filed under the appropriate access points for the respective item. But in an automated system there is only one copy of the description which can be displayed using any access point for searching. The description is now called bibliographic record or just record.

Preparing and maintaining a catalogue require:

- Intellectual activity for the cataloguing process based on selected standards and rules, or for locating and using bibliographic records created externally.
- Choice of an overall organization of records within the catalogue and their specific filing sequence.
- Choice of the physical form(s) for the catalogue and the production of records in that form.
- Developing procedures for adding new records and modifying existing ones.

CATALOGUING PROCESS

Descriptive Cataloguing

This embraces the description of the bibliographic or physical significance of the item except its subject content. The cataloguer also decides here which bibliographic elements should be used as access points for the item in the catalogue and determines the appropriate form of access points used. The description normally has many different elements arranged in standard formats.

The rules that should be followed for descriptive cataloguing in a medical library are the Anglo-American Cataloguing Rules, second edition (AACR2) and its revisions.

As these rules are more or less the most used rules internationally in both manual and automated systems, using them will enable the user to see the same descriptive record format in any library he may use, and enable the library to use records produced in other libraries.

Defining the Subject Content

This is normally done using two types of tools which produce a subject description in a coded form or in the language(s) used in the catalogue, which is the only difference between using them, otherwise the processes are identical. The two processes are:

- *Classification*: Classification, through the notation of the classification scheme used, decides the general area in the collection where the item will be shelved. Most classification schemes lead to an arrangement of items based on their subject content. This allows the user to browse the shelves. Normally, a more specific shelving number or symbol must be added after the class number to give the item a unique place among other items in the same class. The resulting number is called " call number ".

- Standardization in classification, contrary to descriptive cataloguing, has not yet been achieved internationally. The library may choose a generalized scheme or a specialized one.

The general schemes most widely used in medical libraries are:

- Dewey Decimal Classification (DDC), which is now in its 21st edition and the second on CD-ROM.
- Library of Congress Classification (LCC), which is continuously subjected to revision.
- Universal Decimal Classification (UDC), which is widely used in Europe.
- Among the specialized schemes the most widely used one in medical libraries is NLM Classification.
- *Subject Cataloguing or Indexing.* The problem of this process is that it is language dependent and thus no standardization can possibly be achieved.

The process depends on two types of tools:

- *Lists of subject headings:* These may be general or specialized. Among the general ones, the most widely used list is Library of Congress List of Subject Headings (LCSH), while Medical Subject Headings (MeSH) is the most widely used list by medical libraries. It is now available in many languages.
- *Thesauri:* These are more recent than lists of subject headings and are more associated with automated in libraries. Most thesauri are specialized in their nature.

The choice between lists and subject headings and thesauri is mostly dictated by the indexing method, whether it is pre-coordinated or post-coordinated, as the former favours the lists while the latter adopts thesauri. Automated has introduced yet another way of indexing using free text search or selecting keywords as access points. Cataloguing may involve original cataloguing, that is the creation of cataloguing records in the library from scratch, or using existing records elsewhere which is known as copy cataloguing.

This may be carried out manually or automated. The sources for copy cataloguing may be:

- *Cataloguing-In-Publication (CIP)*: The data in CIP is created on the basis of prepublication galley proofs or preproduction information for the item. This data is usually given on the verso of the title page. CIP data has to be handled with care and should be compared carefully with the item itself when it is used as the basis for a cataloguing record, as it may have erroneous elements or is not in conformance with standards and rules adopted by the library.
- *Published Bibliographies*: Whether these bibliographies are catalogues of library holdings or published bibliographies, such as national bibliographies, they may be used for creating cataloguing records.

- *Machine-readable Records on Tape*: Some major libraries, such as NLM, may distribute their records on tapes in MARC format. The subscribing library may get such tapes, then use local computer system to select the records needed for the local catalogue. This approach requires significant local hardware and software. Recent development for this is the use of CD-ROM instead of tapes which is cost-effective.
- *Online Services*: Some files simply offer copies of cataloguing records, other online services allow user libraries to modify or create cataloguing records in a variety of formats for incorporation into their local catalogues. Among these are OCLC, RLIN, WLN, UTLAS, and BCMP. NLM has three online files with cataloguing data: CATLINE (Catalogue-on-line) for printed materials, AVLINE (Audiovisualson-line) for audiovisuals since 1975, and NAF (Name Authority File) for name and series authority records.
- *Service Bureaus*: Several agencies and companies in some countries produce catalogue cards or other catalogue formats on demand. The cataloguing copy is provided in a form that is immediately usable in a local catalogue.
- *Book Suppliers*: Some book suppliers provide catalogue records (cards or otherwise) with the books they ship to their library customers.

Regardless of the source of the cataloguing copy, individual libraries may modify or augment cataloguing records they find in order to make them more useful in local catalogues.

Among such amendments the following are necessary:

- If the copy has subject headings and/or classification which the library does not use.
- If the edition of cataloguing rules used for the copy is different from the one applied by the library.
- If the library may wish to add further access points and explanatory notes to records to emphasize some local interest.

But if the cataloguer comes across an error in an access point or in another part of a cataloguing record, he should write to the appropriate institution and ask for clarification.

Other kinds of modifications are probably unnecessary, such as:

- Eliminating data to simplify records.
- Deleting data that the library feels does not assist users very much, such as ISBN or ISSN.

ORGANIZATION OF THE CATALOGUE

In a manual system, most library catalogues are divided into at least two parts:

Shelflist

The shelflist contains one record for each item in the collection. It is usually arranged by call number in exactly the same order of items on the shelf. It is useful for assigning individual shelving numbers, in making an inventory of the collection, provided it is annotated when the library has multiple copies in the same order. This shelflist may not be available for serials when they are not classified. A list of serials may replace it.

Main Catalogue

The main catalogue contains several copies of the record for each item in the collection. A copy of each record is entered: under the author's name, the names of any of the other persons or corporate bodies associated with the work described, its title, its series title, and various subject headings. It also includes cross-references, guiding users from unused forms of names and subject headings to those that have been used.

Many catalogues may also include guide or special heading to enable a user to determine quickly where in the overall sequence of records a particular catalogue file drawer, page of book catalogue, or part of a microform catalogue is located.

DICTIONARY VERSUS DIVIDED CATALOGUE

There are three major arrangements for manual main catalogues:

- *Dictionary catalogue*, in which author, title and subject access points are interfiled.
- *Divided catalogue*, in which subject access points are arranged in a separate sequence from author and title sequence. Some libraries divide even author and title access points as well.
- *Classified catalogue,* in which the call numbers serve as subject access points and are in a separate sequence from author and title access points. This arrangement usually requires a language subject index to class numbers used in the catalogue, although some libraries may be satisfied with the published index of the classification scheme used.

In an online catalogue there will be no need for such arrangements although the automated systems produce any arrangement as a by-product.

AUTHORITY FILES

The authority file is the file that contains the forms of names (of persons, corporate bodies or places), title, series, or subject headings and descriptors used in the bibliographic record, as well the required cross-references to and from these forms, and their relationship with other used forms.

Authority records may be interfiled in the main catalogue, or may be kept in separate authority files, in a manual system. They must be accessible to cataloguing staff. In automated system, they are usually separate from the bibliographic records database but transparently interlinked with the number or symbol of the authority record.

The following is a brief description of the types of authority files:

- Name Authorities: A name authority record consists of:
  - The authoritative name form chosen for use in the catalogue.
  - Alternate forms of the name, and an indication as to whether cross-references from these forms are maintained in the catalogue.
  - Any related names such as previous names of an institution.
  - Source of the authoritative name.
  - Any historical or biographical information about the name necessary to distinguish it from another name.
  - An indication as to which set of cataloguing rules was used to establish the authoritative form.

Name authorities may be imported from cooperative ventures or from major libraries that have such files, such as NLM. They may be initiated also on cooperative basis particularly among libraries with a common language such as Arabic, because the forms of names may differ among the speakers of that language, and the library in the respective country is the best to verify them. With automated systems, it may be easier to use as a search tool as well if the file is constructed in a thesaurus form.

These systems and the thesaurus structure will enable making the file multilingual.

- *Title Authorities*: These files will be particularly useful if the library uses uniform titles in its catalogue, or when variant titles exist among various editions of the same work.
- *Series Authorities*: A series authority record is required only for a monographic series, where individual works bear individual title and authorship information, in addition to an overall series title. This file should record the decision on how to handle series.
- *Subject Authorities*: The library may consider the list of subject headings or the thesaurus it applies as a subject authority, or restrict the file to the subject headings or descriptors it actually uses. This latter type has been eliminated when an automated system is used as it is going to do both purposes.

Catalogues of Special Collections

Some libraries maintain separate catalogue for special types of materials, such as audiovisuals, in addition to their inclusion in the main catalogue. In automated systems, such catalogues may be produced as by-product from the bibliographic database.

Filing Rules

Records in main catalogue in a manual system must be filed alphabetically according to standard filing rules, while those in the shelflist according to the filing order of the classification scheme in use. In an automated system, the system itself contains filing values for the elements of description that are considered in filing. These values are in fact interpretation of the filing rules adopted. As filing is always language dependent, the rules must cope with all languages represented in the catalogue, whether the characters are in roman or non-roman alphabets.

The major existing filing rules are:

- ALA filing rules/Filing committee, Resources and Technical Services Division, American Library Association. Chicago: ALA, 1980.
- Blaise filing rules/British Library Filing Rules Committee. London: British Library, 1980.
- BS 1749: 1985-British standard recommendations for alphabetical arrangement and filing order of numbers and symbols. London: BSI, 1985.
- ISO 7154-ISO bibliographic filing rules. Geneva: ISO, 1985. and ISO/TR 8393-1985, Exemplification of bibliographic filing principles in a model set of rules. Geneva: ISO, 1985.
- Library of Congress filing rules/prepared by John C. Rather and Susan C. Biebel. Washington, DC: Library of Congress, 1980.

The set of filing rules for Arab libraries discusses the agreement and disagreement of these filing rules and those used in some major libraries in the Arab region as well as standard rules for the region:

- ARIS-Net filing rules for catalogues, bibliographies and directories. Tunis: ALDOC, 1989.

The basic principles behind all these rules are:

- Filing is word by word rather than letter by letter.
- Filing must be strictly as is rather than as if which means that the word is filed as written not as it sounds or means, whether written in full or abbreviated form.
- A numeral files before the alphabet.
- Order of characters must be strictly adhered to.

This order is as follows:

  - Space, dash, hyphen and diagonal slash are given equal filing character and come first
  - Ampersand
  - Arabic numerals
  - Alphabet letters

- Different forms of the same letter have equal value and must be interfiled.

- All records in the same catalogue must be filed according to the same principles-the same rules.

PHYSICAL FORMS OF CATALOGUES

Card Catalogues

This form is still prevalent in medical libraries. It can include all records regardless of their source. Records are on cards which file into drawers housed in cabinets. Standards are 12.5 x 7.5 cm. Rods may be inserted through holes in the bottom of the cards to help retain them in drawers.

Sheaf Catalogues

A loose-leaf binder format providing some of the convenience of the book. Usually each record is on a separate slip of paper. There may be a number of records on each slip.

Visible Index

This form consists of strips mounted in a frame, or cards held flat, hinged, and with the edge of each card protruding to make the heading visible. This form is used for displaying the list of serials holdings of a library.

Microform Catalogues

This is a form in which records are greatly reduced and "printed" upon a film. So a suitable reader which magnifies the film and project it on to a screen is required. It may be a microfilm or a microfiche.

Machine-readable Catalogues

This is a form which permits input and storage for manipulation in a computer. Access may be online or offline. Data are displayed on a screen or visual display, and may also be output to magnetic tape, disk or printed in hard copy. An offshot of the machine-readable form is the CD-ROM. Another is the computer output microform (COM). But the form which facilitates continuous updating, with amended records being available to the user as soon as they are input, is the online public access catalogue (OPAC). It can be accessed from outside the library through remote terminals.

Finally, the form the library decides to choose should possess as many as possible of the following:

- It must be easy to use.
- It must be easy to keep uptodate.
- It must be easy to scan.
- It must be easy to produce multiple copies.
- It must take up as little space as possible.
- It must be easy to guide.

DESCRIPTIVE CATALOGUING

International Efforts

The major contribution in cataloguing at the international level is that of IFLA. This is in the form of international standard bibliographic descriptions (ISBDs) which have influenced almost all existing cataloguing rules.

IFLA has so far issued the following ISBDs and is continuously subjecting them to revision:

- ISBD (G)-General
- ISBD (M)-Monographs
- ISBD (NBM)-Non-book Materials
- ISBD (CM)-Cartographic Materials
- ISBD (A)-Antiquarian Books
- ISBD (PM)-Printed Music
- ISBD (S)-Serials
- ISBD (CF)-Computer file, Machine-Readable files (MRF)
- ISBD (CP)-Component parts
- ISBD (ER)-Electronic Resources (replaced ISBD (CF)

Other international efforts include those of Unesco particularly the creation of the International Serials Data System (ISDS). ISDS seeks to develop a registry of world serials publications. containing sufficient bibliographic information for their identification and bibliographic control.

The cornerstones of ISDS are the ISSN and a corresponding "key title", to which geographic qualifiers may be included in parentheses at the end of the title when necessary to make the key title unique.

Another international organization is the International Standardization Organization (ISO) which is responsible for many relevant international standards, in addition to those previously cited on filing rules:

- ISO 690, Bibliographic references: contents, form and structure.
- ISO 9115, Bibliographic identification (biblid) of contributions in serials and books.
- ISO 2108, International standard book numbering (ISBN).
- ISO 3297, International standard serial numbering (ISSN).
- ISO 3901, International standard recording code (ISRC).
- ISO 2709, Format for bibliographic information interchange on magnetic tape.
- ISO 10444, International standard technical report number (ISRN).

AACR2

AACR2 incorporates the ISBD system aiming at eliminating inconsistency in the descriptive treatment of various types of materials. It allows local cataloguers to choose among three levels or degrees of detail in constructing descriptive cataloguing data and also includes some optional rules. This flexibility improves the utility of the rules by a wide range of sizes and types of libraries.

Levels of Description

Rule 1.OD of AACR2 specifies these levels as follows:

- *First level:* Title proper/first statement of responsibility if different from main entry in form or number or if there is no main heading.—Edition statement.—Material (or type of publication) specific details.—First publisher, etc., date of publication, etc.—Extent of item.—Note(s).—Standard number.
- *Second Level:* Title proper [general material designation] = Parallel title: other title information/first statement of responsibility.—Edition statement/first statement of re-sponsibility relating to the edition.—Material (or type of publication) specific details.—First place of publication, etc: first publisher, etc, date of publication, etc.—Extent of item: other physical details. dimensions.—(Title pro-per of series/ statement of responsibility relating to series, ISSN of series. numbering within the series. Title of subseries. ISSN of subseries. numbering within subseries).—Note(s).—Standard number.
- *Third Level*: All the elements set out in the rules that are applicable to the item being described.

The information stated here is considered the minimum to be given by the cataloguer, as he may add additional elements in the first two levels. Moreover, the cataloguer may use different levels for different materials. if he does he must be consistent. It is noted that a punctuation pattern is used, which is very important element in bibliographic standardization. This pattern is defined for every element of description.

Areas of Description

The description is divided in both AACR2 and ISBDs into eight areas or fields.

They are as follows:

- *Area 1:* Title and Statement of Responsibility Area
  - 1.1 Title proper
  - 1.2 General material designation
  - 1.3 Parallel title(s)
  - 1.4 Other title information
  - 1.5 Statement(s) of responsibility
- *Area 2:* Edition Area
  - 2.1 Edition statement
  - 2.2 Parallel edition statement(s)
  - 2.3 Statement(s) of responsibility relating to the edition

  - 2.4 Statement relating to a named revision of an edition
  - 2.5 Statement(s) of responsibility relating to a named revision of an edition
- *Area 3:* Material (or Type of publication) Specific Details area (Used only for cartographic materials, printed music, computer files, and serials).
- *Area 4:* Publication, production, Distribution, etc, Area.
  - 4.1 Place(s) of publication, distribution, etc.
  - 4.2 Name(s) of publisher, distributor, etc.
  - 4.3 Date of publication, distribution, etc.
  - 4.4 Place of manufacture
  - 4.5 Name of manufacturer
  - 4.6 Date of manufacture
- *Area 5:* Physical Description Area
  - 5.1 Specific material designation and extent of item
  - 5.2 Other physical details
  - 5.3 Dimensions
  - 5.4 Identification of accompanying material
- *Area 6:* Series Area
  - 6.1 Title proper of the series
  - 6.2 Parallel title(s) of the series
  - 6.3 Other title information of the series
  - 6.4 Statement(s) of responsibility relating to the series
  - 6.5 International Standard Serial Number (ISSN) of the series
  - 6.6 Numbering within the series
  - 6.7 Enumeration and/or title of subseries
  - 6.8-The same as for 6.2 through 6.6 for subseries
  - 6.12
- *Area 7:* Note(s) Area (repeatable, each note being a separate area)
- *Area 8:* Standard Number, etc Area (a repeatable area)
  - 8.1 Standard number: ISBN, ISSN, ISRC etc.
  - 8.2 Key-title (associated only with an ISSN)
  - 8.3 Terms of availability and/or price
  - 8.4 Qualification(s) following 8.1 and/or 8.3

Access Points (Headings) and References

AACR2 is of two parts: The first covers descriptions as stated before and consists of (13) chapters where the first covers all types of materials, and chapters 2-12 cover a certain type each, while chapter 13 concerns analytical cataloguing. The second part starts with chapter 20 which is an explanation of the rules of this part, while no chapters 14-19 exist.

Chapter 21 covers the choice of access points, chapter 22 deals with headings for persons, chapter 23 deals with headings for geographic names, chapter 24 deals with headings for corporate bodies, chapter 25 deals with uniform titles, while chapter 26 collects together the various rules for references.

The rules are completed by four appendices:

1. *A:* Capitalization
2. *B:* Abbreviations
3. *C:* Numerals
4. *D:* Glossary

Numerous handbooks and illustrations have been published in different languages, as well as in the local formats adopted such as CEHANET procedures manual.

SUBJECT ANALYSIS

CLASSIFICATION

Classification is basically grouping similar objects or ideas together. This grouping is done through the notations assigned as class numbers from the classification scheme adopted. There are three major general classification schemes that may be encountered in some medical libraries.

Library of Congress Classification (LCC)

This is a general enumerative scheme consisting of 21 classes in individual schemes, although they are now available on CD-ROM as well. The main classes and subclasses are designated by capital letters. Further subdivision is by integral numbers ranging from 1 to 9999, which may be extended decimally.

The classes of this classification that concern medical libraries are:

- *GN:* Anthropology
- *HN:* Social History and Reform
- *QR*: Bacteriology
- *TC:* Hydrology
- *TD:* Sanitary and Municipal Engineering
- *TH*: Building construction
- *TX:* Domestic Sciences

Note here that medicine is assigned class R which is not recommended for medical libraries.

This class is subdivided as follows:

- *R:* Medicine in General
- *RA:* Government Medicine and Public Health
- *RB:* Pathology
- *RC:* Practice of Medicine

- *RD:* Surgery
- *RE:* Ophthalmology
- *RF:* Otorhinolaryngology
- *RG:* Gynecology and Obstetrics
- *RJ:* Paediatrics
- *RK:* Dentistry
- *RL:* Dermatology
- *RM:* Therapeutics
- *RS:* Pharmacy
- *RT:* Nursing
- *RV:* Herbalism
- *RX:* Homeotherapy
- *RZ:* Various Schools and Arts

The LCC uses auxiliary tables for individual classes, but not for the scheme as a whole. There are five types of these tables: form, geographic, historical, topical and mixed.

Dewey Decimal Classification (DCC)

Knowledge in this scheme is divided into ten major classes using arabic numerals 0-9 provided that the number is of three digits. After this base number numbers may be expanded decimally.

Medical sciences are placed in the main class 600-Technology as follows:

- *610:* Medical Sciences Medicine
- *611:* Human Anatomy, Cytology, Histology
- *612:* Human Physiology
- *613:* Hygiene
- *614:* Forensic Medicine, Disease Incidence, General Preventive Medicine
- *615:* Pharmacology
- *616:* Diseases
- *617:* Various Medicine Branches. Surgery
- *618:* Other Medicine Branches. Gynecology and Obstetrics
- *619:* Experimental Medicine

In addition, there is a large number of class numbers relevant to health sciences, among which are:

- *334:* Social Law, Social welfare, Labour, Health, Safety, Education and Culture Law
- *363:* Social Issues and Services
- *574:* Biology
- *628:* Sanitary and Municipal Engineering, Environ-mental Protection Engineering

- *632:* Plant Injuries, Diseases, Pests
- *636:* Veterinary Medicine

The scheme has seven auxiliary tables for using with the various class numbers as instructed in the schedules. The scheme is now in its twenty-first edition in four volumes, of which the fourth volume is an alphabetical relative index and a manual. It is also on CD-ROM.

Universal Decimal Classification

This scheme is originally based on DDC but deviated from it in many aspects particularly the obligation of using the three digits base numbers. But the major classes are nearly the same except for cancelling class 4 to be combined with class 8.

Medical sciences have 61 and its subdivisions are as follows:

- *61:* Medical Sciences (Medicine)
- *611:* Anatomy. Human and Comparative Anatomy
- *612:* Physiology. Human and Comparative Physiology
- *613:* Hygiene in General. Personal Health and Hygiene
- *614:* Public Health and Hygiene. Accident Prevention
- *615:* Pharmacology. Therapeutics. Toxicology
- *616:* Pathology. Clinical Medicine
- *617:* Surgery. Orthopaedics. Ophthalmology
- *618:* Gynecology. Obstetrics
- *619:* Domesticated Animal Diseases. Veterinary Medicine

Class numbers related to health sciences are also scattered in nearly the same way as DDC. The scheme also uses ten auxiliary tables. The latest medium English edition was published in 1993, and its amendments in 1996. It is also on CD-ROM.

NLM Classification

This scheme covers medicine and other related sciences using the classes QS-QZ and W-WZ permanently excluded in LCC. So, LCC may be considered supplementary to this scheme for classifying other disciplines, except QM (human anatomy), QR (microbiology) and R (medicine) in LCC which cannot be used in this scheme.

The classes are subdivided as follows:

- QS-QZ Preclinical Sciences
  - QS Human Anatomy
  - QT Physiology
  - QU Biochemistry
  - QV Pharmacology

  - QW Microbiology and Immunology
  - QX Parasitology
  - QY Clinical Pathology
  - QZ Pathology
- W-WZ Medicine and Related Subjects
  - W Health Professions
  - WA Public Health
  - WB Practice of Medicine
  - WC Communicable Diseases
  - WD100 Nutrition Disorders
  - WD200 Metabolic Diseases
  - WD300 Immunologic and Collagen Diseases. Hypersensitivity
  - WD400 Animal Poisons
  - WD500 Plant Poisons
  - WD600 Diseases and Injuries caused by Physical Agents
  - WD700 Aviation and Space Medicine
  - WE Musculoskeletal System
  - WF Rispiratory System
  - WG Cardiovascular System
  - WH Hemic and Lymphatic System
  - WI Digestive System
  - WJ Urogenital System
  - WK Endocrine System
  - WL Nervous System
  - WM Psychiatry
  - WN Radiology. Diagnostic Imaging
  - WO Surgery
  - WP Gynecology
  - WQ Obstetrics
  - WR Dermatology
  - WS Paediatrics
  - WT Geriatrics. Chronic Disease
  - WU Dentistry. Oral Surgery
  - WV Otorhinolaryngology
  - WW Ophthalmology
  - WX Hospitals and Other Health Facilities
  - WY Nursing
  - WZ History of Medicine

In addition the scheme has two types of auxiliary tables, the first covers form subdivisions which are listed under main class numbers, and the other is list (G) which is common to all schedules and covers the geographic subdivision. This list divides the world into nine geographic regions, and one notation for international organizations that publish materials related to medicine.

It has an alphabetical relative index, which uses terms derived from Medical Subject Headings (MeSH), and includes subjects outside the scope of the scheme and have LCC numbers. The scheme is now in its fifth edition.

CONTROLLED VOCABULARY

There are two types of tools for controlling vocabulary to be used in subject cataloguing and indexing:

- Lists of Subject Headings; and
- Library of Congress Subject Headings (LCSH)

This is the largest list of subject headings in English. It is a general list originally constructed for the use of the Library of Congress. Now it is published annually, as well as quarterly on CD-ROM under the title: CDMARC subjects.

Recent development include:

- The use of accepted abbreviations such as BT and NT, generally used in thesauri.
- Eliminating inverted forms of subject headings gradually.

Gradual elimination of subject headings that have the conjunction " and " or qualifiers.

The list has four types of subdivision:

- Topical subdivision
- Form subdivision
- Geographic subdivision
- Chronological subdivision

The list is not recommended for medical libraries as it is too general and lacks the subject headings required in health sciences.

Medical Subject Headings (MeSH)

This is the largest list of medical subject headings in English and in other languages to which it has been translated. It is published annually by the NLM, and is used in Medline and in most large medical libraries in the world. It is unique in having the following features that are absent in traditional lists of subject headings:

- Subject headings have classification numbers based on the tree structure of the list. Some headings bear more than ten different numbers each.

The major categories of the tree structure are:

- A Anatomy
- B Organisms
- C Diseases
- D Chemicals and Drugs
- E Analytical, Diagnostic and Therapeutic Techniques and Equipment

- F Psychiatry and Psychology
- G Biological Sciences
- H Physical Sciences
- I Anthropology, Education, Sociology and Social Phenomena
- J Technology, Industry, Agriculture
- K Humanities
- L Information Science
- M Named Groups
- N Health Care
- Z Geographic Locations

Each main category is further subdivided once or more as required using arabic numerals and decimal points:

- The list has an index to the tree structure which is published as a separate volume.
- The list has a KWOC index for the terms used. This feature is used in thersauri.
- The topical, geographical, chronological and form subdivisions are not repeated in the list under the related headings but the notes give instruction on their use.
- *The print edition has the following lists as appendices:*
  - Types of publications. The types are also listed in the main list.
  - Topical subdivisions which are only used with main headings. They are also given in the main list.
  - Form subdivisions for cataloguers with annotations. They are also given in the main list.
  - Geographical locations for cataloguers. They are not given in the main list.
  - Language subdivisions. These are not given in the main list.

Entries of MeSH are of three types:

- Entry of the main heading which typically includes the following information as required:
  - The Heading
  - Consider also cross-reference to other terms
  - Tree number(s)
  - Indexing annotation
  - Cataloguing annotation
  - History note
  - Online note
  - See related
  - X See cross-reference, for entry vocabulary
  - XR See related from other headings
- *Subheading:* This is printed in lower case and preceded by a slash.

The entry includes the following information:
- Subheading
- Indexing annotation
- History note
- Online note

- *Vocabulary Terms:* These include synonyms, near-synonyms, abbreviations, alternative spelling and alternate forms that may be more familiar or easier to type. The entry includes the following information:
  - The vocabulary term
  - The word "see"
  - The main heading preferred
  - The tree number(s) of the main heading

Thesauri

A thesaurus is the vocabulary of a controlled indexing language, formally organized so that the relationships between concepts are made explicit.

Fortunately the establishment and development of thesauri have been handled by ISO:

- ISO 2708, Documentation-Guidelines for the establish-ment and development of monolingual thesauri.
- ISO 5964, Documentation-Guidelines for the establishment and development of multilingual thesauri.
- ISO 5963, Documentation-Methods for examining documents, determining their subject and selecting indexing terms.

These standards, the relationship or function of term or note which follows is expressed by the following abbreviations and symbols:

- *SN:* (Scope note). A note attached to a term to indicate its meaning within an indexing language.
- *USE:* The term that follows the symbol is the preferred term, when a choice between synonyms or quasi-synonyms exists.
- *UF:* (Use for). The term that follows the symbol is a non-preferred synonym or quasi-synonym.
- *TT:* (Top term). The term that follows the symbol is the name of the broadest class to which the specific concept belongs. It is sometimes used in the alphabetical part of a thesaurus.
- *BT:* (Broader term). The term that follows the symbol represents a concept having a wider meaning.
- *NT:* (Narrower term). The term that follows the symbol refers to a concept with a more specific meaning.
- *RT:* (Related term). the term that follows the symbol is associated, but is not a synonym, a quasi-synonym, a broader term or a narrower term.

Although these abbreviations have acquired status as generally recognized conventions, some agencies have developed different symbols such as using ® instead of USE, = instead of UF, < for BT, > for NT and—for RT.

The concepts that are represented by indexing terms may be:

- *Concrete entities:*
  - Things and their physical parts
    a. Limbs
    b. Microforms
  - Materials
    a. Adhesives
    b. Drugs
- *Abstract entities:*
  - Actions and events
    a. Treatment
    b. Marketing
  - Abstract entities, and properties of thing, materials or actions
    a. Elasticity
    b. Speed
  - Disciplines or sciences
    a. Chemistry
    b. Microbiology
  - Units of measurement
    a. Hertz
    b. Kilometers
- Individual entities', or classes-of-one, expressed as proper nouns
  - World Health Organization

The indexing term should preferably consist of a noun or a noun phrase. *The latter occurs in two forms:*

- *Adjective phrase:* Handicapped children
- *Prepositional phrase:* Hospitals for children

UNCONTROLLED VOCABULARY

Uncontrolled, or natural language, words and terms can be of considerable value as subject access points when they come from such sources as the title of a document, cataloguer's note on its bibliographic record, abstract or full text.

Such words are often called keywords. Use of these keywords was made for creating KWIC (Keyword-incontext) and KWOC (keyword-out-of-context) indexes particularly by using the computer. In addition they are used for searching databases particularly those without controlled vocabulary. This requires compiling stop-list to identify those words of natural-language text which the computer programme is not to make accessible in an index, thus marking accessible only those words which are highly significant for retrieval purposes.

But natural language indexing compared to that of controlled vocabulary has some stronger and weaker characteristics:

- *Synonym Control:* Suppose that we consider "renal stone" as the keywords to be searched. We must look into several places if our search is to be fairly comprehensive. We have look under renal calculi, kidney calculi, and kidney stones, as well as their singulars. If the system develops some sort of synonym control then searching will be efficient.
- *Singular and Plural:* The same problem occurs here as in synonym control. This has to be solved through truncation and other devices that enable the retrieval of singulars and plurals.
- *Different Spelling:* An important example is the different spelling in British and American English.
- *Hierarchical Relationships:* Prevalent in controlled vocabulary.
- *Specificity:* This is represented better in natural language indexing than in controlled vocabulary.
- Uptodate Vocabulary. Natural language indexing is always uptodate.
- *Ease:* Natural language is easier to use than controlled vocabulary, if the need is for few articles, but is very hard if the need is for comprehensiveness.
- *Lower Cost:* Natural language is quicker and cheaper for the index producer to develop. There is no need for well-trained indexers.
- *Compound Terms:* The controlled vocabulary takes care of this problem fairly easy. Natural language should have the required capability in the system.
- *Inconsistency of the Indexer:* This is not existing in natural language indexing.

CATALOGUING IN THE INTERNET AND DIGITAL ERA

This chapter explores those issues in greater detail. It begins by describing the motivations underlying the reuse of the term "library" to describe the new digital information research area. As will be described, those motivations reflected the expedient interests of each participant community and their respective definitions of a library.

It next describes the influence of that term on the architectures and applications that were produced by the digital library research programme over the subsequent years.

The chapter continues with an explanation of how the architecture of those digital library applications impacts the technical coexistence of digital libraries with the mainstream web.

Finally, the chapter describes how the evolution of the web from Web 1.0 to Web 2.0 has not only increased the technical incompatibilities between the two information environments, but has led to a fundamental conceptual difference in their infor-mation models.

ORIGINS OF THE "DIGITAL LIBRARY"

The decision in the early 1990's to extend the notion of the library forward into the emerging digital information context was the result of the collective and distinctive assumptions of three stakeholder communities: the funders, the technology-focused researchers, and the practitioner library community.

Each community responded to the opportunities offered by emerging networked computing technologies in a unique, opportunistic (and sometimes myopic) fashion. While they all agreed that "digital libraries" was an appropriate term for the new endeavour, they each had a different idea of the meaning of the term and different allegiances to the components of what they considered a library.

The following parts demonstrate this "interpretive flexibility" by describing the different meanings attributed to digital libraries by the three major communities involved in the research effort.

PERSPECTIVE OF THE DIGITAL LIBRARY FUNDERS

The primary funders of digital library research in the U.S. were the NSF, within the Directorate for Computer and Information Science (CISE), DARPA, NASA, and NIH, with lesser contributions from NEH, IMLS (Institute of Museum and Library Services), and the Library of Congress. The notable characteristic of all the primary funders is their focus on technology-oriented science, in contrast to social science, humanities, or arts.

This focus is reflected in a research programme that funded mainly core computer science and its applications to networked information, with very little attention to network information as a sociotechnical phenomenon. In fact, the first phase of Digital Library Initiative (DLI) funding was exclusively technical.

This was moderated somewhat in the second phase. Influenced by the results of a 1996 NSF workshop that called for increased research on the social aspects of digital libraries, the NSF included social science research in the DLI-2 solicitation. An examination of documents published early in the digital library effort reveals the underlying assumptions and biases of the lead agencies that shaped the nature of the funding programmes and their vision of the digital libraries that would emerge from it.

Although it appeared in a visionary 1988 document from Kahn and Cerf, the term "digital libraries" was introduced into the national research agenda in February 1994 in a report from a task force on Information Infrastructure Technologies and Applications (IITA). This report was commissioned by the newly funded High Performance Computing and Communications programme, which was formed to leverage advances in computing and networking for the general social benefit.

The report defines digital libraries as follows:

> "[Digital libraries are] both technologies and applications which will lead to significant advances in the generation, storage, and use of digital information of different kinds across high speed networks. A digital library is a knowledge center without walls, open 24 hours a day and accessible by way of a network. Research areas range from advanced mass storage, online capture of multimedia data, intelligent filtering, knowledge navigation, effective user interfaces, system integration, to prototyping and technology demonstration".

The list of research areas enumerated in this statement is notable for its omission of the implications of eliminating the "walls", or a being open "24 hours a day."

Clearly, the impression of the task force, or at least the only concern, was that the transfer of information to an online form raised only technical issues and that the larger social issues raised by this transfer were either inconsequential, unforeseen, or not worthy of study.

Another report from the same era, authored by Gladney and Fox, demonstrates prevailing thinking of the time that perhaps underlies this decision by the funders to focus only on technical issues:

> "The concept "library" has been refined over several centuries. It would be injudicious to depart from what people expect merely because a digital service is replacing a material one. Except where explicit reasons suggest an improvement that is easily explained to ordinary users (*e.g.*, in query services), library services should implement a familiar model".

Implicit in this text is the assumption that the nature of the institution and the information model it entails should remain as a stable overlay on a changed technical foundation. A digital library should, by nature, imply the same notions of integrity, trust, and quality, historically associated with libraries.

Books might turn into bits, the catalogue might become an online database, and shelves might turn into repositories, but the values, structures, and practices of the "institution" should be based on a "familiar model." Even as the web continue to grow in importance and scale, the notion that digital libraries were the focus for "serious" information-oriented activities persisted.

The web was relegated to a more lowbrow status–an unfiltered mishmash of questionable and frequently objection-able content. For example, a 2001 (U.S.) President's Information Technology Advisory Committee report called the web a "rudimentary" information environment that "only hint[s] at the future of digital libraries".

Even if the funding agencies had decided that the broader implications of the transfer of information to the online environment deserved investigation, it is doubtful whether they were structurally configured to handle such investigations.

In a retrospective on the Digital Libraries Initiatives, Griffin takes note of the problem that agencies such as the NSF have with research that is by nature long-term: "The programme funding models did not work optimally, particularly for the mid-size, longer-term, interdisciplinary research and test bed projects."

PERSPECTIVE OF THE COMPUTER SCIENCE RESEARCH COMMUNITY

The computer science research community had every incentive to follow the funding agencies in this selective interpretation of digital library research. The DL initiatives were a new and relatively large stream of funding for extending their pre-existing database and information retrieval research into a new application area.

As stated by researchers: "The computer scientists] could see, or at least imagine, *how current library functions would be moved forward by an injection of computing insight*". The computer scientists who dominated DL research had little interest in examining the nature of "current library functions" or in understanding how the "injection of computing insight" might affect the foundations of these functions. The library was really only a convenient platform for technically focused work.

Indeed as researchers noted the computer science researchers had little patience for the less technically manageable aspects, and "nagging downsides" of digital library research. For example, issues related to copyright and intellectual property were perceived as an annoyance that interfered with work on more interesting technical problems.

Furthermore, the work often required collaboration with librarians who seemed overly focused on metadata "that the computer scientists felt would be replaceable by just another clever search algorithm improvement".

In hindsight, the attraction of the computer science research community to the field of digital libraries was really not based on special allegiance to the library notion, but was just a case of following the funding. When the funding disappeared and it became obvious that the web was a more attractive, and less restrictive environment for studying and exercising emerging computer science techniques such as machine learning, many of the former prominent members of the digital library community disappeared.

PERSPECTIVE OF THE LIBRARY COMMUNITY

The "real" librarians, those with over a century-long tradition collecting, curating, and preserving books and other materials, entered the realm of digital libraries with a consider-ably more institutionally-focused definition of the library and vision of what the digital library would look like.

From their perspective the library, as an institution, had successfully managed previous transitions to new media (the transition of the printed form from scrolls to the codex book to the printed book, the inclusion of recordings, etc.) and had a track record of incorporating new technology into established practices, such as the computer-based catalogue.

The "digital" library would be just another library and through all, the venerable institution would prevail:

- The functions of the librarian have always been to select the material that his constituents will require. to catalogue it so that those who would use it can know what is available and where it is. and to preserve it so that both contemporary readers and those who will follow will be able to use it...none of these tasks will disappear with the emergence of the electronic library. Somebody will have to perform them: if not the librarian, then his replacement. The anarchy of the Internet may be daunting for the neophyte, but it differs little from the bibliographic chaos that is the result of five and a half centuries of the printing press.

Because of this allegiance to the institutional basis of the library and the belief that it was a necessary component of a useful information environment, librarians vigourously resisted the encroachment of the web on the domain formally dominated by the library.

For librarians the intrusion of the web into the work on digital libraries was much more difficult to integrate.

Initially, they were largely dismissive and disdainful of the web as a serious information space, declaring that the "web is not a library" and likening it to a bookstore in which "the entire stock is just piled up in the middle of the floor". As the amount of valuable content increased on the web, they responded with efforts to fold the web into standard operations, such as cataloguing.

While these efforts to catalogue the web were ultimately abandoned, they demonstrate how persistent traditional practices can be even in the face of a rapidly changing technical landscape. In summary, the application of the library concept to the uncharted and unruly context of networked information reveals the distinctly narrow and flawed assumptions of the three parties responsible for its origin and use.

The funding agencies mistakenly assumed that they could fund (and shape) the development of a new information infrastructure as a mainly technical endeavour.

The computer scientists followed suit by framing digital libraries by-and-large as applications of familiar distributed database problems in which "predictable, repeatable ... access and retrieval is a prime value."

In fact, the unpredictability of the web and its seemingly autonomous dynamism has not only affected our perceptions of information use and management, but it has had a far-reaching effect on computer science shifting it from its deterministic, algorithmic foundations to a more probabilistic and socially-oriented focus.

Finally, the librarians assumed that they could safely wrap radically new technology and traditional organizational values and structures in the same embrace. In combination, these flawed assumptions lead to a research area that by and large treads the middle ground.

At a fine granular level, it produced a number of interesting research results and applications of those results. But, at the higher level, it failed to explore the more far-reaching questions of how putting information online and giving people power over their information might change the nature of the information and the way people use it.

It is useful in closing this part to quote Agre who, "Information and institutional change", spoke of the dangers of naively mixing historical forms with innovations:

- A concept of "library" that is too fully rooted in past historical forms will make innovation impossible, but a superficial concept of "library" that draws out only a few aspects of those past historical forms (for example, a library as a big container of documents) will pass over phenomena whose absence in a newly designed system may be fatal. The middle ground between the maximal and simplistic conceptions of "library" is enormous and is not easily mapped.

INFLUENCE OF THE LIBRARY ON DIGITAL LIBRARY TECHNOLOGY

The previous part described the set of assumptions about libraries and networked information that led to the choice of the term "digital libraries." This part describes the manner in which that term and the presumptions underlying it have affected the nature of the technical artifacts produced by digital library research. This effect is reflected in both the overall architectural framework and on the individual architectural components of that framework.

Table 7.1: Comparison of Digital Library and Web Architectures

	Digital Libraries	Web Architecture
Core Architecture	Repository-centric	Resource-centric
User Model	Portal Searching	Browsing
Content Model	Digital Objects	Resources
Indexing Model	Surrogates	Full-text and links
Identification	Persistent IDs	URIs
Federation Model	Federated Search, Metadata Harvesting	Centralized Indexing

CORE ARCHITECTURE: REPOSITORY-CENTRIC VERSUS RESOURCE-CENTRIC

Digital library systems are by and large based on the notion of the institutionallymanaged *repository* as the central architec-tural entity. The repository acts as the container for storage of and access to "digital objects", the content "within" the library. In this manner, the repository is a virtual boundary defining the locus of institutional management, curation, and preservation of the contained digital objects.

This virtual boundary is the functional equivalent of the physical boundary in the "bricks and mortar" library in which the physical structure defines the limits of library curation and stewardship of the information resources within it. In contrast, the *resource* is the central entity in the web architecture.

Uniquely identified resources are the nodes in a virtual directed graph, in which the edges are the hyperlinks that connect resources. Notably absent from this graph model is the notion of containment or location. There is no first-class entity that corresponds to the repository in digital architecture. Although repositories are sometimes compared to websites, the comparison is incorrect due to the nature of the latter.

A website is an ambiguously defined, second-class technical artifact – it may be all the web pages served within the same DNS domain, or those accessible through a single server. Technically, it has no identity (URI) and therefore it cannot be the target of any protocol requests. Conceptually, it does not imply control or management in the same manner as a repository. The remainder of this part describes the major components of digital library systems that support this repository-centric architectural core.

PORTALS

The portal, or the "front door of the digital library", serves the same purpose as the physical entry to the traditional library. It provides the user with the clear notion of being "inside" the digital library. Services and content within the portal are thereby blessed with the imprimatur of the library, endowing them with a level of trust and integrity. This is commonly known as "branding".

Correspondingly, most digital library applications clearly indicate to the user when they are "leaving the library", for example by traversing a hyperlink to a page outside the boundary of the library. The focus of a portal is usually a search interface, that in most cases is field-based, providing more functionality than the single text box search paradigm employed by most web search engines.

This allows users to search on specific bibliographic fields such as title, author, or subject. This search paradigm reflects the influence of the library cataloguing tradition, which eschews simple keyword searching that is predominant in mainstream crawler-based search engines (*e.g.*, Google) in favour of more targeted search capabilities. Metadata, which is the basis of this field-based searching. In contrast to this "front-door" paradigm, the web user metaphorically "surfs" among linked information resources without regard for their location on the network.

The informal notion of a "homepage" for a website does exist, but there is no presumption or enforcement of this as the uniform entry point to the collection of pages of that site.

The notion of uniform, location-independent sources has proven to be quite powerful. In its simplest form it makes it possible to aggregate information from multiple sources in a single webpage, in the manner that a page may include an image that is stored in some other location on the net. As I will describe later, location independence is leveraged in Web 2.0 in a much more powerful manner in the form of "mash-ups."

METADATA–CATALOGUING IN THE DIGITAL CONTEXT

The shaping effect of the library tradition on digital libraries is perhaps most evident in the focus on descriptive metadata. This focus has its roots in cataloguing, one of the core functions of the modern library. The traditional catalogue developed for a number of reasons. At the simplest level, in a library of physical resources it gave users an easy and compact tool for finding information resources without having to traverse the shelves.

However, describing the catalogue as merely a compact shelf list trivializes its complexity and intellectual content. Underlying cataloguing is the concept of information entities having uniform attributes, such as author, title, or subject classification, and the utility of those attributes for logical organization of those entities. This organization presents multiple *access points* based on those uniform attributes, and allows users to search and browse within those access points.

For example, a user may search for information by author name and then traverse the resources associated with that author, or alternatively they may search for information by subject classification and traverse the resources associated within that class. As a result, the organization of the catalogue and the manner in which it is made available to the user (*e.g.*, cards in drawers or screens in an electronic catalogue) is independent of the manner in which the physical, or digital, resources are organized on shelves, or in repositories.

Furthermore, an individual information resource (*e.g.*, a book) may have multiple catalogue instances, each accessible through specific access points (*e.g.*, title, author, subject, etc.). Efforts to extend the practice of cataloguing into the context of online information reflects an ongoing belief that in a world where even the books that are part of library collections have been digitized and are available for full-text search, structured search over surrogates is more functional and ultimately preferred by users.

This is despite empirical evidence that users seem to prefer the "one text box" search paradigm of Google to the fielded-search paradigm employed in most digital library portals and online catalogs, and decades-old evidence of the frequent superiority in recall and precision of automated full-text search to human-assisted indexing and cataloguing.

Traditional library cataloguing is both complex and expensive, especially when applied to the rapidly expanding and diverse set of digital resources. The notion of metadata emerged as a simpler and less expensive alternative to traditional cataloguing records, perhaps making it possible for nonprofess-ionals to create structured bibliographic information.

The predominant digital library metadata effort is the Dublin Core Metadata Initiative. Ironically, the origins of Dublin Core lie in improving search and retrieval on the general web. However, this effort to develop easy-to-use bibliographic standards for networked information objects has been deemed irrelevant, ill-conceived, or even counterproductive by the mainstream web community and most notably the search engines that dominate it.

As I describe later, the attempts to translate the benefits of cataloguing to the online domain via metadata have been compromised by problems with ensuring the quality of the metadata records that are produced by non-professionals and preventing so-called "metadata spamming" by unscrupulous agents trying to falsely lead information consumers to their sites.

DIGITAL OBJECTS — CONTAINERS FOR COMPLEX DATA AND METADATA

The content model of most digital library architectures is based on the notion of a *digital object*. an identified (first-class) information resource that is an aggregation of multiple information units consisting of multiple formats, multiple subsidiary units, versions, or document components (*e.g.*, the text, data, images, etc. of a scholarly paper).

These are generally known as *compound objects*. These object models reflect an ongoing effort by the library community to account for the complexity of information in both its abstract form and the physical or digital manifestations of it.

These efforts have focused on mechanisms to represent the various relationships among information resources. and to describe those resources at multiple levels of granularity, for various purposes, and in various descriptive formats. Access to compound objects and their components is frequently mediated by protocols unique to the particular repository architecture.

These protocols are usually embedded in the URLs that carry user requests from the digital library portal to the repository. These protocols allow operations such as access a digital object in a specific form, access a portion of a digital object such as its descriptive metadata, and the like.

The proliferation of these architecture-specific access protocols has spawned a virtual cottage industry of repository interoperability initiatives in the digital library community. In contrast, the web architecture includes a quite simple information model based on the atomic resource.

"Interoperability" is defined in the simple terms of the web architecture–resources, URIs, and HTTP. There is no architectural notion of a compound object, or aggregation of resources. Ad hoc and de facto aggregations exist, for example a logical document split into a set of interlinked web pages.

However, these aggregations are not first-class objects. they do not have a unique identity and are essentially ephemeral. There is, in fact, an increased awareness in the web community that more complex information models are appropriate in a number of instances. for example, scholarly publishing.

FEDERATION

The issue of federation arises because digital library systems are conceived as discrete institutionally-managed entities with distinct boundaries accessible to the user through branded portals. Sometimes, a user might want to search across multiple digital libraries when a selected resource is not available in their "local" library. In the physical library domain, this problem is solved by union catalogs such as WorldCat and by interlibrary loan.

Digital library applications employ two mechanisms to allow users to search for and access information outside the confines of a single digital library. The first is federated searching or meta-searching, in which a single search query is multicast to several digital library search engines.

The query is then individually processed at those search engines. the individual result sets are then returned and integrated at the site from which the original query was multicast. Federated searching was the subject of substantial work in the early years of digital library research describes our own work in this area.

Although instances of federated search still exist, the technique has fallen into some disfavour because of problems with dependence on the reliability of multiple search sites and the problems with the ranking of search results from several sources. The second is metadata harvesting, in which bibliographic records from several distributed institutional sources are combined at a single indexing site, which provides a search interface across the resulting "union catalogue".

The most widely deployed mechanism for metadata harvesting is the Open Archives Protocol for Metadata Harvesting (OAI-PMH). That same chapter describes complica-tions with metadata harvesting. Neither of these techniques has achieved widespread deployment in the general web information space.

Boundaries and the repositories that implement them are not a part of the web architecture. Web search engines such as Google crawl the web via graph traversal, ignoring the notion of the location of a webpage, except as a tool for optimizing graph traversal strategies. In addition, ranking algorithms such as PageRank are designed to operate over a centralized index, and are difficult if not impossible in the context of distributed methods such as federated search,

PERSISTENT IDENTITY FOR NETWORK INFORMATION

A final example of the difference between digital library and web architecture is the notion of "persistent identity" for information stored in digital repositories. The attention to this issue in the digital library contexts reflects concerns about both preservation and control of intellectual property. The Handle System is the best known of this class of technologies.

Like many persistent naming systems, the Handle System depends on a hierarchy of identity resolvers, and therefore the notion of a central *root* name server.

These efforts have gained little traction in the mainstream web community, which has historically resisted centralization and has comfortably adapted to the fragility of URLs, deeming identity persistence as a policy problem rather than a technical problem.

COEXISTENCE OF DIGITAL LIBRARIES AND THE WEB

The previous part described the distinction between the repository-centric digital library architecture and resource-centric web architecture. In addition, it described how these different core architectural principles affected the technical components of each architecture.

The digital library applications that have been assembled from these components are indeed quite powerful and include advanced searching capabilities, complex information models, and rich user interfaces.

Ironically, the same architectural features that enhance their functionality have often interfered with the interoperability of digital library applications with the mainstream web and thereby mitigated the impact of these applications in the broader web context.

The problem comes from the fact that the specialized, repository-specific access protocols that provide access to these digital library resources often do not follow the conventions of mainstream HTTP access methods. For example, in many cases the URLs used to access objects are conflated with query predicates, the syntax of which is unique to the digital library and is hardcoded into portal/repository interaction.

This is not a problem when access to the digital library resources occurs through the "front door" portal and through its respective search user interface that generates these query-based access URLs. However, mainstream crawler-based search engines, such as Google, do not access objects through the front door, but rely on generalized graph traversal.

The nature of the access URLs in digital libraries and their interdependence on the respective digital library search interface often makes these URLs unreachable via these graph traversal techniques. This is because the URLs of the digital objects in the repository are not explicitly linked to, but are generated by the digital library based on search engine queries.

These query-generated URLs are not visible in the web graph traversed by mainstream search engines and, as a result, the digital library resources are not crawled and are subordi-nated to an information black whole–the so-called "deep web". They fail to appear in result lists returned by main-stream search engines, which have emerged as the universal tool for discovery of information (much to the chagrin of the library community).

In an effort to increase search engine visibility, digital library providers frequently generate special link pages that expose the individual URLs of repository contents to crawlers as conven-tional hyperlinks. Digital library resources then appear as search results in Google and similar search engines.

As a result, a steadily expanding amount of access to digital library resources occurs through these commercial providers. But this reverse engineering to increase visibility of contained resources subverts the role of the digital library as a control zone, and the intention of the portal as a branded entry to that control zone

The "digital library collection" becomes just another set of web resources, with no joint identity or imprimatur. The digital library becomes "invisible infrastructure", barely evident through a web-dominated information paradigm.

DIGITAL LIBRARIES AND THE EVOLVING WEB

In addition to the technical incompatibilities between the digital library and web architectures that were described in the previous part, there is a widening gap between their underlying information models. The web that Tim Berners-Lee invented in 1989 has undergone an explosive growth in scale, measured in terms of number of URLs, servers, and traffic.

At the same time, it has experienced a radical change in form and impact, referred to as Web 2.0. In contrast to the relatively passive and transactional search/access paradigm characteristic of the library and Web 1.0 in which the delineation between authors and consumers was relatively distinct, information interactions in Web 2.0 are highly inter-active and participatory.

Rather than just browsing and reading web pages, web users, acting as both authors and readers are writing reviews on Amazon, annotating and tagging pictures on Flickr, writing and updating articles on Wikipedia, publishing observations and research results in blogs, and mashing up online content into new content. This part examines the evolving web and the coexistence of digital libraries within that context. The metaphor of versions – Web 1.0, Web 2.0, and the recently coined Web 3.0–is obviously artificial and overly simplistic.

However, it is a useful rhetorical device. The predominant "features" of these versions are as follows. *Web 1.0*–called the document web, the "web of cognition", or the "read-only" web.

The time span of this version roughly extends from the invention of the web until 2000. It primarily consisted of hyperlinked, semi-static, atomic documents (HTML, PDF, GIF or JPEG images). Interaction and collaboration were minimal except for document authoring and querying. Content creation required specialized tools and, as a result, was restricted to a small subset of web users. *Web 2.0*-called the "web of communication" or the "read/write" web.

This "version" includes participation-oriented tools such as wikis, blogs, social applications like Flickr, and instant communication tools like Twitter. Another prominent feature is the notion of a "mash-up" whereby new information objects are created via the dynamic combination of existing information resources.

These features enable a phenomenon that Engestrom calls "object-centered sociality", in which information objects, people, and social exchanges are linked together in web space. This has effected a phase transition in the web's impact on economics, scholarship, learning, and most recently politics.

The effect of this impact on national politics is exemplified by the recent observation that "... Barack Obama's victories in the Democratic primary and in the presidential election would not have been possible without Internet-empowered fund-raising and social networking". *Web 3.0*–called the "web of meaning" or the "contextual web", this currently emerging web function-ality incorporates concepts of the semantic web, the under-pinnings of which Tim Berners-Lee and the W3C have been developing since the late 1990's.

The key features of the semantic web include machine readability and interpretation of web data and the ability to reason over that data. The technological foundation of the semantic web is the Resource Description Framework (RDF) a data model for expressing statements about entities (web resources) and their properties (ontologically defined relationships).

Raffl *et al.* adopt the language of Evolutionary Systems Theory to illustrate how the features of these versions are cumulative: "[E]ach new layer is built upon a preceding one and ...the new stage comprises not only the new layer, but parts of the old one".

As shown, Web 1.0 was primarily a one-way channel from producers to consumers. In Web 2.0, the bifurcation of web participants blurs into consumer/ producers who collaboratively author, manage, and annotate content. This is enhanced in the Semantic Web (Web 3.0) in which machines (agents) process and interpret this collaboratively produced content and contribute new content back on the web. The participatory nature Web 2.0 should not be dismissed as just a popular phenomenon, manifested in increased use of mainly social sites like FaceBook. Many experts in the field, we are witnessing a fundamental change in the prevailing information paradigm that is transforming all aspects of our culture. Notably, this impact extends to the nature of scholarly research and communication, one of the backbones of the research library.

As pointed out by Paul Ginsparg, who create arXiv and is considered one of the icons of Internet-based scholarship:

> ...There are...objective reasons to believe that we are witnessing an essential change in the way information is accessed, the way it is communicated to and from the general public, and among research professionals-fundamental methodological changes that will lead to a terrain 10-20 years from now more different than it was 10-20 years ago than in any comparable time period.

Timo Hannay of Nature, one of the most prestigious scientific journals, makes the following observation of the impact of the current and future of the web on science scholarship:

> For all but a very small number of widely read titles, the day of the print journal seems to be almost over. Yet to see this development as the major impact of the web on science would be extremely narrow-minded–equivalent to viewing the web primarily as an efficient PDF distribution network... Though it will take longer to have its full effect, the web's major impact will be on the way that science itself is practiced.

In addition, there is mounting evidence that, for a number of important informationoriented activities such as education, the participatory information paradigm in Web 2.0 has advantages over the traditional consumption-based model. Fuchs and Raffl argue that Web 2.0 paradigms of collaboration, construction, and participation are more closely aligned with recognized models of human cognition and knowledge development than the more restrictive and controlled library model.

Downes and Ullrich describe the utility of the Web 2.0 model for education because of the manner in which it facilitates activities such as group collaboration, exploration, and manipulation that are key to learning according to cognitively-oriented constructivist theories.

Gee argues that the "affinity spaces" facilitated by the Web 2.0 environment are powerful tools for learning. Black identifies the notion of "beta-reading" in online fan communities where contributors grow as readers and writers based on mutual feedback. Finally, others see the general benefits of the "wisdom of crowds" that is enabled by the collaborative nature of Web 2.0.

ONLINE CATALOGUES AND CARD CATALOGUES: IDENTIFICATION OF AREAS OF SIMILARITIES AND DIFFERENCES

This chapter is prerequisite to the following chapters, in that it provides the background for the study of the possible influences of online catalogues on both the bibliographic record and on cataloguing principles.

A major aim is to explore the development of online catalogues, their basic features and capabilities and also to reveal the major differences that exist between them and manual catalogues.

This comparison will help identify the differences and similarities in the processes by which a bibliographic record and, on a larger scale, a catalogue, is created, manipulated and made accessible to the catalogue user for searching and retrieval.

In this context, the requirements of online systems which may influence cataloguing rules will also be discussed. A thorough understanding of the conceptual as well as the practical and technical differences and similarities between the online catalogue and the card catalogue will then help in an investigation of the relevance of current cataloguing principles and rules to the online catalogue. It is not the intention of the present chapter to discuss the influence of the features and capabilities of online catalogues on individual cataloguing principles or concepts..

In any comparison between the online catalogue and the manual catalogue, it seems appropriate to choose the card catalogue among the other forms of catalogues as an appropriate approach, because:

- The card catalogue has been and still is one of the most important manual systems in use for more than a century,
- It is the basis from which the present cataloguing standards have been developed, and
- It is the basis on which the structure and contents of online catalogues have been developed, *i.e.*, online catalogues are the logical successors to card catalogues.

It is not the intention of this chapter to reject the merits of the card catalogue. A realistic approach in comparing the online catalogue with the card catalogue should reveal advantages and disadvantages in both catalogues.

Although there is overall support among librarians for online catalogues, most librarians consider having knowledge about the card catalogue to be very useful for an understanding of the origins of the present online system, particularly the structure of the MARC format and how individual records fit into the idea of a catalogue system.

This was clearly the case in the general discussions about the card catalogue on the AUTOCAT list, 20 November 1994 to 3 December 1994, commenting on the need to teach the card catalogue in library schools. In fact, an understanding of the origins and underlying concepts from which the present environment has evolved will help us develop catalogue systems based on substantive assumptions.

In short, this understanding and comparison of the two environments will help us to reassess, refine and redesign our standards for the construction of catalogues.

John Hickey states:

> "Even if nobody still uses catalogue cards, more of our professional assumptions that we recognize are based upon unit cards and card displays. it helps to have some acquaintance with the previous technology."

It should be noted that online catalogues and card catalogues can be compared from different perspectives and according to different criteria. However, this study will compare them with regard to the processes by which bibliographic records and files are created, manipulated and organised on the one hand and searched, retrieved and displayed on the other. The differences between the online catalogue and the card catalogue will be explored in terms of the input, manipulation and output processes of bibliographic data.

ONLINE CATALOGUES: WHAT THEY ARE

Online catalogues are a norm today. they are not static. they have developed rapidly and will continue to evolve further. By utilising the various capabilities of computers and telecommuni-cations, online catalogues are adding new features that make them totally different from traditional catalogues. Online catalogues are now gateways to larger information systems or, as Hopkins says, they are the 'one-stop information store'.

The online environment is an environment encompassing a wide range of information tools, both bibliographic and non-bibliographic. Library catalogues are now a small but very important component of the evolving online environment and are accessible through different tools in the networked environment, the *public access computer system* (PACS).

The global network is the Internet including various PACS components such as Gopher, WAIS (Wide Area Information Servers), Netscape and Mosaic and other access modes such as Archie and FTP (File Transfer Protocol) tools. The Webpages created by libraries and other information providers are becoming very pervasive and are often used both by librarians and endusers as linking sources for library information.

The same workstation serves as a means of navigating the whole world of the Internet. In the online environment not only are the information tools different from the traditional tools but also the whole concept of access to bibliographic information has changed. Time and location are irrelevant in searching the online environment.

DEVELOPMENTS AND DIRECTIONS OF ONLINE CATALOGUES

As a result of a significant growth in scientific and technological information after the second world war and a resulting expansion in library collections, manual systems could no longer respond effectively to the ever-growing information needs of society.

In terms of fast and effective retrieval of bibliographic information, the card catalogue had many disadvantages. Its large size, complexity and high costs of maintenance made it more and more difficult for libraries to maintain as an up to date searching tool. It became obvious that a more flexible tool was needed to cope with the new conditions of libraries.

It was thus necessary to think of alternative ways of constructing library catalogues that could be cost-effective, manageable and easy to use. Following on the application of computers in other fields, librarians became assured that the computer's theoretical capability to control library operations constituted adequate grounds for embracing a mechanised approach. As Weihs and Howarth point out, "It was necessary to investigate the computer as a relatively cost-effective tool to provide library catalogs."

Computer applications, however, first occurred in library activities other than the provision of public access to the catalogue. Computers were used in libraries mainly for house-keeping types of activities such as circulation control, acquisitions and serial control. This did not directly affect patrons' access to the library catalogue. Library automated began in the early 1960s with the rationale that "If a job could be done by computer, then the number of staff required to work at a defined level of expertise could be reduced".

Although some evidence of automated of library operations other than cataloguing is reported from the 1950s and 1960s, it is the MARC (Machine-Readable Cataloguing) project that has been considered as one of the most important factors in the development of automated catalogues.

With the beginning of the MARC Distribution Service in 1969, large libraries began to utilise MARC magnetic tapes mainly for automated cataloguing in the standard form provided by the Library of Congress. The usefulness of MARC services in cataloguing, along with the increasing availability of computer technology in the late 1960s, led to more developments in automated catalogues.

In response to the needs of small and medium-sized libraries without access to a mainframe computer, centralised cataloguing services gave way to the establishment of bibliographic utilities in the early 1970s.

The Online Computer Library Center, established in 1971, has been considered to be a significant factor in the development of automated catalogues. With the standard cataloguing services of such bibliographic utilities, libraries were able to utilise the power of computer technology in a cost-effective way.

The proliferation of MARC-based cataloguing led to the realisation of the importance of uniform, standardised bibliographic description as the nucleus of bibliographic services at national and international levels. The growth of bibliographic utilities in the early 1980s as well as developments in telecommunication technology accelerated the move towards centralised MARC-based cataloguing and the need for standardised descriptive cataloguing.

A significant factor further affecting the development of online catalogues was that some libraries began to use MARC bibliographic information for their circulation systems in an online mode. Using short bibliographic records rather than full MARC records for circulation operations, a number of libraries tried to help their patrons in checking whether an item was on loan, on order, or at binding.

This was a form of public enquiry module, which later developed into the online public access catalogue (OPAC). However, as Seal pointed out "The public enquiry module will often replicate the structure of a card or COM [Computer Output Microform] catalogue."

Another major factor leading to the rapid development of online public access catalogues was the contribution, by some library system vendors, of designing and developing public access modules as an important part of their turnkey systems. These vendors tried to incorporate a more sophisticated structure for the public enquiry module with more searching facilities. It should be noted that the early public enquiry systems were not integrated with other library modules, such as acquisitions and serials control.

Due to both the relative success and acceptability of online public enquiry modules, and pressures from patrons and librarians, libraries began to consider developing online public access catalogues (OPACs) with more bibliographic information, *i.e.*, full MARC records and more searching capabilities, such as keyword access and Boolean searching.

The possibility of utilising MARC records as the foundation of bibliographic databases led to the development of the concept of the Integrated Online Library Systems (IOLS) in which "The information that was input at the acquisitions stage would form a basis for the catalogue record which, in turn, would support all library functions. Thus, a number of integrated systems, such as GEAC, ULISYS, ATLAS, DOBIS, NOTIS and VTLS, were established incorporating this modular design.

The overall factors relating to the growing interest in online catalogues have been numerous. It is generally agreed that the most important factors that led to the rapid proliferation and development of online catalogues in the early 1980s were those related to their search, retrieval and display capabilities. Moreover, the opportunity of feedback from librarians and library patrons has provided a continuing momentum for upgrading the structure, contents and capabilities of online catalogues.

Tracing the historical development of online public access catalogues, Hildreth and Matthews identify three generations of OPACs. This categorisation is based on the features and capabilities of online catalogues in the processes of input, storage and output of bibliographic information.

Matthews claims that most of the existing online catalogues are still in the first or second generations and only a few systems have moved beyond first-generation. Added to the three generations identified by Hildreth and Matthews, recent advances in OPACs using graphical user interfaces (GUIs) have introduced a fourth generation to online catalogues.

FIRST-GENERATION ONLINE CATALOGUES

Derived from circulation or cataloguing systems, first-generation online catalogues were in fact computerised card catalogues with almost the same traditional features. In contrast to the patrons' expectations from their use of computerised database systems, these new library catalogues provided limited author, title and controlled vocabulary subject heading access points. For this reason, first-generation online catalogues have been criticised as having no advantages over the card catalogue.

Searching in first-generation online catalogues was essentially based upon pre-coordinated information retrieval principles and was possible only through inputting the exact form of words or phrases. In contrast to searching in card catalogues, the patron had great difficulties as he/she had to input something into the system so that it could respond to his/her query.

As this was possible only through inputting the exact form of words or phrases, which was difficult to remember, searching was not as successful as the searcher expected. Keyword access was not available and refining a search by further limiting it to elements such as date of publication, language or country of publication was not possible. The interfaces, which were usually menu-driven, replicated traditional catalogues in their form of access by providing mainly phrase access to separate subject headings, title, and author indexes. Output and display of search results generally had a single format.

SECOND-GENERATION ONLINE CATALOGUES

With further developments in information technology, it was possible to provide a more sophisticated system for input, storage and output of bibliographic information. Second-generation online catalogues are a departure from traditional card catalogues and incorporate many new features for the provision of effective access.

In contrast to the limited input, storage and output capabilities of first-generation online catalogues, second-generation online catalogues are characterised as being powerful tools for the searching of bibliographic information. Keyword search, Boolean keyword search, cross index search and increasing or reducing of search results are among the features of second-generation online catalogues. Hildreth writes:

Today's second-generation online catalogs represent a marriage of the library catalogue and conventional online information retrieval (IR) systems familiar to librarians who search online abstracting and indexing databases via DIALOG, BRS, ORBIT, MEDLINE, etc.

Improved card catalogue-like searching and browsing capabilities have been joined with the conventional IR keyword and Boolean searching approaches. Many online catalogs support the ability to restrict searches to specified record fields, to perform character masking and/or right-hand truncation, and to limit the results by date, language, place of publication, etc. Also, bibliographic records may be viewed and printed in a number of different display formats.

However, it should be noted that there are a number of major differences between online catalogues and these IR systems that make second-generation online catalogues easier searching tools. With a combination of different search methods, the user is offered possibilities that were not available in first generation online catalogues.

Due to improvements in the design of database management softwares, the structure and content of bibliographic records in second-generation online catalogues may be enhanced by incorporating full records augmented by information such as tables of contents, summaries, content notes, abstracts and links to full electronic texts. Considerable increase in the length of fields was another improvement in second-generation systems.

Interfaces are usually in two modes, menu-driven and command-driven. this makes the interaction between the user and the catalogue more flexible. In terms of user assistance, these catalogues provide more options including, for example, help screens, error messages and suggestive prompts. Ease of use and user-friendliness are two major features of today's second-generation online catalogues.

THIRD-GENERATION ONLINE CATALOGUES

Only a few systems have moved beyond second-generation online catalogues into third-generation online catalogues with enhanced or more sophisticated features. Due to the growing sophistication and availability of technology, new capabilities are being added to online catalogues making them more adaptive to the needs of library patrons. Free text search, enriched database search and simultaneous journal citation searching are among the retrieval capabilities in third generation online catalogues. Furthermore, the mode of interaction has been developed to the point of conversational, adaptive dialogue and the bibliographic format can be tailored according to user preference. Operational assistance such as automatic, context-based correction is also available.

FOURTH-GENERATION ONLINE CATALOGUES

Beginning from the late 1980s, a most recent development in online public access catalogues has been achieved in providing easy access to bibliographic information by using graphical user interfaces (GUIs) such as Windows. These systems, which can be considered as fourth-generation catalogues, have moved away from the traditional menu-type interfaces and are more associated with client server and graphical user interface.

They use WIMP (windows, icons, mouse and pointers) interfaces to speed and simplify searching. With the Windows-style user interface available through PCs (personal computers, *i.e.*, intelligent, and not dumb terminals), there is much more functionality. In these systems the user has the flexibility to click on various buttons, each of which carries a special function.

Nevertheless, these systems do not eliminate but augment the keystroke access. There is also the possibility of using function keys for different purposes when keyboards are involved. In general, access is via mouse or keyboard or a combination of both. Searching capabilities in the Windows version of OPACs are greater than those found in other generations of online catalogues. Pointer capabilities allow the searcher to select exactly the term he/she is looking for, while pull-down menus provide additional options to make searching even more useful. By using scroll bars and pull-down menus, browsing in different indexes is very simple.

With the capability of post-Boolean searching, the search software also attempts to interpret users' search requests in order to present matches of greater or lesser interest to the user. This is called relevance ranking of the search terms. Similar to second and third generation online catalogues, these systems search for terms through using an implicit Boolean 'AND'.

Other Boolean operators such as 'OR' and 'NOT' can also be used to narrow down search results or such search strings can be constructed using the mouse alone. In addition, access has been enhanced by text retrieval qualifiers such as 'language', 'date' and 'form' of the text.

With this feature, it is possible to include new data elements that help in the better identification of the sought item. Integral or add-on text retrieval modules to provide range searching, related term searching, wild card features, adjacency and proximity are supplied by some systems.

One of the recent additional advanced features of fourth-generation OPACs is the 'hypertext' function. Through this function, any word that the user selects or highlights can be used to search all the fields and subfields in all the records in the database for any occurrence of that word. This dynamic feature helps the searcher to navigate the database to find more relevant sources of information.

ONLINE CATALOGUES: HOW THEY DIFFER FROM MANUAL CATALOGUES

There have been some general attempts in the literature of the past decade to briefly compare different types of library catalogues. However, these comparisons have not been concerned with the concepts that underlie the nature and structure of the catalogue. In the following parts, the two types of catalogue will be compared in terms of the creation, manipulation and search/retrieval/ display of bibliographic records.

CREATION AND MANIPULATION OF BIBLIOGRAPHIC RECORDS

Structure and Content of Bibliographic Records

By 'structure of the record' is meant the bibliographic descri-ption consisting of data elements arranged and presented in a given order, such as card catalogue formats and MARC formats. It is generally understood that the medium, via which biblio-graphic records are created, manipulated and made accessible to the searcher, influences their structure and content.

The computer has made possible the enriching of the structure and contents of bibliographic records. While the space limitations of 3" x 5" cards generally restrict the level of data elements to be entered in a record, the content of a bibliographic record in an online catalogue makes it possible and desirable to include more data elements such as those fixed-length data elements indexed in field 008 in the USMARC bibliographic format and even data such as summaries, tables of content, and full texts. This issue has been of major interest to librarians and system designers during the past decade and there have been some proposals in this regard.

User studies of the early 1980s showed that most users of online catalogues would like to have access to tables of contents, back-of-the-book indexes and summaries. Other suggestions have included the titles of essays in collected works or festschriften, book introductions, book jacket material, and the assignment of more subject headings. With the advent and further development of online catalogues it has become possible to assign a larger number of access points to bibliographic records. In comparison to the conventional main and added entries in the card catalogue, any data element in a bibliographic record may be designated as an access point.

MARC Format and Categorisation of Data Elements

As a set of standards for the identifying, storing and communicating of cataloguing information, MARC has significantly contributed to the growth of library automated and to the development of online catalogues. Although the MARC record was conceived as an automated version of the catalogue card, the structure is flexible enough to store bibliographic information in more detailed fields and subfields due to the requirements of automated systems for separate identification of data elements.

While the medium for the card catalogue is the 3" x 5 " card with a fixed, less flexible format, most online catalogues use MARC as a communication format for the exchange of bibliographic information. In this regard, MARC communicates bibliographic information with more flexibility than the card catalogue.

With the machine-readable format, in which the biblio-graphic information on a record has been broken down into fields and subfields, it is possible to separately identify each data element. This approach also allows for inclusion or exclusion of data elements for output as desired.

Based on the MARC format, bibliographic records can be created and tailored according to the specific needs of the library without either discarding standardisation or diminishing the quality of cataloguing.

In the card environment, cataloguing depends on a longer process of manual checking against other catalogues, the ordering of card sets and receiving and interfiling them in the catalogue. This process in online catalogues is done more comprehensively and easily by subscribing to bibliographic utilities or by purchasing MARC products and downloading the needed records into the library's automated system.

MARC records permit a fuller level of description. more data elements to be included in the description and many more data elements to be assigned as access points for retrieval. A MARC record also includes other data, including non-bibliographic data that are used for catalogue maintenance. There is now a trend towards preserving detailed bibliographic records in machine-readable form.

The amount and type of information that constitute a 'full bibliographic record' is certainly open to debate, but since the late 1960s the accepted standard has been the MARC format. The data that can be contained in a MARC record include the entire spectrum of information normally presented on catalogue cards plus a great deal of other potentially valuable categorizing information that can be encoded in fixed elements and elsewhere on record.

However, MARC format has been criticised for being an electronic version of the catalogue card and for its limited accommodation of hierarchically structured information. There are also some problems with the MARC tagging and indexing of data elements that influence retrieval in online databases. Systems may differ from one another in the indexing of fields and it is often difficult to find out what fields are indexed by a given system. This results in retrieval and display problems, leading to user confusion.

Bibliographic Standardization

In comparison to manual systems, the online environment gives much more emphasis to the concept of standardisation. Although the idea of standardised bibliographic description seems to have first appeared with derived cataloguing and the sale of Library of Congress cards in 1898 and later with the introduction of the *National Union Catalogue* (NUC), it was not until the 1970s that the application of computers to library operations and the advent of online catalogues gave to standardisation a much more significant role.

With regard to the description, choice and form of data elements to be included in a bibliographic record, conformity to standards, *e.g.*, cataloguing codes, ISBDs and MARC formats, are vital to online catalogues.

Unlike libraries of two decades ago with their independent card catalogues, libraries of today often create their own catalogue records according to national and/or international standards for the purposes of easy communication of and access to bibliographic information.

Now, it is common for libraries of any size to participate in networks. One result of this, as Wajenberg points out, is an ever-increasing pressure to conform to national and international standards.

Uniformity and consistency are basic requirements for effective bibliographical control. The rapid growth of shared cataloguing systems, developments in bibliographic utilities and the need for bibliographic exchange between databases in the last decade has led to a stronger reaffirmation of the value of standardisation in bibliographic records. Standardisation helps bibliographic records to be uniformly created, manipulated, exchanged and retrieved.

As the cataloguing community moves closer to making the ideal of universal bibliographic control a reality through local, regional, provincial, national, continental and international networks, all libraries assume the responsibility of maintaining standards requisite to maintaining the network. Integration and standar-dization are the keywords in the increasing move-ments towards, and promotion of, interconnected telecommunicating automated systems.

Despite this emphasis on the significance of standardisation in the online catalogue, this concept has been considered only in the inputting of data elements in bibliographic description and not in the output and display, whereas in the card catalogue both input and output are standardised.

For example, both the card catalogue and the online catalogue conform to the ISBD standard for the input format, *i.e.*, the order of areas, punctuation and levels of description. However, in online catalogues the output format is not fixed as in card catalogues and may be flexible.

As Gorman and associates state, the standardisation and formalisation of description and access points is crucial to the online environment and to the effective exchange of bibliographic records. As an important concept that has developed over the last hundred years to meet the changing forms of the catalogue and the needs of the profession, standardisation will continue in the future and as Wajenberg points out, at an accelerated pace.

Input Inconsistencies and Level of Tolerance

A major difference between a manual and an automated catalogue lies in the fact that the creation of bibliographic records for online catalogues demands more precision and logic in terms of typography, spelling, punctuation, spacing, coding of fields and subfields.

This is a critical requirement for computerised systems, since such errors can result in a serious separation or an improper sequencing of entries and therefore can lead to the irretrievability of records. In other words, any errors, even if very small, for instance a faulty keystroke, will be magnified in the online catalogue.

However, in a manual system, when filing catalogue cards or when retrieving information, the human brain can often ignore such minor errors and treat them as if they are correct and file them in the right place.

Errors and inconsistencies can be corrected in the process of filing cards, whereas in the automated catalogue there is a lower level of tolerance towards such errors as variations in format, filing and indexing, and literal and logical inconsistencies within the catalogue. In general, the online catalogue is far less forgiving of cataloguing and typographical errors than is the card catalogue.

CONSTRUCTION AND MAINTENANCE OF THE CATALOGUE

Structure and Content of the Catalogue

By 'structure of the catalogue' is meant how the catalogue is built up, the kinds and content of files and indexes constituting it and the relationships of these files and indexes to one another.

For example, a card catalogue, whether in dictionary or divided form, may include different files such as:

- Authors
- References
- Titles
- Subject headings and
- Shelflists

The advent of the online catalogue has given new dimensions to the catalogue's structure. It is generally main-tained that the online catalogue can support a more complex yet more dynamic structure than that of the card catalogue.

The online file may be independent and self-contained, it may be related to files of similar scope and structure or it may be integrated with other files such as holdings, circulations, acquisitions and authority files.

The online catalogue provides services that were not part of the traditional library catalogue. Access to circulation information, status information, holding information, indexing of special collections, serials and so on have become possible through the development of the contents and structure of the catalogue.

While the structure of the card catalogue is based on the concept of several discrete entries for a single item, the online catalogue maintains a single-entry structure for a single item but with several indexes as access points to records in the master file.

Emphasising what constitutes the structure of an online catalogue, Svenonius states that:

- In its general sense *structure* refers to an aggregate of elements related, or arranged with respect, to each other . . . The structure of a catalogue or catalogue database consists of bibliographic, authority, and holdings records arranged in a given order and referencing one another through a variety of syndetic relationships. Thus, filing rules, together with ordering devices, such as the main entry and see and see also references, define a catalogue structure....The structure of biblio-graphic descriptions consists of data elements arranged and presented in a given order. Thus, card catalogue formats and MARC format represent different but related bibliographic structures, the former intended for display and the latter for communication.

In terms of addition to the contents of the catalogue, the online catalogue has a growing ability to enlarge its own scope. Results of a nationwide survey on the use of online catalogues in the United States revealed that respondents were enthusiastic about accessing journal articles, newspaper articles, encyclopaedias, dissertations, films and government documents through online catalogues.

Other studies showed that users wanted the catalogue to be expanded to include journal titles, government publications and dissertations and journal citations, indexes to collections, content services, abstracts and book reviews. Thus, it can be concluded that the contents of the online catalogue will be expanded in parallel with developments in the technology of catalogue construction.

Integration of the Catalogue

Integration has been considered as an important feature of the recent online catalogue in the sense that different parts of the library automated system are integrated through the use and manipulation of the same record as the basis for different library operations. In such an integration, a single master bibliographic record is tagged and can be manipulated for different library operations, such as acquisitions, cataloguing and circulation. A consequence of integration of the online catalogue, as pointed out by Buckland is that bibliographic information in different parts of a library system, as well as other useful information, can be accessible to users and to other libraries. Such a concept indicates the impor-tance of uniformity and standardisation of bibliographic records in the online environment.

Another interpretation of integration in the online environment is related to various methods of access to bibliographic information. In such an integration, different files and databases can be accessible via the same terminal. This concept has opened up a new era in bibliographic services and is considered as a significant factor in the enhancement of the catalogue. There are increasing attempts to build information systems with integrated access to different types of information services. The trend towards the integration of book trade bibliographic databases and A and I services with the online public access catalogue is an approach which makes the library catalogue a window to the whole bibliographic apparatus, a concept not feasible in the manual catalogue. These different kinds of integration have implications for cataloguing principles.

Authority Control

Authority control ensures the consistent use of names, series and subjects. No bibliographic record can be entered into the system until all assigned headings under which it can be searched are verifiable against the approved authority file. In a manual system, it is a time-consuming and costly operation and requires the services of skilled staff.

There are many advantages to authority control in an online catalogue: in terms of maintaining cataloguing operations, it is particularly advantageous when major revisions to name and subject headings have to be done.

In terms of searching, the actual search that the user does is via an authority control file. What the user inputs to the system is automatically switched through the index to the correct form. In the online environment, the authority records are usually linked with bibliographic records.

There are a number of reasons for the resurgent interest in authority control in the online environment. The various difficulties that users have had with searching names and, as Potter points out, the inconsistencies and errors in the records used to build the databases for online catalogues have led to new attention being given to the concept of authority control. For example, the ability to search personal names in either direct order or through initials has led to the enhancement of the scope and structure of authority files.

Another major difference in the process of authority control between a manual system and an automated system is that correction or change of any heading in the card catalogue is a time consuming operation, whereas this task in some automated systems is to a great extent facilitated through a 'global change' which automatically generates a correction or change in all relevant records.

Although authority control in the online environment is at an early stage of development and, at present, only a few systems have operational authority control modules, the online catalogue's features and capabilities have given a new dimension to the notion of authority control.

Much work needs to be done into the need for authority control in online catalogues. access by name will decrease and the concept of name references will change and the need for authority files in the traditional sense may become less important.

In making the concept of authority control in the online environment clearer, Gorman points out that:

- It is evident that traditional reference structure was designed for premachine catalogues. The ideas that underlie references have been taken over in machine systems and incorporated into the notion of authority files. An authority file consists, very simply, of the approved form of access point for a person, body, or title, together with the references to that approved form and links to other related authority records. We have already seen that, in the computer catalogue environment, the distinction between a main and added entry access point no longer has meaning. The authority record takes this progress a step further. It, in effect, abolishes the distinction between an access point and a reference.... In other words, two of the basic assumptions of traditional catalogue codes—the main entry and the distinction between a heading and a reference—have survived.

Filing Rules and Problems

In any library catalogue, access points are usually filed according to alphanumeric order, which is a conventional arrangement applicable to most information systems accessed by human beings. However, filing is different in the manual catalogue and the automated catalogue.

The arrangement of access points has always been of particular interest to librarians and there have been a number of specific filing rules published to date. The *ALA Filing Rules,* The *Library of Congress Filing Rules* developed by John Rather, and the rules developed by the British Library Filing Committee are among the most important. Although developments in filing rules have been strongly in the direction of commonsense and are oriented towards the intelligent user, users actually have major problems in identifying the exact location of a heading in the sequential order of a large card catalogue.

In a manual system, filing is flexible and can be executed according to the order which seems desirable to the catalogue user, whereas, in a computer catalogue, it must follow the logic of the computer. Filing in a manual system follows the principle of *file as if*: that is, the form and order in which access points are arranged is according to the interpretation of the librarian with the supposition that the arrangement would be the most desirable to the user. For instance, the number *3* can be filed as if it were the word *three*.

The use of the computer has influenced filing practices and it is generally agreed that the principle of *file as is,* which is necessitated by the introduction of computer filing, has more validity in the computer environment. This principle states that characters or words should be filed as they are and not as if they were something else. for example, the number '3' as *3,* and 'three' as *three.* This realisation of the logical as well as the practical differences between filing in a manual catalogue and a computer catalogue came with the earliest attempts in the application of computers to bibliographical work. Current filing rules, which were developed for manual systems, proved not to be effective in a computer environment.

Users of online catalogues can encounter many problems when searching for bibliographic information. Due to different software specifications, computer-based filing has not been entirely standardised and the burden of thinking, for example, about the exact form of access points and the way punctuation and non alphabetic symbols are treated is left to the user.

In manual filing it is possible, by a simple convention, to ignore stop words such as 'the', 'and', 'of', 'a', 'an', etc. at the beginning of titles whereas, in the computer catalogue, this issue demands special programming and in some cases they are difficult to handle. The treatment of punctuation poses another problem for the computer catalogue. while symbols, such as commas, apostro-phes, periods and hyphens, may cause problems in the manual catalogue, they are considered as characters and are located in their 'logical' places by the computer unless software is created to overcome these difficulties.

While the presence or absence of punctuation may be important in access points, they may or may not be important for online display. Diacritics and extended character sets to accommodate non-roman scripts are other important issues in computer filing of entries.

In sum, the logical arrangement of data elements in the computer has implications for the form of access points in the online catalogue. As an example, see the treatment of "Sir," which comes before forenames and thus interferes with filing. This can be seen in the change of some rules for the form of headings in the second edition of the Anglo-American Cataloguing Rules.

In fact, the incorporation/modification of some rules in AACR2 concerning the filing of data elements has arisen in response to the requirements of filing in the computer catalogue. For example, the inclusion of given names in parentheses in cases where the initials are not adequate for identification of authors with identical surnames is to respond to computer filing.

In terms of conference headings the form and order of the number, the date and the location of a conference in parentheses is an illustration of filing relevant to a computer. The place of numeric identifying elements in music uniform titles, *e.g.*, "Pianos (2)" rather than "2 Pianos", is another example of this issue.

SEARCHING, RETRIEVAL, AND DISPLAY OF BIBLIOGRAPHIC RECORDS

User Interfaces

A significant difference between the online catalogue and the card catalogue comes at the stage in which the user interacts with the catalogue, *i.e.*, bibliographic records can be searched, retrieved and displayed. Online catalogues are here considered to be a great departure from card catalogues and it seems that there will be more developments in this regard in the near future.

While the card catalogue is a self-evident medium with a clear physical existence, the online catalogue is not revealed to the users and is not easy to grasp in their first interactions with it. In an online environment, the user cannot immediately understand the catalogue or its structure, coverage and searching mechanisms unless he/she interacts with the system and tries different options for searching and displaying of bibliographic information.

Despite these limitations of the online catalogue, users show a high degree of satisfaction with the variety of features and capabilities it has at the output stage. *Graphical user interfaces* (GUIs) have made interaction with and use of online systems easier and more desirable. It seems likely that, in the near future, new generations of online catalogues will incorporate intelligent interfaces and sophisticated search/retrieval/display facilities.

Interactivity

Online catalogues have often been defined in the literature as 'interactive' catalogues. In the *Dictionary of Information Technology, 'interactivity'* is defined as "system or piece of software that allows communication between the user and the computer in a conversational mode." Interactivity is considered as a major advantage of online catalogues over card catalogues. "It is this interaction between the user and the computer system that really sets apart the online catalogue from the other types of library catalogs"

Unlike in the card environment, if the user does not input a query in the system, the system will not respond to him/her. This process, namely the action of inputting a query by the user and responding by the computer, occurs quickly in real time and in a dynamic and progressive way.

In sum, the concept of interactivity in the online catalogue is well defined below:

> "Online catalogues can be reactive and able to respond to the user in an intelligent way. This can be used to indicate what searching options are available, to correct operational errors, to suggest alternative items which might particularly match the search criteria and to guide the user through a long search. The reader can then be given help and feedback from the system itself, without needing to consult library staff. This approach is impossible in a card or a COM catalogue".

With the introduction of the online interactive catalogue, it has also become possible to record how users interact with the system and search the catalogue. In this way, *i.e.*, through 'transaction log' analysis, librarians are able to check how users approach the catalogue and how frequently search terms appear, as well as to examine other aspects of search/retrieval problems, *e.g.*, users' errors and unsuccessful searches. Many catalogue use studies have been and are being done using transaction logs as a means of data collection.

User's Input Errors and the Catalogue's Level of to Lerance

As pointed out earlier, online catalogues are less forgiving than card catalogues in terms of any kind of error, either in the input stage by the cataloguer, or in the searching stage by the user. A general problem with computers is that they are usually unforgiving of errors. if the user makes the smallest of mistakes, they will not necessarily recognise it as a mistake, and even if they do they will often not offer help in correcting the mistake. However, there are systems being developed that recognise errors, display the type of error, and offer help to the searcher.

User Assistance

In comparison to card catalogues, online catalogues have the ability to provide user assistance in a variety of ways and at different levels. Mitev classifies such aids in four categories as 'retrieval aids', 'linguistic aids', 'navigational aids', and 'semantic aids'. This is a major advantage over the card catalogue in that the system can respond to the user's problems and help him/her as to what the next move to achieve the result would be. Online catalogues have developed, over the past decade, different devices for providing help to their users in the different stages of searching the system.

Most online catalogues have the ability to customise help messages, screen displays and system prompts according to the needs of the user. Online assistance enables the user to influence the dialogue at all times in a clear way. This is not possible in manual systems.

User Satisfaction

It is generally stated that there is a higher level of satisfaction with online catalogues than with card catalogues and that users prefer this new form of the catalogue to the traditional card catalogue. Matthews, Lawrence, and Ferguson, over 90% of users like the online catalogue and almost 75% of users rate the online catalogue as being better than the card, book or microform catalogue.

It is also interesting to note that this high level of satisfaction is consistent across all types of libraries. Lewis, in reporting the results of different user studies, states that: "Users have a strong preference for online catalogs over card catalogs, and they very much want the new technology to succeed". Balaam and Burton and Hawkins report user satisfaction with OPACs despite their shortcomings.

A reason for preference of the online catalogue, even in its primitive form, to the card catalogue is related to its search and retrieval capabilities. It is also safe to assume that, as online catalogues continue to mature in terms of user interface, enhanced content and access, the level of satisfaction will be even greater.

Another point worth mentioning is that the result of different online use studies show that use of the catalogue and use of the collection have increased with the introduction of online interactive catalogues. This, in turn, leads to higher user satisfaction as he/she becomes able to fulfil his/her information needs in easier, faster and more effective ways.

A major group of OPAC users are librarians themselves who are among the strong supporters of such systems. In a series of discussions in the electronic mail discussion group PACS-L@UHUPVM1.UH.EDU, 7-20 April 1994 and in response to Nicholson Baker's "Annals of Scholarship: Discards" published in the *New Yorker*, 4 April 1994, concerning the closing or storing of card catalogues, most librarians supported online catalogues as being superior to card catalogues.

Charles Hildreth considers Baker's article to be a nostalgic approach to the historical value of card catalogues. For Hildreth card catalogues represent a dead-end technology and their maintaining would be very expensive. Instead, online catalogues are open-ended, with a pure potentiality that will never reach its 'final' form.

Walt Crawford asserts that online catalogues are ever-evolving systems that, when reasonably well designed, offer substantially better access and, unlike card catalogues, can be maintained as well as improved.

Robin Alston supports online catalogues for their advantages over card catalogues in many ways and states that a major advantage is that most of the key elements on a record in an online catalogue are searchable, while massive amount of information on catalogue cards are not retrievable. Although there are deficiencies in OPACs, as Baker expresses very well from the point of view of a scholar, online catalogues will keep improving, while card catalogues have not any potential for improvement.

Searching and Retrieval Capabilities

With regard to searching capabilities, the online catalogue is a significant departure from traditional library catalogues. One of its most interesting features and a major advantage over the card catalogue, is the ability of the user to search for the needed item in a variety of ways that are not available in the manual catalogue.

Online catalogues are able to generate both a greater number of access points as well as new searching capabilities that enable the user to search the catalogue with little information to hand. In addition to controlled-vocabulary searches by author, title and subject headings, for which relevant indexes have been created and maintained in the online catalogue, it is possible to search bibliographic records through access points such as other title information, series, standard numbers and any other significant data through keyword searching. In general, although there are still shortcomings in the searching capabilities of online catalogues, particularly in subject searching, the findings of various studies indicate that users show much enthusiasm in online catalogues' searching capabilities. The following types of searches in the online catalogue are not available in the manual catalogue and can help the user to execute a greater variety of searches:

Keyword Searching

Keyword access is a very powerful search tool and can create much greater flexibility for the user to search item(s) of which he/she has not exact information. This is extremely difficult in the card catalogue.

Keywords, *i.e.*, every indexed word in the bibliographic description, mainly headings, titles, other title information, contents notes and subjects, are appropriate alternatives for the catalogue user who cannot match the exact bibliographic information in the catalogue.

When searching the catalogue, it is not necessary for the user to enter the exact form and order of words. while keyword searching is an alternative to controlled-vocabulary searching, it can also act as a complement to it. The potential value of keyword searching has often been highlighted in the literature. For example, reporting the result of a transaction log analysis of the Colorado University Library OPAC, Wallace found that 53% of searches were keyword searches.

In many online catalogues, there are options for limiting keyword searching to fields such as author, title, subject, or cross index. Among these options, title keyword searching provides a useful tool both as a substitute for subject access and for specific items when the exact or full title is not known.

Some online catalogues provide keyword searching of abstracts and a number of systems extend this capability to the entire text of a document, a trend that is becoming common in many online search services.

It is extremely difficult to search authors under their forenames in manual catalogues, whereas in online catalogues with keyword access it has become possible to execute such searches. The same capability is available in the online catalogue for searching compound words of which the exact, full form is not known. However, keyword searching has its disadvantages: in some cases too many records may be retrieved and some records may be irrelevant to the searcher's need.

Boolean Searching

Influenced by A&I (*Abstracting and Indexing*) services, many online catalogues have the ability to run Boolean searches. With the use of Boolean operators, such as AND, OR, NOT, it is possible to define subsets of the desired subject or concept when two or more sets are combined.

Specificity is what Boolean searching offers: the user can combine two or more terms in a search statement and narrow or broaden the parameters of the subject of his/her interest. Matthews points out that:

"In most OPACs, a Boolean 'and' is assumed when two or more terms are entered in a search statement, especially if the search is conducted on a single field or type of information, such as author, title, or subject".

Truncation

As in A&I services, some online catalogues permit the user to broaden the set of records to be retrieved by shortening the search word through entering a special truncation symbol immediately after the shortened search word, or before it, or within the word. Most online catalogues perform right-hand truncation implicitly rather than explicitly. This feature of online catalogues provides greater flexibility for the user to broaden access to the necessary information when character-by-character exact match does not help. It should be noted, however, that users have difficulty in understanding and using this type of searching in online catalogues. In some cases, truncation also results in either too many hits or irrelevant records. This has implications for cataloguing principles and rules.

Browse Searching

When the search aim is not specific, the desired results are not precisely known in advance or the correct terms for representing the user's query are not known at the outset, "browse searching is the most useful and preferred approach". Browsing, which is a good feature of the card catalogue, is becoming available in the form of browsable indexes in more and more online catalogues.

The natural searchability that browsing offers satisfies users. In this type of searching, lists of index terms are usually presented in alphabetical order and the searcher can navigate the database by going forward or backward through the desired index until he/she finds the index term which may lead him/her to relevant records.

A novel interface for browsing, which can improve access and the effectiveness of end-user searching, has been developed very recently. Using a GUI, some advanced online systems offer improved searching functionality by providing a multi-windowed view of data stored on a relational database manage-ment system.

This novel interface can help the user to search bibliographic databases in a multi-windowed environment, each of which represents an index of the catalogue with scrollable windows. This approach has the advantage that the user can browse different indexes on the same screen to filter their content and find the most relevant items. Among the indexes are: author, title, publication date, document type, language and subject headings. It would be possible, therefore, to match different indexes and find related documents which have the same values, *i.e.*, identical data elements. This facility helps the user in appreciating the actual contents of the database through its different indexes and removes the problem of search specification using values that are not present.

Hypertext Searching

A most recent addition to searching capabilities in information retrieval systems, including advanced online catalogues, is hypertext searching or 'hypersearch'.

Non linear, associative hypertext systems offer a search approach that attempts to more closely mimic human thought processes. It is stated that hypertext, when used with bibliographic records, could overcome the static nature of existing catalogues.

The hypersearch facility, such as that one offered by GoPAC from Data trek, can simply be applied by highlighting a term or clicking on a highlighted term in the record. The system will search for any occurrences of the highlighted term in all fields and subfields or all authority-controlled fields in all records in the database.

The number of postings associated with the term will be indicated or the system will show a brief display of those related records which contain the same term. The term is highlighted in the retrieved records so that the searcher can see in which field it is located and can decide on the relevance of the record to his/her information need.

During the display of related records, the possibility exists for the user to shift his/her focus and to continue a hypertext search on new and more relevant data elements. In this way, the hypertext facility helps users to navigate throughout the catalogue to find possible related works.

Author-title Search

In most online catalogues, there is an option for searching a known item through the author's surname combined with any keyword from the title. This is the clearest way to execute known-item searches. However, in those systems which restrict the search to author surname and the first word of the title, this type of search has the disadvantage of retrieving too many records when the author's surname is a common name, such as 'Smith', 'Johnson', and so on, or the title of the item begins with common words, such as 'Introduction', 'History', and so on.

Another disadvantage is that, in most cases, users do not remember the first word of titles and thus fail to use this type of search in online catalogues.

Nevertheless, it is very useful, for example, for searching titles on reading lists and it emphasises the importance of surname field.

ID Numbers

Another type of search in some online catalogues is possible through ID numbers. Among possible ID numbers are: call number. *International Standard Book Number* (ISBN). International Standard Serial Number (ISSN). document number. computer system number, *e.g.*, OCLC (Online Computer Library Center), RLIN (Research Libraries Information Network) or WLN (Western Library Network). local system number, *e.g.*, accession number. These types of search are usually performed by library staff.

Other Searching Sapabilities

Other types of searches in online catalogues include full-text searching, proximity searching, adjacency searching which are available only in a few online catalogues. These new searching capabilities in the online catalogue have revolutionised the way in which users search the library catalogue.

The results of different use studies indicate that the searching patterns of users in online catalogues have changed. In other words, the online catalogue has affected the ways in which users search for bibliographic information in library catalogues.

Output and Display

Display of bibliographic information is another major aspect in which the online catalogue departs greatly from the card catalogue. Surveying OPACs in a number of Canadian academic libraries, Cherry report that screen display is the best developed area in online catalogues.

The last step at the catalogue, viewing a search result through the display of the bibliographic record(s), is what the user actually gains from the system. The quality of such a display affects the overall usefulness of the catalogue. While the form and content of bibliographic records in the input/output format in the card catalogue are fixed, the online catalogue permits a flexible format, with the possibility of displaying bibliographic information in a variety of ways and at different levels.

The ways in which bibliographic information is presented in the online catalogue in response to searches vary from system to system. Each system has its own techniques for manipulation of a search result. This is impossible in the card technology where space limitations and the fixed form of bibliographic description do not permit any flexibility or manipulation of search results.

The level of bibliographic description is usually flexible and can be designed according to the user's needs. On the other hand and from a system perspective, as Boll points out, there is a range of display formats suitable for a computer screen or a page printout rather than a three by five inch card.

Online display formats usually include:

- 'Brief-listing display' which shows, on one or more screens, the overall results of a search through 'author', 'title' and 'date' of publication,
- 'Medium-level display' containing the standard bibliographic description, access points and status and location information, and
- 'Full bibliographic display' which shows full description with all access points, including added entries, and may contain summary and/or table of contents of the item.

Another major difference between the online catalogue and the card catalogue is the way in which data elements in a record make up and represent a bibliographic record. Reynolds points out three functions in this regard: the labelling of data elements, the sequence in which data elements appear and the spacing between them.

The online catalogue can include identifying labels before data elements for distinguishing the bibliographic text in a record. Labels may be highlighted, or displayed in uppercase characters or in a different colour. In relation to the sequence of data elements appearing in a bibliographic record, there is a fairly high degree of uniformity among online catalogues.

As in the card catalogue, the arrangement usually follows the numerical sequence of MARC tags or the ISBD order. Some online catalogues do not incorporate ISBD punctuation on the basis that users do not comprehend such 'secret punctuation'.

However, it should be noted that a number of problems may arise from the differences in the input and output formats in the online catalogue. A problem which would be difficult for the user to understand is that the relationships of headings to bibliographic data may not be clear to him/her.

For example, the role of persons associated with the work or manifestations of a work may not be distinguished in the way these names are displayed on the screen in conjunction with the title of the work. Therefore, the user may miss what he/she is seeking. In short, output in online catalogues is not controlled by cataloguing standards.

Limiting Search Results

Limiting or restricting the search results is a good feature of online catalogues and seems to have been copied from A&I services. Crawford, this capability of online catalogues should be offered or performed only when the search yields a large result.

Matthews points out that assisting the searcher in refining or expanding a search shows the powerful capability of the online information retrieval system over the card or COM catalogue.

In terms of refining the search results, the online catalogue has a great advantage over the card catalogue. When many records are retrieved in response to a search, the user may want to restrict them to certain aspects that might seem more relevant to his/her need.

This is not possible in the card catalogue whereas, in most online catalogues, due to the assigning of some subfields in the MARC format as active and searchable, the user has the opportunity of further restricting, reducing or narrowing the search results.

For example, the searcher can limit all the search results to works in a particular language, in a particular type of material or all the works published prior to, during or after a given date, or even works of a certain level of difficulty. This is done by specifying certain control fields and other MARC elements that can be used for limiting search results.

With further developments in online catalogues it is expected that the limiting of search results will become more sophisticated and more flexible for the user. In addition to the usual access points available in the card catalogue, more data elements are being indexed and more indexes are likely to be created in the online catalogue.

Sorting Search Results

Another feature of online catalogues is the opportunity offered to the user to sort the search results in the way that will best fulfil his/her need. Most online catalogues can sort the retrieved records according to such data elements as the author, the title and the date. This sorting capability requires that, in addition to usual access points, more data elements be indexed in MARC records in the database.

Some systems, such as OKAPI (Online Keyword Access to Public Information) the experimental OPAC developed at the Polytechnic of Central London, SMART, the US National Library of Medicine catalogue CITE (Current Information Transfer in English), STATUS/IQ, CANSEARCH, PLEXUS provide ranked output and relevance feedback.

They sort and display results of a search in order of highest occurrence of keywords. Given the searcher's judgments of retrieved items as either relevant or irrelevant, some of these systems can be asked to perform another search modified automatically by relevance feedback to provide a new ranked output list.

Status, Holdings and Location Information

A major feature of the online catalogue is its ability to link circulation information to bibliographic and holdings information and to show to the searcher the status and location of the sought item(s). The user of the online catalogue is able to see the status of any volume and/or copy of the item and whether the item he/she is looking for is available on the shelf or it is on loan, on order, at binding, missing or is not for loan.

The status information also displays the 'date due' of an item on loan. The online catalogue can also show the location of the item in the library, *e.g.*, on which level and/or in which part it is located. All such information is useful also for stock taking and check-in purposes. These features help the patron, particularly the remote user, saving his/her time in knowing the status and location of the needed item(s).

Access and Availability

Unlike in a manual system, the user of the online catalogue has access to bibliographic, circulation, acquisition, holdings and location information at the same terminal, whether within the library or in other libraries through remote access. Again, this capability may be an indication of the need for uniformity and standardisation of data elements and also the importance of integrity in the structure of different files in the system.

In contrast to the possibilities for online consultation, card technology is a strictly localised medium with many physical restrictions to its use. Almost all libraries have a single set of catalogue cards for a document. To some extent a book catalogue or a COM catalogue might help in making the library catalogue available in different locations but these catalogues are costly to update at regular intervals, particularly when the collection is very large.

Unlike the card catalogue, the online catalogue is accessible through terminals located in different places in the library and outside the library via local area networks (LANs) and wide area networks (WANs). In the online environment it is possible for different users, whether inside the library building or outside it, to use the catalogue online and to even search the same record simultaneously. In terms of access to library catalogues, distance has now become irrelevant. Technology has enabled us to have decentralised access to bibliographic information.

Interconnectivity is one of the most important goals of libraries today and can take different forms. Many library catalogues are now accessible through the different tools in the Internet such as Netscape, Gopher, Mosaic and Telnet. This is a great advantage over the manual system and will continue to expand with further developments in telecommunication allied to a decrease in telecommunication costs.

There is also more flexibility with interconnectivity for the searcher to go from one catalogue to another. This is done through the same catalogue or other catalogues which have a WWW forms-based interface. These developments have brought with them new concepts such as globalisation of catalogues and the 'library without walls'. With the availability of different types of OPAC systems to remote users over networks, for example, over the

Internet, libraries need to conform to a new standard known as Z39.50. This standard is a protocol for information search and retrieval in a client-server environment, and is now moving from a standard to an operational reality. Z39.50 is used by libraries to access and search remote databases.

The WAIS system has implemented the standard to provide a consistent environment with consistent user interface, search and retrieval services. In environments supporting Z39.50 connectivity, the user sees remote catalogues as though they were additional databases available from the local system.

The standard is also being used in different library operations such as technical services, acquisitions and interlibrary loans. In this context, Z39.50 encompasses biblio-graphic databases, full-text documents, even numeric databases. For example, for bibliographic databases, a list of fields needed to exchange information and support those functions has been developed.

With advances in telecommunications and the rapid development of different facilities in the Internet it is now also possible to have access to electronic texts and files stored anywhere in the world. As we move to the end of the twentieth century, more full text services will become accessible through remote databases.

5

National Database

INTRODUCTION

The Indian position has been dealt with at some length because of the variety of existing legislation and the fact that for the greater part of India there still is no legislation. This is not for want of trying. There must be few countries where there has been so much effort, so many reports, such unremitting lobbying of politicians. Dr. Ranganathan has devoted a lifetime to the problem, as well as gaining an international reputation for his contributions to librarianship, and nearly every Indian state has been in consultation with him at one time or another over legislation.

All states have active and persistent library associations, hampered by lack of funds it is true, but making up for it in publications and conferences. The will is there, the sympathy is there, but results have been more than disappointing. The main problem is, of course, one of taxation. The states' governments are reluctant to pass mandatory legislation that will increase the tax burden; the rural and urban areas have not sufficient potential revenue to provide library services; and the states themselves have a limited amount of revenue to disburse.

Finally, the central government, although it has distributed large sums for libraries under successive five-year plans, is reluctant to make permanent commitments. But eventually the problem must be solved by central government contributions to make up the deficiency in the states. It has been suggested that 5 per cent of the amount spent on education should be aimed at as the total. This would not provide expensive buildings and equipment, but it would provide a basic public library service. The difficulty is that the longer the central government hesitates to insist on mandatory state legislation, the more difficult it will be to provide this basic service.

A start must sometime be made on bringing the many semi-public libraries into a system and possibly channeling and consolidating the small sums they spend. Grant-in-aid to them altogether must amount to a respectable sum and a large part of it is wasted so long as these libraries are independent, using untrained staff and decrepit premises. The attitude is that they are better than nothing, but this is not true if they give the impression that they are a library service. There is also a danger that more states will pass defective legislation, and the more that do, the longer it will take to bring them into line.

The only Act which is reasonably acceptable so far is the Mysore Act and it is the only one to create a state-wide service. It is now nearly ten years since the Advisory Committee reported and gave a comprehensive view of the situation. It is surely time for the Government of India to make a definite move, if only because otherwise they may be faced with a series of defective and conflicting Acts by the states.

LIBRARY LEGISLATION

The Nature of the Problem

It would appear at first sight that provision and public maintenance of a system of public libraries would be an obvious step in any country where education and the promotion of literacy were considered important. Education, after all, is not an end in itself; the individual must not only have access to the printed word during his period of formal education, he must have the means of enlarging his experience after school and university, and this necessarily implies organized collections of printed materials. If a library is an essential adjunct to school or college, it is an essential adjunct in the world outside.

One would also think that the legislative base for such a system of public libraries would be a comparatively simple matter, and that those libraries would automatically be free for all to use.

It is almost universally recognized that education should be compulsory, and that it should be free up to a certain level. True, cost can be a limiting factor but few countries today do not devote a large proportion of their resources to educational provision. Neither of these assumptions is in fact correct. Systems of public libraries, as against individual public libraries, have only recently been recognized as essential, even in advanced countries, and many countries, some with a secure basis of culture and education, do not have generally applicable public library legislation. Examples are France, Belgium, the Netherlands and Italy.

Even where public library legislation has been long established, it can be seen from the examples studied here that, in the framework of the modern State, public library law is noticeably defective. The development of public libraries has probably been hampered by the paradox that they were in fact recognized as instruments of popular education and social welfare long before the conception of compulsory education and before the legal framework of the modern State was established. The concept of the public library has been essentially that of a local community project.

All countries have public libraries, buildings where books are provided for general reading, either free of charge or for a small subscription. They have been provided in thousands all over the world by charitable bodies, educational, social and religious organizations, by philanthropic individuals, as memorials to a person or to commemorate an occasion.

The public libraries in England and the United States in the early nineteenth century were typical, but they are not always a passing phase of development. The traveller interested in the phenomenon will come across examples almost anywhere: in Asia, for example, the Hardinge Library in Delhi, the Connemara Library in Madras, the Raffles Library in Singapore; in Africa, the King George VI Memorial Library in Tanga, the Connaught Library in Nairobi. Some become moribund.

Some are being or have been incorporated by good fortune into a national or local public library system. Some operate even today with some success. But they are not public libraries in the modern accepted sense, nor were they, for that matter, in the nineteenth century.

Edward Edwards, pioneer of the public library in Great Britain, summed up their built-in failure over a hundred years ago, in evidence to the Select Committee on Public Libraries of the House of Commons in 1849:

- Without some assured provision of the means of continued increase, as well as simple preservation-no man ever secured to posterity the true advantage of a public library. To those persons, therefore, who took thought of such matters, two principles to start with seemed plain. The one that new libraries should be formed in a catholic spirit. The other, that they should be freed from all dependence either in gifts or in current 'subscriptions', for their permanent support. The first principle involved the corollary that the new institutions and their management should stand entirely aloof from party influences in politics or religion. The second principle involved the corollary that the maintenance must be by rate, levied on the whole tax-paying community, and administered by its elective and responsible functionaries.

This statement quite obviously implied that a legal basis was necessary, if the public library was to be a permanent institution and on the implications of this statement most of the public library legislation of the nineteenth century and early twentieth century was founded.

In 1949, Unesco issued the first international declaration on the need and the functions of the public library, and in it was contained the same principle:

- This manifesto, by describing the potentialities of the public library, proclaims Unesco's belief in the public library as a living force for popular education and for the growth of international understanding and thereby for the promotion of peace.

- The public library is a product of modern democracy and a practical demonstration of democracy's faith in universal education as a lifelong process.
- Though primarily intended to serve the educational needs of adults, the public library should also supplement the work of schools in developing the reading tastes of children and young people, helping them to become adults who can use books with appreciation and profit.
- As a democratic institution operated by the people for the people, the public library should be: established and maintained under clear authority of law: supported wholly or mainly from public funds: open for free use on equal terms to all members of the community, regardless of occupa-tion, creed, class, or race.

The manifesto goes on to define the purposes and list some of the services of the public library. It did not, however, attempt to deal with a problem that was already engaging the attention of public librarians and those concerned with the spread of education and literacy, that there must not only be a legal base, but that that base must give equal opportunity to all citizens to use the services of public libraries. In other words, the legislation must be mandatory and cover the whole of the area falling within the scope of the legislation.

The legislation must also provide for something more than opportunities for voluntary co-operation between libraries-it must provide for a nation-wide service, even though the public library remains a locally rooted institution. In 1953, Unesco organized its first seminar on public libraries in developing countries, at Ibadan, in Nigeria. Eighteen countries were represented, mostly in West Africa. Legislation was one of the primary subjects discussed, and in the general report of the seminar, the following statement of principles was included:

- Only legislation can empower the appropriate authorities to provide the service and ensure adequate financial support and efficient administration according to a national standard. Only legislation can define the functions of the providing authority, create the conditions in which it may fulfil those functions, and ensure development.

Library law for national schemes should include the following elements:

- General authorization of expenditure without fixing a maximum.
- Compulsory implementation whenever conditions become favourable. The basis of favourable conditions, it is suggested, is the possession of necessary finance and all requisite material by the providing authority, the existence of a tested organization and the presence of trained and experienced personnel. Compulsory provision is never likely to precede compulsory primary education.
- The obligation to employ only qualified and trained personnel as librarians, and to authorize development only when professional librarians are available to administer the service.

- Service for the entire population in some form or other.
- The inter-lending of books between libraries so that the book resources of the whole territory shall be available to all.
- The book stock shall embrace every shade of opinion, without prejudice to anyone.
- The national scheme in all its parts shall aim at free service.

An addendum to this statement pointed out that there was great difficulty in arriving at a conclusion regarding compulsory legislation, since it was recognized that permissive legislation might well allow for a high standard to be set by enthusiastic authorities, which would act as an inspiration to others. This, and other proposals of the Ibadan seminar, were an act of faith at the time they were published, in view of the conditions of West Africa at the time, just beginning to emerge from colonial rule, with very few African librarians. But the statement was the beginning from which can be traced the rapid development of public library services in Ghana, Eastern Nigeria and Sierra Leone, based on simple but mandatory legislation. In 1955, the Public Libraries Section of the International Federation of Library Associations published a memorandum on the development of public library services, of which one section was devoted to legislation:

Each State should adopt library laws which will include the following provisions:

- Appropriate local authorities must be empowered to expend public funds for public library purposes.
- The amount of local expenditure should not be limited: local authorities should be able to expend as much as they are willing and able.
- The public library purposes for which funds may be expended shall be so defined as not to restrict development.
- Local authorities should be empowered to enter into arrangements with other local authorities for joint schemes for providing the whole or any part of the service, and to contribute to the cost of schemes for cooperation and mutual assistance.
- Each local authority should appoint a library committee directly responsible to the local council.
- Each local authority should have power to appoint staff who shall be employed in accordance with the conditions and regulations applicable to other local government officers.
- The use of all the services provided must be available to all inhabitants free of any charge whatsoever.
- Though each local authority provides services primarily for the use of its own inhabitants and those who work or study in its area, other persons living outside that area should be able to use those services

if they wish... when adequate library services are provided generally in a country or region, however, they should be available to all, regardless of place of residence, without payment.

As soon as practicable, all appropriate local authorities should be legally obliged to maintain adequate public library services. The document was adopted as a statement of policy, with the recommendation that it be sent for study to all governments and appropriate agencies concerned. One further example may be given of the continuing concern with the importance of library legislation. In October 1955, Unesco organized a further seminar on public libraries, this time at Delhi, India, where a successful demonstration project had been founded. The seminar was held in the Delhi Public Library and twelve Asian countries were represented by forty-six librarians and educators. Again, public library legislation and its nature were under discussion, and the following proposals were accepted:

Over-all control and co-operation of development, to provide for a permanent and progressive national public library service, can be obtained only by legislation, which should provide for the following:

- Opportunity for the development of public library service which will be available to all people on the basis of free and equal access.
- An independent service, and not one attached to another department.
- The constitution of a governing body, to be referred to in this report as the central library board, or in a federal state a number of such bodies, subject to a national body with advisory functions.
- Provision for adequate public finance.
- The constitution of district library boards responsible for administration of units of public library service.

Other parts of the report pay tribute to the work done by private bodies in founding and maintaining public library services, but affirm that planned direction and control are now required, and that these cannot be achieved by subsidy to private organizations. On finance the report states: It is of fundamental importance that finance should be by public funds, whether national, state or local, or a combination of these... differences in the structure, powers and financial resources of government at local, state, and national level are such that a simple statement of general applicability cannot be made. It can be said however that sources of finance must be adequate for the support of the service established. The proportion of local funds to national or state funds is a matter for decision by individual governments.

On the unit of service:

- At an early stage in the establishment of a national public library service, the question arises of the convenient administrative unit. This may be defined as the smallest autonomous unit of public library service... the selection of this unit as the real basis for the

> development of public library service, is a matter of some importance. It should be a viable area as regards finance and administration, and should conform as for as possible to existing local government boundaries... for ideal development, the area chosen should contain both rural and urban districts.

It is illustrative of the complexity of the problem that these four authoritative statements on public library development, issued over a short period of time, should vary so greatly in their emphasis. The Unesco Manifesto concentrated on the value and use of the public library, but said nothing about its financial or legislative base. The Ibadan seminar defined as a first principle that only legislation could provide the necessary secure and permanent foundations. It said nothing about the administrative unit on which implementation must depend, or financial problems, but it did prescribe mandatory legislation under favourable conditions.

The IFLA statement, though it defined the nature of public library service, proposed what was in fact permissive legislation, and it did not make any proposals about central control, the size of the administrative area, or financial viability of local authority areas. Although it said there should be no upper limit on expenditure, it did not mention the vital problem of minimum expenditure. The Delhi seminar proposals, with the previous statements before it, went much further, and proposed legislation which would provide for over-all control, viable areas and financial support at national and local level. But it found itself in difficulties when it attempted to define the nature of the viable area. Any acceptable general statement must be vitiated by the enormous differences between countries in national administrative and executive structure, local government and its relationship to central government, the powers existing at different levels of government, and above all, the financial capacity of these different levels.

The stage of educational and technical development of a country must also be taken into account, but this is possibly not quite as important as it may appear. While literacy is obviously a primary requirement of public library use, most countries now have an extensive programme of primary and secondary education, and in many countries, too, advanced technology exists side by side with primitive standards of living in some areas. It should also be remembered that in the last century, in some countries, notably the United Kingdom, public library legislation actually preceded general legislation on education. It would be a mistake, also, to assume that the problems of public library legislation are confined to the developing countries. If there is one thing that emerges quite clearly from this study of public library law, it is that the problems of an adequate and effective library law are just as great in the more advanced countries as in the developing ones, apart from the fact that some advanced countries do not yet have a general public library law.

In some countries, such as the United Kingdom, the United States and Canada, the problem is primarily one of reshaping law which is defective and inadequate to meet the need of the user of the public library in the twentieth century, who requires access to the enormous and increasing flood of printed material, numbered in books by the hundred thousand, and periodicals by the thousand.

These requirements create in their turn a need for more and more specialized and trained personnel. The search is for a legislative base for viable units which can meet the readers' needs, and provide not only the material, but the technical services, equipment and staff required.

In other advanced countries, such as Norway and Denmark, the problem is not one of the viable unit, which in fact cannot be provided, but of compulsory co-operation to give the same results.

The problems facing the developing countries may be different, but not so very different. It has often been stated that in social legislation, some African and Asian countries are at the stage others had reached in the nineteenth century. This is only superficially true. We are all living in the twentieth century. If the legislation of the nineteenth century is to be repeated, there is a long road to travel. Not only long, but unnecessary. The example of the past is to be learned from, not repeated.

Basic Principles and Practical Considerations in the Framing of Legislation

Assuming for the purpose of this chapter that new legislation is being considered, the first consideration in the framing of legislation is, of course, the nature of the State itself and the place that legislation takes in its structure. Particularly in social legislation such as the establishment of public libraries, which has primarily a local impact, account must be taken of the nature of the authority by which national government passes on its responsibilities, the basis of taxation at local and national level and in a federal State, the constitutional rights of established organisms within the State.

Even where there is no general legislation, in countries where the doctrine of ultra quires does not apply and organs of local government may establish any service they are not specifically forbidden to do, public libraries may exist perfectly legally by local legislation, and this in turn will cause difficulties in framing a general law.

This is the case in the Federal Republic of Germany, and to some extent in the Netherlands and Belgium. Apart from this, there are patterns in the relationship of local government to national government which must be taken into account. H. F. Alderferl in his study of local government in developing countries, identifies four basic patterns, which are established in developing countries either through adoption or by passing on of previous colonial development. The French pattern, which exists in a large part of Africa, carries the doctrine of ultra vires much further than in England or the United States. Local government has no powers not granted to it by constituted authority.

Local government also is subject to executive jurisdiction which is independent of the administrative and legislative branch to a great extent. Generally, he states, French local government is characterized by centralization, chain of command, hierarchical structure, executive domination and legislative subordination. The English pattern, as defined by Alderfer, is characterized by decentralization, with local decision-making bodies with more or less independent powers, as against concentration, in the French pattern, where all power lies with the central government with local units acting as agents.

The English pattern generally implies also legislative dominance, the committee system and voluntary citizen participation. The Soviet system is one of 'democratic centralism', with all organs as links in one continuous chain of governmental power.

Communist Party direction and leadership exist at all levels, and local agencies are not law-making or executive bodies in their own right, but subject to correction not only at the next higher level but at other levels. The 'traditional' form of local government is non-Western, though in Western forms there are traditional residues. The pattern is one of a chief or local leader, or a group of people, having jurisdiction over a village or group of villages. Essentially the form is non-urban, but it has deep roots and cannot be ignored as a working unity.

The Indian panchayat system of local government is an example of a traditional form being incorporated into the local government system of a modern State, organized generally on the English system. The clash between two systems, and the different types of law that may be produced, was illustrated in Africa when, at a UNESCO seminar at Enugu in I961, the question of a model Act for African countries was discussed. The Act proposed was on the English model. This was simple and mandatory, giving almost unlimited authority to an independent board, subject to central government control. It was this type of legislation which has been successful in practice in Ghana, Eastern Nigeria and Tanzania.

The delegates from the French-speaking countries could not accept this since it was not an acceptable type of legislation for their countries, and they proposed a different model Act for their purposes. Without quoting this in full, it can be said that it was at once more detailed and less specific. Though it set up a directorate attached to the Ministry of Education, and advisory bodies, it could be said to be rather a statement of intention than a legislative instrument. Subsequent decrees in the various territories have similar structure. Thus, the decree for the Ivory Coast goes into some detail on expenditures and staff required, but does not provide for means of raising the necessary funds or an organization charged with continuous development.

The differences may be more apparent than real, given a determination to create a public library service, but it does seem that in Europe, the Scandinavian countries, the United Kingdom and Ireland have been more successful, through planned co-operation between local and national government, than for instance, in France. A recent survey in Le Monde of the public libraries of Paris showed enormous variations in expenditure on libraries in the various communes, with seemingly no co-operation or standards imposed centrally. A generous system of subsidies for building is offered by the central government, but there does not appear to be any way of forcing local authorities to take advantage of them if they do not wish to provide their share.

There are other, important factors to consider in pre-consideration of legislation. Some investigation must be made of the practical problems, and a body of facts built up. While the survey is important, it must be a practical move towards action, and not an end in itself or a means of delaying action. One of the most successful librarians in charge of a library service in a developing country has said that until a service is provided it is impossible to say what sort of service is needed. A careful analysis at grass roots level involves a detailed statistical examination of a community-its growth rate, its educational levels, its literacy rates; it involves the testing of different types of reading materials and a survey of existing places for reading and studying.

Such an approach overlooks the complete lack of basic statistics on which to base the survey. And above all, it ignores the sense of urgency which permeates any developing country trying to pull itself into the twentieth century by its bootstraps. I am sure that these critics would produce a magnificent report. . . and that report would probably conclude that the contemplation of any form of library service was premature.

By the time it appeared it would have been overtaken by events, such is the speed of development of Africa today. This may be overstating the case against survey, but it is true that a survey should be made after decision-to discover specific problems and how they might be overcome.

These problems can be summarized as follows:

- *Educational Situation:* The provision of libraries depends on adult literacy, and is also concerned with the provision of primary education. Literacy rates based on averages are deceptive-for instance, the adult literacy rate in India is less than 20 per cent, but in Delhi in 1954 it was nearly 40 per cent and is now over 50 per cent. The Government of India report of 1959 did not consider that a literacy rate of 20 per cent was any barrier to a nationally organized public library service, but of course one would assume that a low average literacy rate would suggest concentration on urban areas. In terms of cost relative to use, there would be no point in providing for an elaborate system of mobile libraries to serve rural areas.

- *Language and Book Production:* The number of languages in use and their relative importance is a factor in pre-consideration. Allied to this is the matter of book production. Lack of book production in the national language is an extreme limiting factor, though the establishment of public libraries may well stimulate production and in fact has done so in some countries. But it must be observed that the success of public library development in some African countries has been due largely to the fact that English is the established language of communication, thus giving immediate access to an abundant source of material.
- *Population Density and Concentration:* It goes without saying that a rural and scattered population is more difficult to provide for than an urban one. The problem therefore is not one so much of over-all density as of concentration, and this can well affect the unit of administration
- *Communications:* This also affects the matter of the unit, and administrative arrangements. Decentrali-zation may well be necessary. This may be a problem of organization rather than legislation, but it must be considered.
- *Income and tax structure:* This affects the time factor during which legislation can be expected to come into effect, and also the proportion of cost to be met from various sources.
- *Existing Legislation:* This may exist nationally or locally, and consideration must be given to its possible incorporation in new legislation. In some countries, Ceylon is an example, effective public libraries exist in some areas through local legislation, and a new library law must take into account their existence and their legislative base.
- *'Trained Librarians and Training Facilities:* While most countries will have trained librarians, though not in public libraries, pre-consideration must take into account the availability of trained librarians to implement legislation. Opportunities for training abroad must also be considered. While it is an important consideration, the availability of trained librarians is no more than a temporary limiting factor, since there is little point in training unless there are opportunities for employment. In India and Pakistan, facilities for training and qualification are in advance of employment possibilities in the public sector-not only bad planning but wasteful public policy.

These are some of the major items For pre-consideration and survey. The objective is to determine what a country can afford, how great is the need, what structure is required, and how legislation can assist rapid development, without placing too great a burden on financial ability or the administrative structure. None of them should be over-emphasized. The objective remains the same; the limiting factors affect how it is to be attained and at what speed. In this connation, the object by E. M. Broome repays careful study. Nearly all these limiting factors were present, but none of them deterred the Government of Tanzania from passing legislation and implementing it with determination and success.

As was reported at the Delhi seminar:

- In all countries represented at the seminar, public library service is already being provided in some degree, and the time is ripe for further development. In no country do the material difficulties appear to be unsurmountable, nor is a low literacy rate a decisive adverse factor. The rate of development may vary with the speed of overcoming these problems, but the basis for public library services should be laid now. The major deficiencies in present provisions are: lack of over-all control, and the existence of small unco-ordinated units; lack of, or deficiencies in, existing legislation; lack of sufficient funds and government interest; and lack of trained and experienced librarians.

Practical Considerations in Framing Legislation

It has been said that it is easier to pass a law than it is to change it, and this is a lesson to be learned from existing legislation. In the United Kingdom, for nearly seventy years only minor amendments were made to the enabling legislation, despite the fact that under the existing law there was no means by which county councils could set up public library services for rural populations.

Legislation should therefore be flexible and allow for changes in social conditions, in local-government structure and in the tax base. It should be capable of immediate application, but with progressive application. Study is made of the comparative merits and defects of existing legislation, but certain basic problems can be enumerated for primary consideration.

The Public Library as an Independent Service or Part of a National Library Service

In any country which can even consider the foundation of a public library service, there will already be in existence many libraries of high standard: university libraries, libraries of institutions, government departmental libraries, technical libraries and almost certainly a national and probably state libraries. It is tempting to think that there is an advantage in creating an integrated library service of which such libraries are a part.

But it must be remembered that public libraries are for the whole community, whereas all other libraries are designed to serve a section of the community for a special purpose, and that purpose must be their prime consideration. Techniques are similar, but basic purposes are different. Uniting all libraries in one piece of legislation at an early stage is hardly practical, since not only would it tend to stifle the growth of the public library, but it would also entail bringing independent libraries under the legislation, and this would undoubtedly be resisted.

At the same time, there is an obvious need for provision for cooperation and some co-ordination, probably best organized around the national library. Bibliographical and interloan functions should be of value to all libraries. The national library could therefore be usefully linked to the central public library authority.

The Central Authority

The need for a central authority charged with carrying out the provisions of legislation is clear. Should it be an independent body or one linked to, or subordinate to, a government department? This is a matter for decision at governmental level. There are advantages in making the central authority part of the department of education, with a department for libraries and controlling body, which should have more than advisory functions. The central board or authority is a modern device of government much used in developing countries, and experience of its past success in other circumstances will affect legislation for public libraries. But the implementation of legislation should not be left to any other body but education, and if education is chosen as the implementing and organizing department, then a section including trained librarians is essential, with advisory and inspecting functions.

Permissive or Mandatory Legislation

It has been shown that permissive legislation is of limited effectiveness, even when accompanied by financial inducements. Legislation should therefore require action to be taken, wherever the ultimate source of action. But provision should be made for progressive implementation at a rate to be determined by resources.

Relationship Between Local and Central Authority

It is generally accepted that the public library is a local community service. In fact, this becomes less and less true with the explosive growth in production of information material and technical developments in library organization. The answer must be sought in the local government structure of the country concerned. In some countries, a nationally controlled public library service has been created, with provision for some devolution to local government at later stages. The existence of federally organized states also presents some problems. But it must be stated that local interest is desirable and must be stimulated. This implies the passing over of some authority, or the creation of local advisory bodies.

The Size of' the Unit

Assuming that local authority interest is essential, the question then arises: what unit, what size and with what authority? The lbadan seminar, speaking for the situation in Africa, concluded that since recognition of local authority was only beginning, the sole public authority should be the national or state agency. At the same time, the appropriate local authority must eventually be given a responsible place in any national scheme of book service. The roots of the service must be in the local community rather than in the state, regional or national headquarters.

The size and authority of the local unit are important questions, even when there is a suitable urban authority. An urban authority should never be the sole local unit, since its economic and social catchment area is equally important for public library purposes. The requirements for a viable unit, as we have seen, were well stated in the report of the Delhi seminar, but it is already clear, fifteen years later, that they are expanding. In developed countries for example, much larger units than previously thought necessary are now postulated, and the basing of a service on too small a unit can be disastrously hampering in later development. Apart from size, there are other considerations. Whatever the attachment at national level, it is generally conceded that at local level the public library service should be executively independent of other agencies, whether education or other departments such as cultural affairs or social education.

The public library serves all, but is not solely a part of any, SO it should remain independently governed and administered. The question of policy control is a matter of the form local government takes. There is much to be said for the board system, independent but responsible to the local-government system, but this is not always legally possible. But it should be possible at all times to bring into consultation persons of knowledge and goodwill.

Finance

It is generally now accepted that financial support for public libraries should come from public funds, that is, taxation. It is also generally recognized that the service should be free to the user, though this is not always the case in practice. In most developing countries, this means major support at national level, with assistance at local level so far as practicable, having regard to the limitations of local taxation in most developing countries. The acceptance of this principle has been a major limiting factor in public library progress, even in advanced countries, as will be demonstrated in study of existing legislation. It follows, therefore, that any unit at local level must be a tax-raising body, and provision for funds from taxation at a national level must be written in to any legislation. In a federal system, of course, another stage of financial support will be introduced.

Various calculations of the cost of a public library service have been made, but they are of little value in view of changing needs, and could not sensibly be included in basic legislation. No one would expect a public library service to spring armed and ready from the ground, like Jason's dragons' teeth, and financial provision must depend on the rate of implementation of legislation. The Government of India report of 1959 postulated a period of twenty-five years for the creation of a full service, but its calculations as to cost are already completely out of date. Given progressive implementation, standards of service required are also a matter for progressive regulation, and not a suitable one for inclusion in legislation. The power to make regulations on standards and other matters should, however, be given.

Other Considerations

There are several other considerations which may have to be taken into account in framing legislation, but their importance will vary according to country. In some countries, there will be a problem of fitting in private or subscription libraries to the system. There must also be some provision for co-operation between libraries, but this again will vary with the primary decisions already taken. If a linkage with the national library, for instance, is envisaged, or if the unit of service is the whole country, then these provisions can be taken care of automatically under regulation. But if existing resources, as provided by various agencies, are to be fully utilized, then some provision for co-operation and inter-lending must be made. Although university and institutional libraries may not be fully integrated, their resources, after their first priorities are met, should be circulated generally. Whether library education, or the encouragement of library associations, should be incorporated in legislation is a moot point.

It could be fairly argued that if opportunity for employment of qualified people is given by the provision of a public library service, then educational institutions will provide the necessary further education facilities for training librarians and technicians, without any legal requirement to do so. Library associations, also, should not be too dependent on legislative assistance. Again, the provision of a service will itself exert the necessary stimulus for the creation of an active body of professional librarians. And if such associations are to encourage further progress and technical improvement, they should be independent. All these problems and others applying to particular countries will need to be closely considered before framing suitable legislation in terms which will create a permanent, expanding public library service available to all people, whatever their age, status or geographical situation.

The way in which the problems have already been approached and the answers embodied in legislation is the subject of the next stage. There are many lessons to be learned, and the gap between intentions and results is often a depressing commentary on how the goodwill of legislators can be frustrated by circumstances unforeseen or unsuspected. Government and legislation are, alas, by no means an exact science. But in the framework of the modern State, legislation as an instrument of authority is necessary. In the case of public libraries it can truthfully be said that no successful public library system can exist without legal authority, but that many devices have been necessary to get round defective legislation. Public libraries happen to be the subject of this study, but no doubt authorities on law and government could produce better examples of problems caused by legislation rather than solved by it.

The Pattern of Legislation Comparative Solutions

The main body of this study consists of summaries of the existing legislation in fourteen countries, and taking into account the federal countries, twenty Acts are considered, with others mentioned in passing. More could have been chosen, but in fact, not more than thirty countries have effective general library legislation, less than a quarter of the independent nations of the world. Of the countries chosen, four are developing countries, two are countries with centrally planned economies and three are federally organized.

This, therefore can be considered a reasonably representative sample, ranging from the most advanced countries, where coverage is complete and basic standards established, to a country which has only just become independent, Botswana. They all have one thing in common; in none of them is legislation, even now, entirely satisfactory and effective, in that it encourages development to the point of greatest efficiency and maximum results. All have problems to some degree, despite the fact that in most of the countries considered there has been revision of law in the last ten years. The advanced countries, most of which have had public library legislation in some form for many years, but with varying effectiveness, have no great problem of financial ability to provide a nationwide system of public libraries, if that ability can be brought to bear.

The problem is rather one of an inadequate and unsuitable local-government structure, and the supplementation of local resources, or in some examples, replacement of local initiative, by central-government intervention. A pattern clearly emerges in nearly all recent legislation, first of a search for a larger and more viable unit of service, which must be both geographically and financially able to deploy larger resources for public library service, and second of the creation of a central advisory body to encourage improvement of public library service. One can see similarities in the solutions adopted, but there are also wide variations.

It is proposed in this chapter to show by comparison the major similarities and variations of the law as it stands in advanced countries. There are important lessons to be learned by the developing countries in framing their own legislation, and it appears that the advanced countries could also learn from their neighbours. In making these comparisons, it must of course be borne in mind that though public library law is evolutionary in character, it cannot be separated from the general body of law of a country, and it must be set in the executive, social and geopolitical structure of the country concerned.The fact that some countries with a high educational and cultural standard have not so far been able to enact general mandatory legislation on public libraries proves this to be the case. Permissive legislation has been replaced by mandatory legislation in most countries. The appropriate local authorities are now required rather than permitted to provide a public library service.

In some countries, notably the United Kingdom, Finland and Sweden, mandatory provision is not necessary, since coverage is already complete. In Norway, obligatory provision is laid down in the Act, and in Denmark a date is set for all communes to provide public libraries. In Canada and the United States, though provision is not mandatory, the problem is no longer one of provision but of viability, and this could be said generally of all the countries considered, except the countries having centrally planned economies, where the law has nothing to say on this. But it would appear that in Hungary, at any rate, there is complete coverage.

Central Government and Advisory Bodies

In all countries, the intervention of the central government, either at state or federal level, or both, has led to the setting up of a central body to guide future progress, and this is the most common feature in all recent legislation. These central bodies may take many forms, either advisory or executive. They may be independent, or responsible to a department of State. Their membership may be drawn from organizations or individuals. Their constitution and powers can be summarized as follows:

Czechoslovakia

The Central Library Council is an advisory body in the Ministry of Education and Culture. There are two bodies, one for Bohemia-Moravia and one for Slovakia. Membership consists of representatives of authorities and expert librarians. All proposals concerning libraries are submitted to them, and they have the right to initiate proposals themselves.

Denmark

The Library Council consists of sixteen members representing all sections of the Danish Library Service. They are appointed by the Minister of Cultural Affairs, are consulted in all matters of importance to the working of the Libraries Act, and have the right to initiate representations. The chairman is the Library Director, head of the State inspectorate.

Finland

The library delegation is an advisory body responsible to the Central Board of Schools. There are twelve delegates, representing the Department of Education, local authorities, library training and other organizations working for libraries and adult education. The delegation can take the initiative in submitting proposals to the Central Board of Schools.

Hungary

The National Council for Library Activity, responsible to the Ministry of Culture, has a section for public libraries. It has also a working organization, the State Institute of Libraries, similar in some respects to the State inspectorates of Scandinavian library systems. The functions of the National Council are advisory and technical, but being a direct organ of central government, it obviously has great prestige.

Ireland

The Library Council has as its main purpose the operation and supervision of the Irish Central library, and a secondary purpose of assisting local library authorities to improve their services. Its membership is by nomination, and a majority of the members are nominated by universities or the National Library. The powers of the Library Council are considerable, since it considers applications for grants from local authorities and its functions are much more than advisory. In view of the form of local government in Ireland, it can be said to be an executive body with potentially great powers. In fact, the original secondary function has become the primary one.

Qntario

The Provincial Library Council is an advisory body responsible to the Minister for Education, and it consists of nine members appointed by the minister, and one for each regional system. It has certain functions under the Act and may also make recommendations regarding development and co-ordination of library service.

Quebec

The Quebec Public Libraries Commission is responsible to the Minister for Cultural Affairs. Its membership is six persons nominated by the minister, whose qualifications shall be their interest in the development of public libraries, and the Director of Public Libraries of the Province. The powers and duties of the commission are wide, in that it is generally charged with the study of the best means of developing public library services, and it must report every three months on its findings regarding the working of the Public Libraries Act.

United Kingdom

The Library Advisory Councils, set up by the Minister of Education under the 1964 Act, one for England and one for Wales, have no set number of members, nor any stated qualifications for membership. They are nominated directly by the minister, and actually the representatives are drawn from local authority members, university and public librarians representing all the major interests of local government and various sizes and types of library. The function of the councils is purely advisory, and their main work is in connexion with the achievement of standards and the general working of the Act. But by their existence, they have become the advisory bodies for libraries in general, and on such matters as librarianship training.

Washington State

The State Library Commission is an executive commission appointed by the Governor, and responsible for administration of federal and state funds for improvement of public library services. It operates through the state library and appoints the state librarian, who acts as secretary to the commission. Though its main functions are executive, it also has advisory responsibilities. The functions of these bodies are mainly advisory, and as will be seen generally from their constitutions, are intended as a source of expert opinion on public library development.

They are useful bodies, but equally important, their existence creates a secretariat, and that secretariat, whether clearly laid down in legislation as in Quebec, or not, as in England and Wales, inevitably assumes supervisory functions. Those functions can be of inspection and control, as in Finland and Denmark, or they can be limited to advice to the appropriate minister and the right to ask for regular reports and give advice to individual library authorities. Even where there is no central coordinating body, there is invariably a central coordinating government department.

In Norway, the State inspectorate is recognized by the Act, and the State Inspector is a direct appointment of the Crown, though responsible to the Ministry of Church and Education. In Sweden, there is a Library Section of the Central Board of Education, and its functions include supervision of State grants, approval of building plans, and supervision of the School of Librarianship. With the change in local government law, its functions are now more limited, being more advisory than supervisory.

In the United States, in addition to the state departments concerned with public libraries, now established in most states, there is an office in the Department of Education in Washington charged with supervision of the very substantial grants under the Library Services and Construction Act. Except in Scandinavia, where they have been in existence for many years, the emergence of these bodies and the departments attached to them is comparatively recent, and their influence on public library development is bound to increase. It will be noted that the usual attachment of the library councils and their civil-service bureaux is to the Ministry of Education, in some cases to the Minister of Culture. But this attachment at central-government levels does not necessarily imply any attachment of public libraries at lower levels of government to any particular department.

Provision for Co-Operation

In most countries, legislation shows a marked preference for the provision of public library services within the existing local-government framework, and an equal reluctance to interfere with those existing agencies, even when they are clearly not viable. The only exception to this in recent legislation, where smaller authorities are required to give up their powers, is in England and Wales, where there is provision for the compulsory surrender of library powers by authorities of less than 40,000 population.

Even here, the clauses have not so far been used, since a major local-government reform is expected to make them unnecessary. Local-government reform in Sweden and Denmark is also making the problem less urgent, though it will still exist.

Failing the forcible creation of larger public library authorities, the search for the larger unit must take the form of co-operation, and recent legislation is characterized by the creation of a superstructure of co-ordination, often at two or three levels, either mandatory or permissive. Library authorities are either to be persuaded to join with others in a library system, or a superstructure of co-operation is created above them, in which they have the opportunity, or are compelled, to take part. Financial assistance is usually given. Some examples of this kind of provision are as follows:

Denmark

A number of suitable libraries are designated as county libraries, serving a district. Their functions are to assist the local libraries in the district by lending or obtaining for them books and other suitable materials they cannot provide themselves, and by giving advice and technical assistance.

In the present legislation, the Library Director recommends which libraries shall be recognized as county libraries, and the minister shall ensure that the district served is of a suitable size and that the county library is able to carry out its functions. In the past, it is thought, too many county libraries were designated, and the districts were too small.

The provision is mandatory, that is to say, all libraries must join a district, and an advisory committee is formed to direct the work. National grants are made to the county libraries, and the county or counties must also contribute at rates laid down. The communes themselves do not contribute directly.

Norway

The system of regional central libraries is similar, except that the designated libraries have wider functions in super-vision of their local libraries. The problems of establishment, and suitable areas, are very great in Norway, and though nineteen regional libraries have now been established, they vary greatly in resources. Again the inclusion in an area is mandatory, and grants are made to meet the cost, with supplementary grants from the areas covered.

Sweden

In addition to the establishment of county libraries on similar lines to Denmark and Norway, a further superstructure has been added of three inter-library loan centres, which lend to the county libraries and receive grants for their services from the State. It must be emphasized that in the Scandinavian countries, the aid-giving libraries are the larger libraries in their area, and though they may establish special departments for their additional functions, in no sense, except in a limited way in Norway, do they administer or supervise the other libraries in their area.

Quebec

The regional libraries in Quebec are quite different from others, and serve a different purpose. They are intended, not to superimpose an additional system, but to encourage the provision of public library service in those sparsely populated areas which cannot provide for themselves, even with grant aid. The system is fully described in the appropriate section, but briefly, when a minimum area containing 25,000 inhabitants can be defined, an ad hoc committee is formed. The kind of service depends on the size of the area and other factors, but generally, grant is 85 per cent of the total cost. Such a system is only required under extreme adverse conditions, but the similarity to the Norwegian system in its northern area is obvious.

Ontario

The Ontario method of creating larger areas is in effect a three-tier system. In a county, a combined library system can be formed at the request of 75 per cent of the authorities in the county, then a county library service is formed, and a separate public library board set up.

But it is only responsible for that part of the county which has asked for inclusion. The system has obvious defects, but it does have the effect of helping some at least of the smaller authorities to combine.

Superimposed on this system of county libraries and independent libraries is provision for regional library systems, working roughly on the Scandinavian pattern, and having similar responsibilities. Substantial grants are available from state funds, but regions are not necessarily inclusive of all the libraries in their area since, throughout the legislation of Ontario, there are no mandatory powers.

United States of America

There are no mandatory powers in the United States, and most recent legislation, both federal and state, has written into it an injunction that the independence of the community library is to be respected and preserved.

The creation of the larger unit therefore is by the voluntary amalgamation of independent libraries into 'systems', in which service is often provided by contract between one library and another. It is interesting to note that current thinking puts the minimum viability of a system at 150,000 population.

United Kingdom

A voluntary system of co-operation has existed for many years, with member libraries paying subscriptions usually on a per capita basis. The country is divided into fourteen regions for this purpose. The 1964 Act legally recognizes this system, and provides for compulsory membership by all library authorities, and for amalgamation of the regions where necessary.

Two of the largest regions, comprising London and the south-east of England, have already amalgamated, with the authority of the Ministry of Education. The purpose of the regions is principally inter-library co-operation, and for this purpose provision is made in legislation for bringing into the system other than public libraries.

NATIONAL POLICY ON PUBLICLIBRARIES

Pre–Five-Year Plan Period

The programmes executed by provincial and central governments since 1910 for the social and adult education of the populace have paved the way for the enactment of library laws and rules for grants-in-aid in the country. Hence, public library finance is part of the education budget.

The level of literacy in 1941 being as low as 16 per cent, universalization of elementary education and eradication of illiteracy in the nation were the aims of the education policy of the government. To fulfil this goal, a variety of programmes were undertaken such as extension services, continuing education, social education, part-time education, refresher courses, non-formal education, and adult education.

In order to accelerate the pace of socio–economic development, the government considered public libraries to be an integral part of development projects. In 1948, the first public library bill was passed in the state of Madras, mainly due to the efforts of the eminent librarian S.R. Ranganathan. One of the earliest Advisory Committees-the Sinha Committee, appointed in 1957-

recommended that public libraries be developed on the basis of a hierarchical network. The hierarchy should have the national central library at the apex, followed by state central libraries, district libraries, block libraries and panchayat libraries. This is the foundation upon which the public library system has been built.

First Five-Year Plan (1951–1956)

The first plan provision was ₹ 140 million for social education, physical education, and youth welfare, out of the total budget for education of ₹ 1.33 billion. Libraries were considered to be part of social education. ₹ 5 million was set aside for establishment of the national central library, but this sum was not used.Improvement of library services was mentioned in this plan for educational development. The essence of the scheme was to establish district libraries in each state, which were to be supplemented by a state central library. The government of India also initiated a scheme, "Integrated Library Service," with the support of the state government. The scheme targeted units in every area selected by the governments for intensive educational development.

The experimental project was meant to monitor the impact of a number of educational institutions in areas covering 100 villages. Each area was to have five model community centers, plus a main library with branches to distribute books to 20 villages. This pilot project was implemented in 29 areas in the country. Nine states made plans to open state central libraries, and some others were in the process of setting up district libraries in about 100 districts. This cost approximately ₹ 10 million, of which nearly two–thirds was contributed by the government of India. Thus, libraries were considered to be an essential part of the Community Development Programme that was launched during the first plan period.

Other important developments included establishment of the Delhi Public Library in 1951. The Central Reference Library in Calcutta was established in 1955. Connemara Public Library, in Madras became the State Central Library in 1950 under the provisions of the Madras Public Libraries Act of 1948; in 1955, it became one of the three depository libraries. At the end of March 1954, the country had 32,000 libraries with a book stock of about 7.1 million volumes; an amount of ₹ 9 million was spent on library services. By 1951, the level of literacy had risen to 18.33 per cent.

In 1954, the Delivery of Books Act was passed to include newspapers. The act obligated every publisher in India to deposit a copy of its publication with the National Library in Calcutta; the Asiatic Society Library, Bombay; Connemara Public Library, Madras; and the Delhi Public Library. On the basis of books received under this act, India has a national bibliography which is published by the Central Reference Library, Calcutta. The bibliography, however, does not include textbooks, musical scores, maps, and atlases.

Second Five-Year Plan, (1956–1961)

Of the ₹ 2.040 billion budgeted for education, ₹ 100 million was proposed for social education, physical education, and youth welfare. This plan contained the same provisions as the first plan, plus additional provisions for establishing integrated library service. There were three objectives. First, state and district libraries were to be set up in each state. Second, the library services were to be organized on the basis of legislation. Finally, district libraries were to form the link between the state central library and village libraries. As a result, nine states in India established state central libraries and 254 district libraries. But the national central library was still not established. In 1960, the state of Andhra Pradesh enacted library legislation.

During this plan period, a total of ₹ 2.040 billion was spent on educational development, of which ₹ 9 million was spent on library development. Even though ₹ 18.6 million was provided, the states only used 48.6 per cent of this amount. Thus, the number of libraries nearly doubled in 1964 as compared to 1951, and the expenditure on public libraries in this period increased three–fold. A UNESCO report published on the occasion of the Public Library Seminar held at Delhi in 1955, India had 24,086 public library service points at the time. The level of literacy in 1961 increased to 28.31 per cent.

The Advisory Committee for Libraries was appointed in 1957 by the Government of India, with K.P. Sinha as the chairman.

The committee drafted a Model Library Bill and drew up a 25-year plan. In 1959, the committee submitted a report with recommendations, some of which follow:

- Enact library legislation, in all constituent states, to establish public libraries;
- Build nationwide library service with detailed suggestions for financing through the state and central governments;
- Extend public library service to the blocks, panchayats, and villages; and,
- Create an independent Department of Social Education and Libraries.

Third Five-Year Plan, (1962–1967)

The amount of ₹ 5.6 billion was budgeted for education in this plan period, but the amount to be spent on libraries was not clearly indicated in the plan. Of this amount, ₹ 620 million was expected to be available for social education. During this plan period, the system of central government assistance to the states was changed, and funding for libraries was kept to a bare minimum.

Thus, it was up to the individual states to take the initiative and develop their public libraries. With the beginning of this plan period, the scheme to assist state governments in establishing state central libraries, district central libraries, and block development libraries was abandoned. The central government decided to let the states decide on the development; the decision was a major setback that hindered the development of public libraries.

During this plan period, four national libraries were to be established at Delhi, Calcutta, Bombay, and Madras. District–level libraries were to be established in all the states. A sum of ₹ 32.3 million was made available to the states for this purpose.

In 1962 the central government sent a model Public Libraries Bill to those state governments which had not adopted any library legislation, hoping to persuade these states to show an interest in passing the legislation.

A Working Group on Libraries was appointed by the Planning Commission in 1964. Group recommendations included:

- By the end of the Fifth Five Year Plan, set up libraries at block headquarters and in every village having a population of 5,000;
- Encourage the Programme of Adult Education to use the services of the public libraries to eradicate illiteracy.

As of January 1, 1965, according to the information received from the states by the Working Group:

- Twelve of 18 states/UT had state central libraries;
- 205 of 327 districts had district central libraries;
- 1,394 blocks of 5,223 had block development libraries;
- 28,317 villages out of 566,878 had village libraries.

Library legislation was passed in two states during this period: Karnataka in 1965, and Maharashtra in 1967.

Fourth Five-Year Plan, (1969–1974)

The education budget was estimated at ₹ 7.120 billion of which the social education component was ₹ 100 million. Thus, the tempo that had built for the development of library services slowed. However, ₹ 130 million was provided in this plan period for provision of information services, which included information centers, radio transmitters, film production, mobile cine vans, and other media.

The literacy level rose to 34.45 per cent in 1971.In 1972, the Working Group on Development of Public Libraries was constituted by the Government of India Planning Commission to make recommendations for library development. These recommendations were to be included in the Fifth Five Year Plan.

The group submitted detailed proposals for:

- Allotment of ₹ 310 million for the development of public libraries; but the amount actually provided was a meager ₹ 20 million;
- A network of libraries to cover the whole country, and other recommendations similar to those made earlier by the Advisory Committee.

Figures provided in 1973 concerned the number of public libraries, and read as follows:

- Fifteen of 21 states/UT had state central libraries;
- 235 of 376 districts had district central libraries;
- 1,500 of 3,100 sub–districts had sub–district central libraries;
- 50,000 villages of 566,878 had village libraries;
- 1,800 of 2,641 towns had town libraries.

In 1972, during this plan period, the central government established the Raja Rammohun Roy Library Foundation. The foundation was created as an autonomous body under the Department of Culture, controlled by the Ministry of Education, for the development of public libraries in India. This foundation matches the funds of the states for purchasing furniture and books, organizing conferences and seminars, and providing mobile library service to the rural areas. It also advises the central government on all matters relating to library development in the country.

Fifth Five-Year Plan, (1974–1979)

An adult education programme was the emphasis of this plan. The programme was to be supported by a network of libraries at the village and block levels, and various community centers. Thus, steps were taken to strengthen not only the village and block libraries, but also the central and state libraries, and the district libraries. The states were assisted by the Raja Rammohun Roy Library Foundation, which was established in 1972. During this plan period, the amount of ₹ 15.620 billion was allocated for general education, and ₹ 350 million was budgeted for social education.

The only state that enacted a public library law during this plan period was West Bengal, in 1979. In 1978, the government adopted the National Adult Education Programme, but it did not recognize the public library as an agency that could be assigned a role in solving the literacy problem. Rather, the public library was relegated to the role of post–literacy work. This view was also promulgated by the Draft National Policy on Education (NPE), 1979. However, the need for the rural public library system to play a role in continuing education in the villages and rural areas was recognized.

In 1979, the Ministry of Education in the Department of Culture established a library section under the charge of an under secretary. The goal: to promote development of public libraries in India. Since then, libraries have not been part of the social education budget. Instead, they have been included in the art and culture component of the budget.

Sub–Sixth Five-Year Plan, (1980–1985)

This plan emphasized minimum essential education of all adults, to be achieved by inter-sectoral cooperation and interand150; agency coordination. These efforts were to be supported by post–literacy, continuing education through a network of rural libraries as well as instructional programmes conducted through mass communication media. The amount allocated for general education was ₹ 21.622 billion. The art and culture component was ₹ 839 million.

During this period:

- Twenty–six states/UT out of 31 existing in 1982 had established/designated state central libraries;
- Out of 401 districts, 291 had district central libraries;
- Out of 5,027 blocks, 1,798 development blocks had block libraries;
- Out of 575,936 villages, 41,828 had village libraries;
- Out of 2,643 towns, 1,280 had town libraries.

Of the 29 metropolitan cities with a population of 400,000 and above, only four — Madras, Hyderabad, Bangalore, and Delhi — have city public library systems with central libraries, branches, and deposit stations. Thus, it is estimated that approximately 20 per cent of the literate population has access to public library service.

A Working Group on Modernization of Library Services and Informatics in the Seventh Plan was appointed by the Planning Commission in 1983. In its 1984 report, the group recommended formulation of a National Policy on Library Services and Informatics in support of similar recommendations made earlier by other committees.

From its establishment in 1972, to 1982, the Raja Rammohun Roy Foundation provided funds of ₹ 250 million to assist 15,000 rural libraries. In 1982, the Delhi Public Library became a copyright library. The level of literacy increased to 43.56 per cent in 1981.

Seventh Five-Year Plan, (1985–1990)

During this Plan period, the Planning Commission's objective was to address the needs of 90 million people, ages 15–35, in the Adult Education Programme. The network of libraries was to play a role in the development of literature for neoliterates. Library systems were to be strengthened with specific attention given to improvement of facilities at the national-level institutions. The general education budget was ₹ 47,753 million; ₹ 4.821 billion constituted the art and culture component.

An important development during this period was the 1986 adoption of the National Literacy Mission, which emphasized the education of women and also the establishment of rural libraries.

In 1989, there were 7,180 main libraries and 18,000 service points. The collections of the National Library of Calcutta were increased significantly. The Central Secretariat Library started creating a database on the epic "Mahabharata." The Raja Rammohun Roy Foundation set up an "Integrated Research Cell-cum-Computer Unit" for promoting research in librarianship, and also started a database of public libraries in the country. A Committee on

National Policy on Library and Information System was appointed in 1985 by the Government of India, Department of Culture. The resulting final report was submitted in 1986. This policy stressed the need to establish strong links between a village's community library and primary school. If the school lacked a library, the community library was to provide the children with adequate resources. Furthermore, a children's section was to be organized in every public library.

The National Policy on Education, 1986 barely mentions libraries. It states that a nationwide movement for improvement of existing libraries and the establishment of new ones will be taken up, provision will be made in all educational institutions for library facilities, and the status of librarians improved. The school library programme, "Operation Blackboard," was initiated with the provision of essential teaching and learning materials.

The National Book Policy–1986 also had an impact on libraries, as it recommended:

- Provision of reading material for children by all the agencies involved;
- That 10 per cent of the annual education budget of the governments be used to purchase books for libraries.

During this plan period, these states passed library acts: Manipur in 1988, Assam in 1989, Haryana in 1989, and Kerala in 1989.

Eighth Five-Year Plan, (1992–1997)

The money allocated for this period for general education is ₹ 168.133 billion; for art and culture, ₹ 7.276 billion has been allocated. Universalization of elementary education, eradication of illiteracy in the 15-35-year age group, and strengthening of vocational education in relation to emerging needs in urban and rural settings are the major thrusts of the plan. These goals are to be achieved by using formal, non-formal, and open channels of learning. The plan states that in those states with an advanced library system, rural libraries should become the focal points for post–literacy and continuing education programmes.

Book promotion is also emphasized in this plan, to be promoted by the organization of a National Centre for Children's Literature, which should produce 3,000 titles annually. Important books are to be translated into the various Indian languages, and books for neoliterates published. Publishers and voluntary agencies will be given assistance, and the school library programme, undertaken as part of the "Operation Blackboard" scheme of the National Policy on Education-1986, will continue.

Public libraries of national importance are to be provided funds for improvements/innovations such as the following:

- The Khuda Baksh Public Library proposed establishment of an Institute of Oriental Studies and open regional units for research on Indo-Islamic and comparative religion;

- The Rampur Raza Library would acquire sophisticated equipment for preservation of its collections;
- The Asiatic Society, Calcutta, is to open an art gallery, introduce a desktop publishing system, and construct a new building;
- The National Library proposed making microfilms available, producing a national union catalogue, and providing book production statistics;
- The Central Reference Library is to be reorganized into a National Bibliographical and Documentation Center with a computer center; and,
- The Delhi Public Library is to open two new libraries within its service area.

The Raja Rammohun Roy Foundation proposes assisting state central libraries in their quest to obtain reprographic equipment. The Foundation also hopes to assist certain libraries in the processing of rare books, and to provide assistance to rural libraries, and to those public libraries that have completed 100 years of service.

The Model Public Libraries Act is based on the national seminar on this subject, which was held February 14, 1990, in New Delhi. The seminar was organized by the Indian Library Association in collaboration with the Raja Rammohun Roy Library Foundation. This excellent document encompasses all aspects of legislation important to the establishment of public libraries.

The National Cultural Policy, 1993 is the new policy designed by the Government of India. It was created by merging the National Policy of Library and Information Science, the National Book Policy, and other related policies dealt with by the Department of Culture of the Ministry of Human Resource Development.

LIBRARY LEGISLATION IN INDIA

India became an independent republic in January 1950. It is a federal union of states, there being seventeen states and ten union territories. The form of government is democratic, with a president and two Houses of Parliament. The Upper House, or Council of States, is indirectly elected, the members being elected by the legislative assembly of each state. The Lower House, or House of the People, consists of 500 members directly elected by adult suffrage. Each state has its own legislature, directly elected.

Certain legislative powers are retained by the central government, but education, the most important function so far as libraries are concerned, is reserved to the states, though there is a central Ministry of Education with co-ordinating powers, including that of making grants for specific purposes.

These powers have been increased by the very large sums made available under successive Five-year Plans. The area of India is 1,262,275 square miles, and its population approxi-mately 5II million.

Local Government

Local government is in the hands of some 2700 municipal authorities which have primary functions relating to their own areas and frame their own budgets, though usually, however, these require approval at state level. For rural areas there is a three-tier system of panchayats, or local councils-at village, block and district levels.

Generally speaking, the block panchayats consist of groupings of village panchayats, but this does not apply to the whole of India, There are nearly 4000 block panchayats, and some 212,000 village panchayats. The district is the taxing authority below the state. The system is virtually complete and one can therefore say that local administration proceeds from state to city, district or municipality, and right down to its roots in the villages.

Education

The literacy percentage is approximately 24 - men 34.5, women 13. Despite this very low rate of literacy, very great progress has been made in education, and the rate has been improved by 8 per cent since 1951. Over ₹5,000 million were spent on education in 1964 and over 750,000 primary and secondary schools were in operation. The official national language under the Constitution is Hindi, but under the Official Language Act of 1963, English will continue to be used as an official language for an indefinite period alongside Hindi. The regional language of the state is also taught at various levels. There are fourteen officially recognized regional languages.

Library Provision

In the light of the facts the problems of public library provision are very great. India is a very large country with a predominantly rural population, a small per capita income and a number of recognized languages. There are other problems, arising from the local-government system and the relations of the central government to the states. India is a federal State and, as in Canada and the United States, provision of public libraries is reserved to the states and is their sole responsibility.

Even grants under the Five-year Plans, given specifically in the past for public library development, were changed under the third plan to block grants to be spent at the discretion of the states. The central government has therefore no coercive powers to enforce legislation by the states, or to dictate the form of such legislation.

The legal powers to take over the many private or association libraries are also limited. To bring them into the public sector would require separate legislation which is unlikely to be voted. In view of the numbers of such libraries, this is important. Given a government determined enough to create a nation-wide public library system, the position could, of course, be changed.

There is a national Ministry of Education, and it could be given coordinating functions. In fact, the Advisory Committee of I 959 proposed this in the form of an All-India Library Advisory Council, with an executive committee nominated by the Minister of Education, and a secretariat consisting of a division of libraries in the Ministry of Education.

It also suggested that the Government of India should contribute to the library funds of the state an amount equal to funds raised by property tax. Presumably, these proposals would require legislation at national level. Despite many obstacles, India has a strong and continuing literary tradition, and there is a thirst for knowledge which is evidenced by the fact that over 10,000 periodicals and newspapers are published in India. Book production, although its organization is chaotic, flourishes and there is not in fact, any shortage of libraries. Very few Indian towns or even large villages are without a library of some sort, provided by a charitable foundation, by an educational organization or by executive action on the part of state, municipal or district authority.

Very few of these institutions are well endowed, many are little more than reading-rooms. In this connexion, the statement by the Advisory Committee on Libraries, which reported in 1959, is of value in estimating the true position:

- In India the phrase 'public libraries' is used in a very loose sense. It is used to denote any library which permits members of the public to use its material for reference or borrowing on payment of fees or rent. In this sense, all kinds of libraries, national, university, schools and subscription libraries, etc., would be public libraries. Because of the loose connotation of the term, it would appear from the statistics published by Unesco in 1956 that India leads the world in the number of public libraries, which is given as 24,086. The statistics are flattering; they express the aspiration rather than the achievement of the country. The internationally accepted definition of a public library is that it is a library which is:
  - Is financed out of public funds;
  - Charges no fees from readers and yet is open for full use by the public without distinction of caste, creed or sex;
  - Is intended as an auxiliary educational institution providing a means of self education which is endless;
  - Houses learning materials giving reliable information freely and without partiality or prejudice on as wide a variety of subjects as will satisfy the interests of readers. Were such a definition adopted, the number of public libraries in India could not be counted by tens, let alone by hundreds or thousands.

A framework of library provision does, however, exist, and it has been expanded by grants under successive five-year plans, at national level. In the first five-year plan, 1951-56, a scheme of improvement of library service was included calling for a network of libraries to be spread over the whole country. The kernel of the scheme was the establishment of district libraries, which would circulate books throughout the district. These were to be supplemented and supported by a central library for the whole state, or for a whole linguistic region. A supplementary scheme to set up integrated library units was also commended to state governments in connexion with the areas selected for intensive educational development. Under successive Five-year Plans, the schemes have been developed but have not so far been backed up generally by a legislative base, despite strong recommendations by the Advisory Committee in 1959.

These recommendations were for a comprehensive state library law, which would provide for free library service for all. Funds would be provided by a library rate on property tax, the income to be covered by a matching State grant. The unit of library service would be the district. Proposals were also made for legislative action by the Government of India to collate the various Copyright and Book Deposit Acts and to make them viable for a national library service. The Act should also provide for assistance to state governments for public library service. Since provision of public libraries by executive action is an important feature in public library provision in developing countries, a typical example in India, that of West Bengal, is worthy of brief examination.

West Bengal Library System

West Bengal not only contains the largest city in India, Calcutta, but also India's National Library. Its population is over 65 million, and the principal language is Bengali. The literacy rate is 30 per cent. The first public library was opened in Calcutta in 1836 and it was followed during the nineteenth century by the founding of many other libraries on a subscription basis. After independence, small grants were made by local authorities and from state funds, and in 1950, about 1,000 subscription libraries were receiving small grants. In 1956, a coordinated scheme was sponsored by the state government, with financial assistance on a 50 per cent basis from the Government of India.

In 1969-70 a sum of ₹4,313,000 was given in annual grants. All the districts of West Bengal now have a district library and much progress has been made in the provision of buildings, furniture and equipment. A reasonably coherent library system has now been established, with a state central library in Calcutta, over 68 district and area libraries and 579 rural libraries, with total staffs of over 1500. Many of the libraries are still subscription libraries, and grants in fact are still given to many subscription libraries outside the system. While it is a source of satisfaction that public library service has been created, it cannot be denied that it is far from ideal. Since the entire service is under the Department of Social Education, district librarians have no real executive powers, and there appears to be little co-ordination of book stocks. Above all, the lack of a legislative and tax base necessarily makes for uncertainty in future planning.

The Delhi Public Library

Another example of executive action is the Delhi Public Library. This was founded by joint action of the Government of India and Unesco as a demonstration project applying Western concepts of book provision, furniture and equipment in a developing country.

In the final terms of agreement between Unesco and the Indian Government, the terms of reference for the project were set out:

- "It shall provide a public library service for the people of the City of Delhi and shall be a model for all public library development in India, and in all other countries where similar development of public libraries can be undertaken. The library shall be designed to carry out the policy of the Unesco Public Libraries Manifesto and to serve the needs of popular education."

The organizers of the library had, therefore, to plan for a library which would have complete open access to the shelves, which would make no direct charge to readers, and would be organized not for preservation, but for use by readers of all ages and all levels of education. These concepts were not new to India. They had been propagated by the devoted work of Dr. Ranganathan and his disciples. But between concept and execution there was still a wide gap, and the Delhi Public Library was the first in India, and probably the first in Asia, to apply these principles. The library was opened in 1951 by the Prime Minister, Mr. Nehru, and the present author was consultant to the project during the first year of its life. The government of the library is by the Delhi Library Board, an autonomous body acting on behalf of the Ministry of Education.

It is a well-balanced body, now with fifteen members. The Ministry of Education, the Finance Ministry, the Delhi Municipal Corporation, the Delhi Administration and the New Delhi Municipal Committee are all represented and four experts with technical qualifications or library experience are co-opted.

The director of the library is secretary of the board and ex oficio member of it. Finance was jointly from the two sponsoring bodies in the first two years, but is now the sole responsibility of the Indian Government, with small grants from the municipal bodies. The story of the Delhi Public Library has been told many times, and it is not proposed to repeat it here. From its inception it was an enormous success, enrolling over 10,000 members in the first few months and lending over 70,000 books.

In 1966-67, membership had increased to 136,000 and annual issue of books to nearly 2 million volumes. Book stocks have increased from 14,000 to 350,000. It is still, in the words of a recent Indian writer, 'the only public library in India worth the name.' In 1955, the author was invited by Unesco to make a detailed evaluation of the project. This was published by Unesco in 1957. In 1956, the Government of India notified its acceptance of this evaluation, the preamble of which began with the statement: 'During this period of five years the library has made gratifying progress and it has, therefore, been decided to place it on a permanent basis. ' After twenty years of existence, this statement is still the only basis on which the library operates.

Its functions have never been more clearly defined than in the original terms of reference as a pilot project, and it is still not a statutory body. More curious still, though it spends over I million rupees a year, by far the greatest expenditure of a single Indian public library unit, it still has not been given over-all responsibility for providing public library service in Delhi.

In 1964, a further evaluation of the library was made by the board itself, which has this to say about the area of the library's responsibility:

> "A rather peculiar feature of the situation regarding public library service in Delhi is that in addition to the Delhi Library Board, three other bodies, *viz.*, the Delhi Administration, the Delhi Municipal Corporation and the New Delhi Municipal Committee operate a few libraries and reading rooms, and the New Delhi Municipal Committee proposes to open small lending libraries in the area within its jurisdiction. There is no co-operation at all between the several authorities administering these libraries. The fact is stated here because of a possible wasteful duplication of effort and money."

The fact that Delhi is the seat of government and has no state administration possibly accounts for the perpetuation of this rather odd situation. But one would have thought that a short enabling Act would have been possible giving the Delhi Public Library responsibility for providing all public reference and lending services in the Delhi area. Nevertheless, the Delhi Public Library has shown and continues to show that a modern public library can exist and can flourish in India.

Model Libraries Bill

In 1960, following the recommendations of the Advisory Committee on Libraries, the Government of India appointed a committee for drafting a library bill. This was submitted to the Ministry of Education in 1963 and in 1964 the ministry circulated the bill for comments to the various state governments and professional organizations. No further action has yet been taken. The bill is intended for adoption on a nation-wide basis. It would therefore need to be adopted by each state and presumably general legislation by the Government of India would be necessary to define the rights of the citizen to access to libraries, similar to those he has to education, to provide for some form of co-ordination of the various state library services and to provide for financial assistance for the state public library services as envisaged in the Model Bill.The exact form of such legislation, in view of the states' rights, is difficult to foresee, but a similar problem was solved in the United States with the Library Services Act. A long process of legislation is therefore obviously involved, and an equally long process of organization. The integration of the present systems of public libraries provided by executive action will in itself present certain problems.

State Legislation

The Model Bill has been discussed at length because it is presumably the basis on which future legislation will be founded for all the states. But four Indian states have already passed legislation: two, Madras and Andhra Pradesh, before the publication of the Advisory Committee Report and the Model Bill, and two, Mysore and Maharashtra, after the publication of the Model Bill.

Madras Act

Madras State (capital: Madras) has a population of 37 million. The literacy rate is 30 per cent. Tamil is the principal language. Madras was the first state to pass legislation to create a public library system, in 1948. This was largely due to the unremitting efforts of Dr. Ranganathan, but the bill was watered down in its various stages to make it acceptable and it is generally agreed that in its present form not only is the Act defective but that its implementation has been unsound.

In the words of S. K. Mookerjee:

> "The Madras Act and its implementation in the sphere of library organization have taught us all a very good lesson. It has shown how completely the intentions of the legislature can be flouted and the public needs neglected when such implementation is entrusted to the wrong agency."

The main provisions of the Madras Act are as follows: A state library committee is formed for the purpose of advising the government. Its membership includes the Minister in Charge of Education, who is to be president of the board, representatives of universities and local library authorities and three persons nominated by library associations in the state. But the Director of Public Instruction is named as being ex officio Director of Public Libraries and a 'Special Officer' assisting the director in the administration of the Act is secretary of the committee.

It is quite clear that it is not intended that the special officer shall be a librarian and there is no place in fact in the Act for a state librarian with technical qualifications.

It has been stated that the 'Special Officer', not a librarian, was in fact appointed with some haste. The Director of Public Libraries is charged with managing the State Central Library, superintending the work of local library authorities and superintending and directing all matters relating to public libraries in the state. The Act creates local library authorities, one for the City of Madras and one for each district, each district authority being given full powers of management of libraries within the district.

This is a much more sensible arrangement than the one in the Model Bill, in that it creates, in theory at any rate, more viable authorities. There are thirteen districts in Madras, so the average effective literate population of a district is around I million. The powers and duties of district library authorities do not, however, include provision for the appointment of a librarian, and there is no provision for a librarian on the committee.

The power to make regulations also includes clauses: to 'provide for the admission of the public to public libraries in its area on such conditions and on payment of such fees as it may specify'; and 'requiring from persons desiring to use such libraries any guarantee or security against injury to, misuse, destruction or loss of the property of such libraries'.

These sections of the Act do, of course, nullify the whole function of public libraries if acted on, although they are permissive. Each local library authority is empowered to levy a library cess in its area, of six paise per rupee. This can be increased by an authority with sanction. The principal defects of the Act, apart from the omission of a requirement for trained staff with some status and the out-of-date provisions for access to the libraries, are that the Act does not in any way create a system of libraries. The State Central Library has no duties in relation to the district libraries and the district libraries have no duties in relation to each other. A parallel system of libraries is also created under the Act, since one of the duties of the director is to declare what libraries are eligible for government aid.

In the rules made under the Act, the director is to maintain a register of such libraries and conditions are laid down for eligibility for grant. There appear to be no provisions, as in the Model Bill, for eventual merging of these libraries within the public libraries administered by district authorities. Despite the defects of the Act, and its slow implementation, in recent years the public library service has obviously made some impression.

In 1965, total expenditure reached over 7 million rupees as against I,685,000 in 1957, and of this sum I,897,000 was raised in library cess. Over half the total expenditure in 1965, however, was by special grant, under the five-year plan, and it is not known whether this has been maintained since. Book stocks are reported as being nearly 2,500,000, visitors to the libraries nearly 18 million.

But one notes with surprise that there are in the whole state only 15,000 registered borrowers and only 143 trained library staff, of whom only I have full library qualifications. But however suspect some of the statistics, and it must be noted that criticism of the Madras library service by Indian librarians has been very severe, it is undoubtedly true that some progress has been made which would not have been made without a legislative base.

It is to be hoped that the efforts of Dr. Ranganathan and others to improve the Act will eventually bear fruit and that Madras may then emerge as not only the first, but also the foremost, Indian state with a tax-based, legally founded, public library service.

Andhra Pradesh

Andhra Pradesh was a linguistic state formed from Hyderabad and parts of Madras State. A Telugu-speaking area, it has always had a strong library and literary tradition. In the words of an Indian librarian, 'the library movement has had a vast influence on the social and political life in Telugu land'. The population is over 40 million. When the new state was formed, there was already an Act in force for Hyderabad, while the parts of Madras taken over were covered by the Madras Act. In 1960 an integrated Act was passed for the entire state. In many ways the Act is similar to the Madras Act, in the provision of a state library committee, the constitution of local library authorities, the levying of library cess and the matching of the funds raised in this way by grants from the state government. But generally the Act is a great improvement on the Madras Act, and corrects many of its defects.

The Act creates a separate department of public libraries, although the Director of Public Instruction may be the director in charge of the department. But the librarian of the State Central Library has a place on the State Library Committee. In the provisions for the district authorities and the city authority it is laid down that the District Librarian and the City Central Librarian shall each be secretary of the respective committee. The amount of library cess is fixed at four paise, which may be increased to eight paise at the discretion of the district authority. It is prescribed in the Act that no fees for admission to any public library shall be charged, but it is not clear whether a fee can be charged for borrowing of books. Again, a parallel system of libraries is formed, since under the definitions, a public library can be 'a library established or maintained by any local body or co-operative society and declared open to the public', or 'a library declared to be eligible for aid and receiving aid from the Government or from the Library Fund'.

The duties of the Director of Public Libraries also include a declaration of what libraries are eligible for aid and under the rules of the Act conditions for such aid are laid down. It is clear that these are libraries outside those provided directly by the library authority, but there are no provisions, as in the Model Bill, for taking them over. The Act has been rapidly implemented, and appears to be working fairly satisfactorily.

Mysore Act, 1965

This Act has taken features from the Madras Act, the Andhra Pradesh Act, and the Model Bill and is a great improvement on all of them. Mysore is a

Kannada-speaking State formed under the States Reorganization Act. The capital is Bangalore and the population is approximately 27 million. The literacy rate is 25 per cent (36 % males). The preamble of the Act states that it is:

'To provide for the establishment and maintenance of public libraries and the organization of a comprehensive rural and urban library service for the State of Mysore.'

The State Library Authority includes a member representing the State Library Association, but the State Librarian, though *ex officion* secretary of the authority, is not a member. A department of public libraries is formed under the Act, with the State Librarian at its head.

This clause takes the administration of the public library out of the province of the Department of Education. The State Librarian is also specifically stated to be a whole-time officer with qualifications to practise as a librarian. All posts in the Department of Public Libraries are to be filled by appointment of persons employed by the state library service. This may seem supererogatory, but is obviously intended to prevent appointment of persons already in other departments of the civil service. It is one of the grievances of Indian librarians that posts are often filled by people without library qualifications, coming by promotion from such departments as social education and community development.

Local library authorities are specified for cities and urban areas with populations of more than 100,000, and for each district authority. The chief librarian of the city or district is *ex officion* secretary of the local library authority. Development plans are to be prepared for each district and advisory committees formed by branch libraries and mobile libraries under the plan. The library cess is not confined to a levy on property, but is also levied on other taxes in city areas.

It is limited to three paise in the rupee, subject to increase at discretion, with an upper limit of six paise. It will, of course, raise much more money, though the rate is the same, than property tax.

The grant from the state to districts is met from land revenue tax, at the rate of three per cent. In addition the whole of staff salaries in the library authority is met by the state. The State Central Library has, among other functions, the task of providing facilities for the blind. This is not mentioned in any other Act. The Act also specifies a number of public libraries owned by societies which are to be taken over under the Act. Whether this is by prior agreement or not, it is an immense step forward. The Mysore Act, it will be seen, is in many respects an improvement of the Model Bill, particularly in its creation of an independent library service and the widening of the tax base for urban libraries. The provision that all staff are employees of the state library service and paid by the state creates, for the first time in any of the Indian legislation, an integrated library system with the State Central Library at its head.

Maharashtra, 1967

Maharashtra, a Marathi-speaking State has a population of 46 million. Literacy is 30 per cent (males 42%). The Maharashtra Act, passed in 1967, has some of the features of the Mysore Act in that it creates a state library council, with a director of libraries who is a member of the council, acts as its secretary and must be a qualified librarian. A department of libraries is established and a state library service with staff salaries to be paid from state funds. There the resemblance to the Mysore Act stops.

A state library is to be established and a divisional library for every division. But provision for library service in a local area can only be made if the director is not satisfied that a local authority, society or trust is willing or competent to provide a public library service. No such library however shall be established without an opportunity being given to the local authority, society or trust to show because why the state authority should not establish a library. The Act gives no powers of taxation; the Library Fund is made up solely from general and special grants, and central government grants. The general state grant is to be not less than 2,500,000 rupees, not a large sum. It is difficult to see from this how the Act can work satisfactorily, even though a functioning department and qualified staff are provided for.

6

Library Automated and Problems in their Implementation

INTRODUCTION

Do we need library automated now? In developing countries the problems are many and though they are not insurmountable, they are certainly very difficult to face and live with. The most pertinent question for our profession in this regard, however, is whether we really need computerised library services on a large scale. A colleague from Bangladesh said: "The library and information sciences are a 'least-priority area' in this country. Only 20 percent of the people can write their names. There is an acute shortage of readers.... Most of the nation's resources are utilised for food, shelter, flood control and health problems."

Although the Indian situation differs from that of Bangladesh in many ways, the first priority of any developing country is to provide the basic necessities to its people. Litreacy and education are still at the primary level. Information of a very basic nature, such as the essentials for healthful living, must be presented in simple terms and communicated through media which will reach the people. Library activities of even the most primitive nature will not be within the intellectual grasp of most people unless the library is turned into a proper communication centre. We cannot take as our model the community information centre as developed in the West. The economic and social problems here are so acute and diverse that no one model for all parts of the country can be established.

As discussed earlier, library facilities may have to cater to a sophisticated and highly academic clientele in different organisations even though it is a minority. Libraries have had a long tradition here, but academia has yet to develop a tradition of data-oriented search for knowledge. The concept of libraries as storehouses of books remains very strong. Information is still sought in books rather than in microform. Because profundity in knowledge is the tradition of Eastern culture, the modern trend towards fast, accurate information is still not expected. That is exactly what a computer is supposed to provide for a scholar. Information is often treated as a commodity in the West. In industrially developed countries it is believed that any information which is economically profitable should be considered worthwhile and made quickly available.

Can the same be said of the Indian situation? In highly developed industries, such as Hindustan Machine Tools, Ltd., a survey of the information needs of engineers revealed that the time factor was not important. Even if the information were received a day or two after it had been requested it would still be accepted and used. The competition in the industrial field is not sufficiently keen to require immediate information. Industrial research is done in a relatively leisurely fashion in India.

At the documentation centre of SIET, the need for computerising library and information work has not been perceived. I quote: "As of today, there does not seem to be adequate justification for computerising library and information work here. Our intake is not that sizable, nor are the demands on us yet so enormous that we should think of using computers."

The genuine need of the country is to provide usable resources for spreading litreacy and to develop libraries at the school and college levels in order to give students the opportunity to acquire the taste for information. I do not intend to belittle the efforts to build a sophisticated information system such as NISSAT. India is a country in which the levels Proposals of development are varied in different areas. Its planners must therefore cater to the needs of each area in its own right. On the whole, however, our priorities still differ. Both librarians and clientele must be made information- conscious before anything as expensive, sophisticated and dumb as a computer can become a tool in their hands.

PROBLEMS OF LIBRARY AUTOMATED

Presently, the system of computerised library activities is growing, although it is still in its infancy compared with system in developed countries. While at the sophisticated research level there appears to be general acceptance that computerised library activities will lead to increased efficiency, the hindrances to such a goal are many and any efforts to achieve it are the exception rather than the rule. Computerised library service is likely to be beset with technological, economic and attitudinal problems peculiar to most developing countries.

TECHNOLOGICAL PROBLEMS

Technological problems include both the hardware, *i.e.*, the computer as an instrument for information processing, and the software, *i.e.*, the methodology which is applied. The major problems faced today in terms of the hardware are due to the variety of computers being used in different types of research and business institutions. The computers, manufactured by various firms are not compatible. Developing countries sometimes receive sophisticated technology like computers as gifts from more developed countries; these often become obsolete from the manufacturer's point of view.

Such machines are not only unsuitable for most complex work but any technical problems which come up cannot be repaired. Information retrieval work requires machines more sophisticated than those manufactured indigenously, and few imported machines are capable of handling information retrieval applications. The random access facility and disks large enough for storage of bibliographic information are not readily available.

In most institutions, organisational goals receive priority over the library's requirements, meaning that the librarian must use the computer available rather than what is actually required according to specifications. Library activities in all institutions are done through sharing disk space as well as computer time. Therefore, when the storage capacity is not large enough to accommodate various types of data, bibliographic data are given the lowest priority. On-line facilities are rare in India. In fact, only TIFR's library has access to an on-line terminal for bibliographic data, the DEC-1077 computer of the National Centre for Software Development and Computing Techniques.

The communication infrastructure of India is still not suitable for extensive on-line information facilities; the telephone system is not reliable enough to support an effective network facility. Software problems arise because programmes must be developed in terms of the machine on which they are to operate.

Therefore, the incompatibility of equipment tends to make the software incompatible as well, especially when programmes are written in machine or assembly language. While using languages which are not machine-bound, such as FORTRAN, COBOL, ALGOL, etc., may seem like a solution, in actual practice such languages cannot be interchanged without suitable modifications.

A software package developed for the IBM 360 model 30 would require many changes not only in the programme but also in the programming language if it were to run on any other computer. Development of a programme suitable for the available machine is therefore preferable to acceptance of a package programme. This makes the development and use of package programmes difficult and leads to a lack of standardisation in programming language as well as in output. Machine-readable data bases are byproducts of international information network systems and are available on magnetic tapes.

These are useful in building information resources and for retrospective search and current awareness services. Again, however, the tape service is expensive and suitably sophisticated computers are scarce. The data bases have a standard format which requires extensive changes to fit existing hardware and other system requirements. Also, relevant bibliographic information has to be selected from the data base and stored. Often this storage space is scarce and expensive.

ECONOMIC PROBLEMS

The major obstacle for any innovations in developing countries is the lack of resources. The initial cost of establishing a computer system is beyond the reach of most organisations and institutions. Library and information processing is done either with spare computer capacity made available by the institution itself, or with computer time hired from another institution. The cost of hiring computer time and storage space is very high and often cannot be justified at the management level by cost-benefit analysis. At IIT, for example, CPU time per hour costs ₹ 1000 for educational purposes and ₹.2000 for business and industrial use.

Moreover, the computer provides only paper printout, and the paper often costs more than the processing. Few developing countries can afford the machine-readable data bases, either. The tapes are very expensive and because foreign exchange is involved in subscribing to them, it is even more difficult for most organisations in India and other developing countries to afford them. The annual subscription rate of one data base is now $8000. Library tasks often overlap and their peculiar nature seldom makes the advantages of computerisation seem very convincing in the light of cost-benefit analysis.

In India, libraries and information centres are attached to government organisations or research institutions, so library services cannot be calculated on a profit/loss basis. Long-term benefits have to be kept in mind while justifying such services. The libraries that have computerised some of their services or operations often have not taken such steps as a result of serious thought. Computerisation has a glamour of its own in the minds of many librarians. Overly enthusiastic librarians often run uneconomical programmes, producing lengthy listings, for instance, in the name of computerised service.

Often the manual method is used concurrently with the computerised system because of a lack of faith on the part of staff and users. The duplication of work and the cost involved in these cases is obviously unjustifiable; the librarian should know which aspects of service should be mechanised. An example of an economically viable computerised library activity is the centralised acquisition of periodicals in operation at INSDOC. This facility serves thirty laboratories, which not only frees the facilities from the tedious task of periodical acquisitions but also eliminates the cost of duplicate purchasing.

ATTITUDINAL PROBLEMS

Computers appear very awesome to developing countries. They are powerful machines which can perform many functions and therefore offer a solution to the many types of manual inefficiency which often plague the developing countries. Among librarians there are two different attitudes towards computerised facilities. One group is taken in by the glamour of modern technology and believes that computers can perform miracles. Members of this group often give insufficient thought to the real value of the computer to the organisation/institution and make uneconomical, haphazard use of the facility.

The other group, still the majority in developing countries, lacks knowledge of the potential and consequences of library automated. There is constant tension between this traditional librarian group and the 'new-wave' librarians. Professionals of the majority group do not realise that computers cannot replace human intelligence. Due to the accuracy essential for data input in library services, the librarian/information scientist is indispensable. The National Library of Calcutta conducted an experiment to computerise the Indian National Bibliography in 1968.

The scheme failed, however, because labour unions opposed it fearing retrenchment of library staff. Among developing countries, the attitudes of India's librarians are typical. They are not confident about automated services. Library staffs should therefore be trained in programming and thus be made aware of the work involved in automated. They will then realise that automated will not take away their jobs.

They will also realise that computers are machines which have their limitations as well as their advantages. The communication gap between the librarian and the computer specialist is another major hindrance in establishing any effective automated system in a library.

There is often disagreement among the librarian, the programmer and the systems analyst. Librarians should be trained in computer programming and computer specialists should be versed in the special needs of library automated. Only then can a common language evolve among the three and a project be started. Administrative personnel assume a very important role in decisionmaking. Their enthusiasm, support and conviction can help realise any new plan, just as their apathy and lack of understanding of the need for accurate and speedy information can jeopardise any effort. Although many things have taken a favourable turn in India, the majority of those at the management level unfortunately are not conversant with the development of information science and are unaware of the important role of information in all areas of national development.

This very often results in insufficient planning, which in turn curbs the enthusiasm of imaginative information scientists and librarians. Due to this lack of appreciation, priorities are poorly ordered and funds are not well allocated. Administrators also have a tendency to underestimate or overestimate the capacity of automated. Any information system or service is planned for the best possible benefit to its users. Unless the users are mentally prepared to accept a new system, however, it cannot be effective. Indian users are still unfamiliar and overawed by computers, so computer awareness and interest has to be fostered to enable proper utilizaton of a system.

They should neither overestimate computer capabilities nor be afriad of interacting with the computer systems. Another obstacle is that, because batch processing systems are still in use in India, there are bulky printouts in monotonous type faces and formats which prove to be a headache not only for the librarian, but also for the user. There is no dearth of manpower in systems analysis and computer programming in India. We are already exporting software packages to countries that find them less expensive than developing their own. Library automated is still neglected, however; it is an area which has not attracted young people with appropriate expertise. Training should be given to both the librarian and the computer specialist about each other's functions and possibilities. Both INSDOC and DRTC conduct courses on automated systems in libraries. Under the forthcoming NISSAT plan, steps are being taken to build the requisite technical manpower.

Moreover, the Indian government's Department of Electronics is developing training programmes for the National Informatics Centre. There are two main objectives in training for library automated: to orient the programmers and system analysts to writing programmes suitable for automating library facilities, and to persuade librarians to accept the utility of automated and teach them to prepare accurate inputs to make the system worthwhile.

RECOMMENDED IMPROVEMENTS

- The computers used in India should not vary so widely. Production of computers with special capacity for library automated should be taken into consideration.
- Government policy has taken a positive step in establishing large computer systems, with one sophisticated central computer capable of handling complex information to be connected to indigenous minicomputers. The National Informatics Centre project dealing with agricultural and other governmental data processing is designed along similar lines. Such plans should be pursued.
- Indigenous, inexpensive library package programmes are very necessary. These should be usable on a large variety of machines and be capable of handling different activities in the library. The MARC format would be ideal if it could be adapted for the smaller indigenous computers. DRTC is currently involved in preparing software packages for information retrieval.
- The international data bases are being used by some organisations. However, these are expensive and often not applicable to Indian research needs. Indigenous data bases with our specific requirements

should be prepared. Core periodicals in each subject relevant to India, and litreature from important Indian periodicals, should be used as input for such data bases.

- A national standard or common language for bibliographic information exchange is necessary. Efforts are being made to achieve a standard language compatible with any international standard.
- Training of personnel, *i.e.*, proper communication among the librarian, computer programmer and systems analyst is very important. Courses offering training in library automated are being taught, but there is a general need for better understanding among these three architects of library automated.
- User awareness and orientation is very much needed. The users comprise managerial policy-makers as well as the research scholars and regular clientele of a library. The need for, as well as the possibilities of, automated library facilities have to be highlighted by professionals and experts in this area. A few seminars and workshops have been conducted at New Delhi and Bangalore, namely the UNISIST workshop in August 1975 and the Indo-U.S., seminar in 1977; however, little else has been accomplished in this area.

NATIONAL SCENE ON LIBRARY AUTOMATED

Elaborate automated library systems are still far off in the context of any developing country. The priorities of each country may vary, but the emphasis is mainly on providing the basic necessities of life to its people. The use of computers started in India with the establishment of computer centres at the Indian Institute of Technology and the Tata Institute of Fundamental Research during 1963-64. At present, there are about 400 computers installed at different places. The size and variety range from a Honeywell 400 to the large IBM 370/155 and DEC-1077.

These computers are used mainly for scientific calculations, business applications and data processing for decision-making. Computerised library activities are found in very few organisations, and consist primarily of the use of spare capacity of available computer facilities suitable for off-line use. Although the number of institutions which have computerised library applications is still very small, the awareness of quickly and easily available information is gradually increasing.

I conducted a short survey in this connection through a questionnaire and personal letters sent to different institutions and business houses outside Delhi which have automated library facilities. Like most questionnaire surveys, this one did not prove very successful, although the personal letters I received from some heads of institutions were encouraging. I then visited some of these major institutions in and around Delhi, and interviewed many of those who work with computerised systems or have plans to do so in the future. The institutions visited were: Indian National Scientific Documentation Centre (INSDOC) and National Informatics Centre, New Delhi; Bhabha Atomic Research Centre (BARC) and Tata Institute of Fundamental Research (TIFR), both in Bombay; Documentation Research Training Centre (DRTC), Hindustan Machine Tools, Ltd. (HMT) and Central Machine Tools of India (CMTI), all in Bangalore; and Small Industries Extension Training (SIET) Institute and the Administrative Staff College of India in Hyderabad. Altogether, twenty-five organisations were contacted. While this survey may not have been comprehensive in its coverage, the extensive discussions gave a good picture of the problems facing Indian organisations using library automated.

INSDOC, NEW DELHI

Automated is used for indexes, a union catalogue of serial publications, data processing of Indian periodicals on science and technology, directory compilation, and the centralised acquisition of periodicals for thirty laboratories. The IBM 360 model 44 and IBM 1620 are used on a rental basis.

TIFR, BOMBAY

Automated operations include recent additions list, cumulative classified catalogue of books, weekly list of preprints/reports of TIFR, catalogues of progress serials and periodical holdings, and evaluations of journals from the user's point of view. The CDC 3600/160-A and DEC- 1077 computers are available in-house.

NATIONAL INFORMATICS CENTRE, NEW DELHI

Bibliographic citations are available so far only for books in its library; periodical articles are to be added. The centre is a member of INSPEC tape service and a subscriber to a patent bibliographic information system since, 1978. The HP 2 I/MX is used.

INDIAN INSTITUTE OF TECHNOLOGY (IIT), MADRAS

In collaboration with INSDOC, IIT handled the CHEM/SDI project, a computer-based SDI system using the IBM 370 model 155 system and the CA Condensates data base. The CHEM/SDI uses a subset of CAN/SDI software made available by CISTI through UNESCO for its regional pilot project. The project was also handled by NISSAT during 1976-77. The project has been upgraded into a national SDI service using CAC, INSPEC and Compendex data bases; there are more than 500 users.

DRTC, BANGALORE

This group provides education and training, and researches methods for designing and developing computer-based information systems and services.

A set of fourteen programmes have been developed in COBOL for creation and updating of the data base, retrieval of bibliographical references in response to specific queries, provision of current awareness and SDI services, retrieval of factual data, provision of a referral service, the semi-automatic generation of a microthesaurus, indexing, and so on.

BARC, BOMBAY

The computer unit of the Library and Information Services of BARC uses the in-house computer Honeywell 400 and BESM 6 for information processing. Computerisation activities include: preparation of a monthly current awareness bulletin, Bibliography of Current Reports; an SDI service offered regularly to some seventy-five users since, May 1972; retrospective litreature searches based on stored data on request from BARC scientists; subject bibliographies; documentation lists; compilation of periodical holdings; loan and issue system of the library; and inventory.

An SDI service using the DEC-1077 computer of the National Centre for Software Development and Computing Techniques and TIFR and the magnetic tape output of the International Nuclear Information System is being developed and will be in operation shortly.

SIET, HYDERABAD

This group has automated its Index to Product Profile, which is a list of literature available in the library to April 1976. A TDC 12 is used on a rental basis.

CMTI, BANGALORE

Here work is being done on automating an in-depth index of periodical articles to compile a data base. They have a PDF/ 11 in-house. Future plans include classifying the trade catalogue.

HMT, BANGALORE

Currently under consideration is computerisation of the comparative product profile and the issue system. The computer used is ICL 1903.

PHYSICAL RESEARCH LABORATORY, AHMEDABAD

This laboratory has a mechanised catalogue of its publications holdings and information retrieval facilities. They have discontinued CAS and plan to start SDL In use is the IBM 360 model.

OTHERS

Some industrial units, such as Asian Paints India, Ltd., Hindustan Zinc, Ltd., and Institute of Armament Technology have automated catalogues of holdings. Along with all these ventures in automated library services, a weeklong on-line demonstration of the ESRIN/RECON data base system used at Frascati, Italy was arranged at TIFR during September 1976, with the assistance of UNESCO and the European Space Agency. The Frascati centre had 10 data bases and provided access to about 7.5 million references at the time.

NISSAT: SECTORAL SYSTEM

Although these organisations and some other institutions have plans for future automated, the most important plan in India is the National Information System for Science and Technology (NISSAT). In 1971, for the first time, it was seriously felt that a strong national network of documentation and information services was necessary to meet the evergrowing need of scientists and research scholars. The Indian government created the high-powered National Committee on Science and Technology in October 1971.

A report submitted by the committee in 1973 recommended the establishment of NISSAT under the Department of Science and Technology. The NISSAT network comprises a sectoral system, a regional system and other specialised services.

All major areas of science and technology are classified into information sectors based on discipline, mission and product, *e.g.*, leather technology, machine tools, drugs and Pharmaceuticals, etc., Organisations of national stature, such as INSDOC, Defence Scientific Documentation Centre, BARC and Small Enterprises Documentation Centre, will continue to provide services at the national level.

REGIONAL SYSTEM

Because of India's size, more than one sectoral centre for each discipline is necessary. Therefore, regional centres will act as NISSAT contact points. These will be located in major areas of research, development, educational and industrial activities, *e.g.*, one centre is in Delhi and another in Bangalore. Similar centres will be started in Bombay, Calcutta, Madras and Kanpur.

OTHER SPECIALISED SERVICES

Efforts such as the experimental computer-based SDI services of IIT and the on-line demonstration of ESRIN/ RECON at TIFR fall into this category. The ESRIN/RECON demonstration was a success and attracted considerable interest, and there is now a proposal to provide permanent terminals at Bombay and Delhi. NISSAT also includes plans to create and maintain data bases on themes of national importance, and technical and statistical data banks on such topics as minerals, resources, etc. NISSAT is the most ambitious information network plan in India today. Although the social sciences have also been brought within its fold, its emphasis is mainly on science and technology.

Therefore, social scientists are of the opinion that a parallel system for the social sciences and humanities would make the circle effectively complete. India's library system, as described earlier, can make use of automated in different ways for more effective functioning.

Thus far, the specialised libraries and documentation centres have laid emphasis primarily on information retrieval, which has been substantially developed in many areas. The major need for computerised bibliographical control has not yet been satisfied.

Table 3.1 Possible Computerized Activities for Different Types of Libraries

	Type of Library			
Activity	**Public**	**Academic**	**Special•**	**National**
Acquisition and distribution	x	x	x	x
Management and administration	x			x
Cataloguing and bibliographies	x	x		x
Periodical holding		x	x	x
Information retrieval		x	x	
Circulation	x	x	x	

•Special libraries include documentation centres

IN THE END OF THIS STAGE, WE CAN SAY

In old civilizations like India and other Asian countries, libraries have been in existence since, early times. Recent political and economic developments which have brought about various types of changes in these countries are also reflected in the evolution of information systems. India's educational system had a definite elitist slant in mediaeval times and the legacy of feudalism during the British period nurtured this trend. Libraries with very rich collections of manuscripts and other rare reading material were mainly the property of the elite.

The infrastructure of the country was, moreover, not congenial for the kind of wide-ranged library system which one can envisage today. Library development has shown a marked change since, 1947. It is estimated that India now has approximately 90,000 libraries of different types. The Indian library system can be divided into four broad categories: public, academic, special and national libraries.

PUBLIC LIBRARIES

India is divided into states, union territories, districts, sub districts and villages. The state central libraries serve as public libraries. There are also district central libraries, but village libraries are few and far between. Libraries and library development are included in the broad category of education which, under India's constitution, is considered the responsibility of each state. Some states, namely Tamil Nadu, Karnataka, Andhra and Maharashtra, have very progressive library legislator! which provides the necessary framework and finances for developing good state public library systems. Despite this, only a very small percentage of the total population of India has access to public libraries.

ACADEMIC LIBRARIES

There has been some improvement in the standards and status of university and college libraries in recent years. At present there are more than 100 universities and 8000 colleges throughout the country. Most of these have library facilities which are in different stages of evolution. School libraries, however, have not been given sufficient attention. Primary and middle-level schools rarely have library facilities, and barely 20 per cent of the secondary schools have adequate library facilities.

SPECIAL LIBRARIES

These are mainly the boon of the post-independence period. Government departments, research institutions, business and industrial houses have established libraries for their own research and development programmes. Currently there are approximately 1500 of these special libraries in India; they are also at different stages of development.

NATIONAL LIBRARIES

Under the national library system, the National Library of India is situated in Calcutta. There are regional libraries of national stature at Bombay and Madras. Some libraries on special subjects are now being given the status of national libraries, *e.g.*, the National Medical Library and the Indian Agricultural Research Institute Library.

The major activites of the different categories of Indian libraries are mainly routine work, such as acquisition, circulation, management, processing, reference and bibliographic service, periodical holdings, information retrieval, inventory, and so on.

The services and techniques utilised in the different libraries, however, tend to make these activities very cumbersome and slow. The acquisitions of most libraries are done independently, and involve unnecessary duplication of work and lengthy procedures.

Cataloguing and classification methods differ from one library to another and are generally time-consuming and labour-oriented. This is very confusing for the users as they must thus switch from one classification and cataloguing system to another when using more than one library.

There is also a lack of bibliographic control at the national level. The Indian National Bibliography suffers from a large time lag. Almost all library activities involve long hours of manual work, tending to make library service very unpopular. Therefore, users still cannot envisage a librarian as a giver of information but consider him or her a custodian of books. In order to improve the services of libraries, application of newer methods, such as information, computer and communication technologies, will be needed. I am only concerned here with computer applications in libraries and believe that for efficient functioning of our library systems, as suggested, need automated services at some point. But serious thought must first be given to which areas will be automated, while keeping in mind the national need.

7

Structure and Syntax of an Indexing

GENERALIZED FACET STRUCTURE FOR SUBJECTS

Analysis into constituent ideas and structuring of several thousands of subjects in a variety of subject fields for the purpose of designing and developing of schemes for subject classification, preparation of feature headings and subject headings, and for indexing of subjects have helped in:

- Categorizing the constituent elements in a subject into three types: Facet, Modifier, and Relations.
- Sub-categorizing each of the three types of constituent elements into a few kinds.
- Developing a typology of Basic Subjects, the modes of formation of Basic Subjects, and the arrangement of Basic Subjects.
- Developing a typology of Modifiers for basic facet and for isolate facet in different subject-fields.
- Recognizing the relative strength of bond between the first context specifying element and other types of facets in subjects.
- Formulating principles for helpful sequence among
- Facet s of a subject
- Spectators to a facet
- Compound subjects falling in a particular subject-field
- Subjects falling in different subject-fields.
- Developing a Generalized Facet structure of subject, with specific models for different subject-fields.

The main developments are briefly outlined in a recent FID/CR report. Subject structuring obtained using the Generalized Facet Structure has been found to give a co-extensive representation of subjects and arrangement of subjects helpful to majority of users.

The chart in figure shows the interrelation between subject- structuring, designing a classification scheme, generation of subject indexes, etc. Depth classification schemes for over a hundred subject-fields have been designed and several hundreds of articles, technical reports etc., have been classified using these schemes in each subject-field. The structuring of subjects and the sequence in which the subjects get arranged have been found to be acceptable to a large number of users. In a small-scale experiment, subject-headings each with several components, structured in the manner, were presented to about a hundred persons for indication by them of the subject that each of them perceived in the structuring.

For Example:

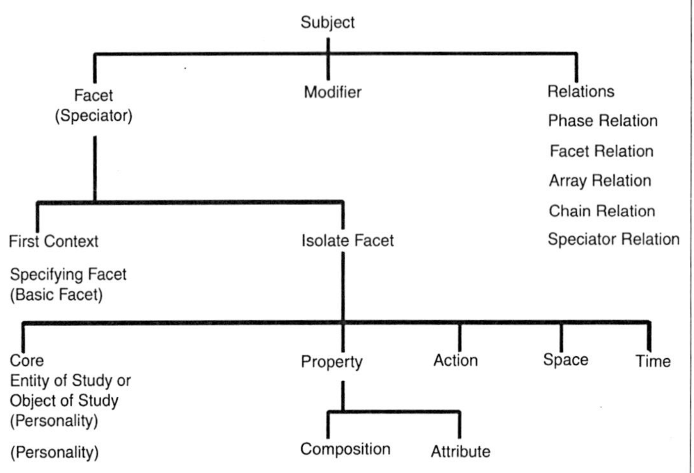

Although there were more than one way of representing each subject in the natural language, the subject perceived was the same in all the cases. That is, there was no homonym. Large scale experiments with other types of structuring of subjects has been planned. Translation of the subject heading terms into different natural languages did not give rise to any difficulty in interpreting the subject represented by persons knowing the language concerned. The facility of rearrangement of given terms into the preferred sequence and synthesis of class number given the descriptors, using computer, have been demonstrated.

These experiences indicate that the structuring of subjects conforming to the model developed according to the General Theory of Classification:

- Helps to secure a facet syntax parallel to that of the absolute syntax;
- Gives a "standard format" for representing information considered helpful by Anderson and Bower; and
- Provides a frame work for an intermediate or linking language that is helpful and consistent.

STRUCTURE AND PATTERN

The kind of pattern one perceives in a representation of an entity lies in the perceived structure. For instance, in a pictorial representation, the idea of "triangle" can be conveyed by 300 dots, or 30 dots, or 3 dots. Of these three representations, the last mentioned is deemed to be the most efficient, because it uses the fewest number of elements to convey the same amount of information as those using more number of elements.

This indicates the important role of structure of a representation in relation to the perception of its "meaning". Structure is the way in which the components of an entity are put together. Lancelot Whyte defines the concept of structure as "effective patterns of relationships in any situation". In a general sense, structure denotes logical form. The content of a logical form may be physical, musical, psychological, temporal, or in some other way non-physical. Anything that has structure has parts, properties or aspects, which are in some manner related to each other.

Thus, in every structure one can distinguish the relations and the items which are related.

The items may be qualities, values, or any conceptually distinguishable feature called elements of the structure. An idea is a pattern, a structure, a gestalt, a form, a kind of picture that one perceives. A subject is constituted out of a combination of ideas that is, a combination of patterns. In understanding a complex structure, the human intellect finds it helpful to identify the substructures and categorize them. Such pattern recognition, pattern formulation, and categorization have been found to be involved in the human learning process and information handling.

Anderson and Bower point out that the representa-tion of knowledge-structures is an important problem in cognitive psychology:

- "..what are the primitive symbols or concepts, how are they related, how are they to be concatenated and constructed into larger knowledgestructures, and how is this 'information file' to be accessed, searched and utilized. The choice of a representation is central, since how one handles this issue causes widespread effects throughout the remainder of his theoretical efforts. As computer scientists working on problem solving have known for years, a good structural representation of the problem already constitutes half of its solution".

Therefore, the structure of representation of subject that is, surrogate of subject has a crucial role in conveying information about the subject denoted.

ABSOLUTE SYNTAX

A POSTULATE

At the International Conference on Scientific Information, S. R. Ranganathan suggested that "to help in the establishment of a fairly longlived helpful scheme for classification, a team of epistemologists, psychologists, linguists, reference librarians, classificationists and statisticians should investigate the way in which the human mind thinks that is, the Syntax of Facets that will give the greatest satisfaction to the greatest number of readers".

In 1966, in his valedictory address to the Maryland Symposium on Relational Factors in Classification, Ranganathan postulated such a syntax of facets and named it as Absolute Syntax. Absolute syntax in the sequence in which the component ideas of subjects falling in a subject-field arrange themselves in the minds of a majority of normal intellectuals, for instance when they think and communicate about the subject. Ideas are largely products of intellection.

Intellectual activity is known to be controlled by brain. There is considerable similarity in the structure and, therefore, in the functioning of the brain in a majority of normal human beings.

Thus, a majority of normal human beings have more or less a similar mode of thinking and learning that is, in forming ideas and in combining them to build knowledge-structures. It is further stated that biologically man has not changed to any appreciable extent since the emergence of Homo sapiens; for, the structure of the genetic material has not appreciably changed since then that is, for some 500,000 years although we have changed culturally. Therefore, the probability of a sudden change that is, a mutation in the mode of thinking and learning of a majority of normal persons in the immediate future is quite low.

Hence, if the syntax of the representation of the component ideas of subjects is made to conform to, or parallel to, the Absolute Syntax, then the pattern of linking of the component ideas that is, the resulting knowledge structure is likely to be:

- Helpful to majority of normal intellectuals;
- Consistent in pattern in subjects falling in different subject-fields;
- Relatively more stable and continue to be helpful to a majority of normal intellectuals so long as there is no mutation in their mode of thinking;
- Free from the aberrations due to variations in linguistic syntax from the use of the verbal plane in naming subjects;
- Capable of representing and indication of subjects co-extensively with a minimum number of variety of component elements;
- Helpful in recognizing the less explored and unexplored regions in the universe of ideas; and
- Helpful in probing deeper into the pattern of human thinking and modes of combination of ideas.

ANALOGY FROM SEARCH FOR LINGUISTIC UNIVERSALS

It was pointed out that the formulation of a generic framework for structuring subjects has a parallel in the search for universal linguistic forms such as that expounded in the works of Chomsky, Fodor, Katz, and the generative grammarians. Birnbaum suggests a multi-layered syntactic structure between the deepest of the deep structures and the surface structure. He points out: "As a result of the general trend towards a generative semantic framework, a new slightly modified model of generative grammar seems now to be taking shape.

This model can be thought of as comprising three independent components:

- A Semantic Component which will define the relations obtaining between semantic units or, rather hierarchically ordered clusters of semantic features such as:
  - ⊛ (Thing),
  - ⊛ (Concrete),
  - ⊛ (Countable),
  - ⊛ (Animate),
  - ⊛ (Human),
  - ⊛ (Personal),
  - ⊛ (Male),
  - ⊛ (Adult);
  - ⊛ (Predication),
  - ⊛ (Agent),
  - ⊛ (Definite),
  - ⊛ (Action),
  - ⊛ (Patient ¾ Oriented),
  - ⊛ (Time-Determined),
  - ⊛ (Aspect ¾ Determined), etc.,
- A Transformational Component which will convert the semantic deep structure representations into surface structure representations.
- A Phonological Component."

Fillmore points out that "there may also be some psychological reasons that argue for the use of predication as a data-base language in a model of memory... Perhaps 'thinking' represents operations at the level of the semantic base structure, before it has been transformed into actual sentences through the application of syntactic rules".

The case categories suggested by Fillmore include the following:

- "*Agentive* (A), the case of the typically animate perceived instigator of the action identified by the verb.
- *Instrumental* (I), the case of the inanimate force or object causally involved in the action or state identified by the verb.
- *Dative* (D), the case of the animate being affected by the state or action identified by the verb.
- *Factitive* (F), the case of the object or being resulting from the action or state identified by the verb, or understood as a part of the meaning of the verb.

- *Locative* (L), the case which identifies the location of spatial orientation of the state or action identified by the verb.
- *Objective* (O), the semantically most neutral case, the case of anything representable by a noun whose role in the action or state identified by the verb is identified by the semantic interpretation of the verb itself.."

Vleduts and Stokolova also propose structures ¾ standard phrases at different levels for subject - representation in different disciplines. Leibniz's ideal language and the Whorfian hypothesis that "Every language contains terms that have come to attain cosmic scope of reference that crystallize in themselves the postulations of an unformulated philosophy.. such are our words 'reality, substance, matter' and.. 'space. time, past, present, future", are worth noting here.

BIOCYBERNETIC VIEW

In his book on Systems Philosophy, Ervin Lazlo mentions about "basic modes of thinking".

- "..It is also becoming evident that all men, regardless of the culture they happen to belong to, have basically similar nervous systems, are equipped with analogous sense receptors, command like patterns of response, and use patterns of thought which obey very similar laws or regularities. In other words, there appear to be some "universal" traits underlying cultural cognitive relativities: Chomsky could locate "linguistic universals" and Kluckholn discovered a number of" universal categories of culture

"Finding such universals is rendered difficult if not impossible, by arguing out of one's own culturally or individually relativistic categories. In that light, every other world-model becomes but a special case of one's own, and is forced into the latter's structural scheme. But, in using the neutral frame work of a cybernetic mode, one is no more arguing out of his own culturecategories than out of that of a thermostat. Conceptualizing the cognitive process with such categories, we can reach universal structures, for we are not dealing with particular contents. Regardless of whether a person conceives a sensory pattern as trees, meaning "standing peoples, in whom winged ones built their lodges and reared their families" or interprets the very same pattern as obstructions to be cut down and burnt; he is using a construct which endows his perceptual input with meaning. And the development of constructs and gestalts obeys some general regularities, already manifest in biological evolution and set forth in cultural development".

Lazlo further points out:

- Regardless of the genetically and empirically induced differences, however, basic modes of thinking characterize all human beings, and indeed all higher biological species. These are rooted in, and explained by, the fact that all such organisms are self-maintaining open systems using a specific mode of reproduction, and forming part of some similarly specific social structure. The mental capacities needed to maintain such systems in their environments are adaptive functions; they crystallize as cognition in the more evolved species, and culminate in man.

The most immediately pertinent to human cognition make up an ascending ordering of categories, universally human in principle but variously evolved in different real individuals.

These categories may be listed as follows:

- Gestalt (invariant patterns with established meanings to which the input patterns are assimilated);
- Rational constructs (theoretic entities postulated through abstract reasoning and connected to the input patterns by means of some established rule of correspondence); and
- Aesthetic construct (non-discursive meanings discovered in the input and illuminating some part of the knower's "felt experience"). These are the types of constructs which represent the limits of human cognition, given the kind of perceptions, cognitive organizations and effective output channels at our disposal. I argue that many forms of human experience do not constitute disjunctive culture conditioned categories, but a set of universal structures which transcends individual and cultural differences and relativities, and accommodates as subclasses, the many varieties of cognitive patterns as environment mappings and constructions of natural cognitive systems on the specially human level of nature's hierarchy"

SYNTAX OF KNOWLEDGE AND EPISTEMICS

Meredith suggests the existence of a "syntax of knowledge".

The argument runs as follows:

- "At a multi-lingual conference.. with a community of disciplines, experience and thought, the translators have no difficulty in transforming, virtually instantaneously, the most elaborate syntactic forms of one language into the quite different forms of another whilst reserving the essential structure of information and conceptualization in the speech. Thus, there is a 'syntax of knowledge' which, even if not entirely independent of the particular languages, can and does, in practice, follow its own course alongside the syntactic sequence of language. It may serve to sharpen the difference if, provisionally, we think of the latter as governed by temporal relations (by the sequence of words in the sentence) and the 'syntax of knowledge' as primarily a spatial structure only shredded into temporal filaments in order to conform to the sequential character of speech.

- "This is a big step forward. Even though the syntax of language cannot be entirely divorced from the syntax of knowledge, we can pragmatically separate them by treating the one as a temporal sequence and the other as a spatial pattern. But, it may be objected, what about the temporal character of knowledge itself? Our knowledge of history, our under- standing of sequential operations, of industrial processes, of astronomical events etc., all of which involve time. Two points may be noted here:
- Even though in a narrative the sequence of paragraphs normally follows the time-sequence of the events narrated, this correspondence scarcely holds at all within the limits of a single sentence. And what is called linguistic syntax is largely based on the analysis of the single sentence. 'The assassin shot the President at the end of his speech'. In the actual event, the speech came before the shot; in the sentence after it. Thus, 'epistemic time' and 'linguistic time' are partially independent.
- We speak a sentence sequentially, that is, at the beginning we have not yet spoken the end but what we are talking about even though it may be temporal event, is known to us throughout.. 'Epistemic time' is in fact 'dead' time, the completed past history, fossilised, and hence not "time" at all in the linguistic sense. It has a discernible sequence but no flow. Our knowledge of it is a geometric knowledge of evidence spread out in space or held in memory".

Constance Amsden commenting on Vygotsky's ideas on "inner speech", also suggests a "syntax of thought".

COMMON STRUCTURE

Arturo Rosenbleuth postulates a "common structure" in preserving the message received through a set of transforma-tions:

- "When a person hears a symphony, the messages sent by the orchestra reach the listener as air vibrations. These vibrations stimulate mechanically the receptors of the organ of corti, and these receptors set up nerve impulses along the fibres of the VIIIth nerve. It is clear that at this stage the physical events that are taking place are of an entirely different kind from those occurring in the instruments of the orchestra. Yet the message is preserved because there are similarities in certain features of the two series of events sounds emitted by the orchestra and nerve impulses traveling over the auditory nerves. The existence of these similarities of relations is precisely what is called a common structure. The mental decoding, which is the perception of the symphony, again preserves the corresponding relations. A common structure thus implies the quantitative preservation of the relations that exist between the independent constituents of an event or message through a set of trans- formations".

LOGIC OF EXPOSITION AND LINGUISTIC SYNTAX

Rosenbleuth also comments on syntax of thought and linguistic syntax thus:

- "As a further example of the fundamental difference between the mental events and the correlated neuro-physiological processes, let us consider the processes that would develop in my brain if I presented verbally a specific relatively complex, argument on three different occasions in Spanish, English, and French, respectively. Although the neurophysiological correlates corresponding to the logic of my exposition might be similar or identical in the three cases, clearly those corresponding to the selection of words and their syntactical organization, a very important aspect of the presentation of the argument would be absolutely dissimilar. If I should want to use dictionaries to translate from the language of the introspective data to that of the physical processes, I would need in this instance three different dictionaries, and more, if I were capable of using fluently other languages"

CONCEPT AND CONCEPTION

Suzanne Langer points out that the psychological context of our thoughts may be private and personal. Therefore, two persons talking about the same thing may perceive it in different ways. They are then said to have different conceptions. But, if they understand each other, then their respective conceptions embody the same concept. A concept is an abstracted form. Abstraction is the consideration of logical form apart from content.

REPRESENTATION OF SUBJECT

An information system handles discourses. A discourse may be verbal as expressed in a query of a user of an information system. It may be in a recorded form as in a conventional document such as, a book, an article in a periodical, and a technical report or on magnetic tape, film, etc., all of which may form information sources.

Finding information and/or documents containing information co-extensively matching the subject of a user's query may depend, in a good measure, on the capacity of the system to identify and specify coextensively the subjects of discourses that is, subjects embodied in queries and those embodied in information sources.

The representation of subjects expounded in discourses for example, subject headings, class numbers, data structures, algorithms or other kinds or surrogates may provide the first point of entry into an information retrieval system. An information system of this sort may form a node or component of a hierarchy of increasingly larger network of local, national, regional and global information systems. To facilitate the integration and collaborative functioning of the information systems developed in different contexts, it would be helpful if the "languages" used for representation of subjects in the different systems are syntactically consistent, compatible with each other, and inter-convertible at a reasonable cost. Thus, the representation of subject of discourses in the form of surrogates is central to the designing of information files for information storage and retrieval purposes.

FRAMEWORK FOR REPRESENTATION

PROBLEMS OF TRANSFORMATION

The second one is the more practicable at present stage in the development of information systems throughout the world. However, in either of the methods, an important consideration relates to the framework elements, relations, and structure to be used for the analysis and representation of subjects of discourses that is, subjects embodied in information sources and in users' queries. This stage mentions some of the suggestions about a common knowledge structure and framework for representation of subjects and discusses one such framework. There are various methods of representing subjects, such as, class numbers, subject headings or strings of words, multi-dimensional arrays, tree-structures, etc.

These arise from the process of analysis of subjects of discourses into constituent elements; recognition of the relevant relations among the elements as they obtain in the context of the subject concerned; and assembling the elements in a preferred pattern so as to represent as coextensively as possible the subjects. Representation of subject by a subject heading or a class number is equivalent to transforming the n-dimensional configuration of the subject into a linear configuration. An arrangement of the component elements in each subject falling in a subject-field among themselves, in a sequence helpful to a majority of users requires keeping invariant every Immediate-Neighbourhood relation among all the subjects while transforming or mapping the n-dimensional configuration of subjects on to a line.

The number of subjects falling even in one subject-field is quite large and continues to increase rapidly such that it is difficult to arrange them in a helpful sequence consistently without the aid of guiding principles. In the transformation, only one of the many Immediate- Neighbourhood relations can be kept invariant. Determining which should this be, and which components should come respectively as remove 2, remove 3, etc., with respect to a reference component is a difficult decision. To depend, for this purpose, on the conjecture of different classificationists as to what is helpful to a majority of users may not yield a consistent pattern of arrangement of components of all subjects. But, such a consistency in pattern is helpful and necessary to the users, as well as the designers of the information system.

CRITERIA FOR CHOICE OF FRAME WORK

Meredith summarizes the problem of transfer and trans- formation of knowledge-structures, as follows.

- "The long-term task is not merely to analyse the problems but to design methodological instruments for carrying out practical researches into problems of communication.
- These may be treated as problems of mapping. Given an original territory of factual phenomena how does this territory become mapped in the brain of the investigator? How does this map become transformed into a verbal or symbolic expression a linguistic map? How is this map transformed again into a language adopted to the needs of the ultimate recipient, the learner? Finally, how is this third map introjected into the learner's brain to form a pattern of knowledge?
- If we can establish a cartography for these maps, we can formulate "projective equations" leading from one map to the next. Each map will be a pattern of definable variables under appropriate controls and observing changes in the next map, the equations can be solved and laws of projection may be discovered."

Anderson and Bower have listed the following considerations deemed helpful in the choice of a "standard format" for representing information:

- The representation should be capable of expressing any conception which a human can formulate or understand.
- The representation should allow for relatively efficient search for and retrieval of information. That is, specific information should remain relatively accessible even when the data-files grow to encyclopedic proportions.
- The representation should saliently exhibit the substantive information extracted from a given input. It should not be influenced by the peculiarities of the particular natural language in which that information was communicated.
- This hope for language-invariance amounts to a wish for a universal interlingua in which any conception in any language could be expressed, but for which the format would not be specific to a particular language...

- For reasons of parsimony, the representation should involve a minimum of formal categories. That is, it should make a minimum of formal distinctions at the outset; more complex distinctions would be built up by the construction rules for concatenating primitive ideas.
- The representation must allow for easy expression of concatenation operations, by which "duplex ideas" can be constructed out of "simple ideas". This means, for example, that the representation should allow easy expression of conceptual hierarchies, or multiply embedded predications, or allow one to predicate new information on any old information- structure".

MINIMIZING THE CONSTRAINTS

HELPFUL FEATURES OF AN INFORMATION SYSTEM

Some of the features of an information system that may help in minimizing some of the constraints and difficulties are as follows:

- Providing access to information on the subject of interest to the user by the name of the component idea(s) he may bring up in using the surrogate system.
- Providing facility for browsing and selection of information to compensate for the dissimilarity and non-coextensiveness between the subject perceived and expressed by the user and the at perceived and understood by the information scientist at the time of query negotiation or user-system interfacing. This may involve providing access to:
- Subjects greater in extension but subsuming the subject of the user's interest at the moment.
- Subjects greater in intension but containing a substantial portion of it devoted to the specific subject of interest to the user at the moment.
- Subjects in some other manner related to the specific subject of interest to the user at the moment.

INTERSYSTEM CONNECTION AND COMPATIBILITY

In order to facilitate switching over or movement from one information system to another with the longrange goal of establishing system interconnection on a global scale, there are at least two approaches.

These are:

- To use the same or very nearly the same information storage and retrieval language in all the information systems; and
- To use an intermediate language or switching language through or by which one moves from one information system to another.

PROBLEMS IN THE EFFICIENT USE OF THE LANGUAGE OF SURROGATE

The following are some of the factors which raise problems for the user of an information system in the efficient use of the language of the surrogate system.

For various reasons, it may be difficult for the user to perceive precisely and express coextensively the subject of his interest at the moment. Therefore, the total semantic domain represented by the expression of the subject of his query may not be coextensive with the semantic domain of the subject of his interest as perceived by him.

The information scientist's perception of the semantic domain of the subject of interest of the user derived on the basis of the latter's expression of his interest at the moment, may not be coextensive with what the user purported to convey.

A user may not and, perhaps, cannot be concentrating attention or work on at one and the same time on all the component ideas potentially falling in the subject of his interest, even if it be a narrow one. He may study and concentrate attention only one or a few of the component ideas at a time. The recall value at the moment that is, the likelihood of being retained and recalled from memory for this component idea would be relatively greater than that for the other component ideas in the subject of his interest.

Therefore, he is more likely to bring up the name of this component idea in searching for information on the subject of his interest at the moment. The information scientists' knowledge and understanding of the subject of interest to the user may be inadequate. For various reasons, it would be difficult for the information scientist to perceive precisely and express coextensively the semantic domain of the subjects embodied in information sources. Therefore, the surrogate system prepared by him for representing the semantic domain of subjects embodied in information sources may not be coextensive with the semantic domain of the subject(s) purported to be described by the author of the work.

- User's perception of the semantic domain of his subject interest-at-the moment
- Actual semantic domain of the subject as expressed by user
- Librarian/Information Scientist's perception of the semantic domain of user's subject interest-at-the-moment

TERMINOLOGY

The following are the operational definitions of some of the technical terms used in this paper:

- *Idea*: An idea is a product of thinking, imagining, etc., got by the intellect, by integrating with the aid of logic, a selection from the apperception mass, and/or what is directly apprehended by intuition, and deposited in memory. Alternative term: Concept.

- *Entity*: An entity is any existent, concrete or conceptual that is, a thing or an idea.
- *Discourse*: A discourse is an expression of ideas, especially systematic or orderly expression in speech or writing.
- *Subject*: A subject is an organized or systematized account of a body of ideas, whose extension and intension are likely to fall coherently and comfortably within the intellectual competence and the field of inevitable specialization of a normal person.
- *Example*: A systematized account of "Conduction of heat" is a subject; and so may be deemed a systematized account of "Thermo-dynamics", and of the ideas in "Physics". But, not all the discourses embodied in the McGraw-Hill Encyclopedia of Science and Technology, taken as a whole can be deemed to be a subject; for, the totality of the subjects embodied therein cannot form an inevitable and convenient field of specialization of a normal person.

CONCLUSIN

Switching from one information system to another would be convenient if the information languages ¾ that is, the method of representation of subjects and other information content of discourse used in the systems are syntactically consistent, compatible with each other, and inter-convertible at a reasonable cost. In this connection, the development of an intermediate language through which the switching from one information language to another is an important consideration.

An idea is a pattern, a gestalt, a form, a structure that one perceives. A subject of a discourse of an information source or of a user's query is a combination of ideas, that is, of structures; therefore, the structure of a subject representation that is, of a subject surrogate has a bearing on the user's 'perception' of the subject represented.

Some characteristic features of an information structure helpful to users, the problems of transformation of information structures, the linear structuring of subject surrogates, and some criteria for the choice of a 'standard format' or framework or model for such structuring are considered. Absolute syntax is defined as the sequence of the component ideas in a subject helpful and acceptable to a majority of users.

The helpfulness of structuring of subject parallel to the absolute syntax is indicated, together with supporting information based on postulations and research on deep structure of languages, biocybernetics, syntax of knowledge, common structure in preserving messages in a set of transformations, etc. The generalised facet structure of subject representation obtained on the basis of the general theory of classi- fication and the guiding principles for helpful sequence formulated thereof is found to be helpful and acceptable to a large number of users of information systems, and therefore, conjectured to parallel the absolute syntax. Work done in this regard and in the development of specific schemes for classification and for the formulation of subject headings in different languages within the general framework is mentioned.

8

Unicode Support Serials in Library Automated

INTRODUCTION

As we described earlier, despite the fact that there are several OPACs supporting the automated of retrieving bibliographic information, only a few of them support some kind of bilingual or even multilingual access to libraries catalogues.

In this chapter, we presented a system that aims at solving this problem. Translib allows multilingual search as well as multilingual presentation of the query results and consists of an integration of state-of-the-art existing information tools and tools built from scratch. The integration of these tools was a difficult task, since, the former were built for different purposes and, some of them, for different operating systems.

The multilingual functionalities of Translib help the user, to a high degree, improve significantly the results of a query and allow him/her to select the presentation of the results in the preferred language. For all these reasons, we feel that libraries, book trade enterprises, appropriate consultancy services and library schools can directly benefit from a system of this type. Translib should have a remarkable impact on the improvement of library services as well as on the easy access to the wealth of knowledge held in libraries. The results of its performance on the Greek library database and its pilot installation in the Central Library of University of Patras strongly encourage us to believe that it will have a successful commercial exploitation in the near future.

Our short-term goal is to endow Translib with the capability to support bibliographic information retrieval from remote databases through INTERNET servers. In addition, we plan to further improve the present system by adding new languages in the existing framework. Our long-term goal is to enrich it with new AI tools. In particular, we intend to provide the translation of entire abstracts rather than just the titles and improve the accuracy of the search results based on intelligent information extraction.

EVALUATION

The Translib system has been tested in the library databases in both Greece and Spain under real life conditions.

Two parameters were evaluated:

- The subject search, *i.e.*, the proportion of citations found by the user referring to a given subject, and
- The user satisfaction, *i.e.*, the impression of the user with respect to the quality of the service provided.

The first parameter was measured by means of the standard 11- point average precision for our DICT method. The 11- point average precision is a conventional performance measure for evaluation of text retrieval systems. Given a query, for recall thresholds of 0 per cent, 10 per cent, 20 per cent..., 100 per cent, the system assigns in decreasing score order as many titles as needed until a given recall level is achieved, and computes the precision value at that point. Then, the precision values of individual queries are averaged over all test queries.

Table 4.3 Recall- Precision Values for the DICT Approach

Monolingual Retrieval		Multilingual Retrieval	
Recall	**Precision**	**Recall**	**Precision**
0.0	0.90	0.0	0.63
0.1	0.86	0.1	0.50
0.2	0.83	0.2	0.45
0.3	0.80	0.3	0.39
0.4	0.77	0.4	0.34
0.5	0.72	0.5	0.30
0.6	0.68	0.6	0.23
0.7	0.59	0.7	0.21
0.8	0.52	0.8	0.18
0.9	0.50	0.9	0.12
1.0	0.35	1.0	0.10

These averaged precision values can be further averaged over the recall thresholds, to obtain a single-numbered global measure. The resulting global average is referred to as the 11- point average precision. We carried out the measurement of the first parameter in the Greek library database, initially with the previous OPAC system and then with the Translib system.

We used 1,000 test queries from the scientific domain of engineering and computer science. The input language for these queries was either Greek or English, and the search criteria comprised either a unique search field or a combination of two or more search fields.

The vast majority of these queries consisted of isolated words or short phrases. Only 15 per cent of the above queries formed long phrases. The DICT approach proves efficient enough for queries consisting of isolated words or at best short phrases. The second parameter was evaluated by means of a short questionnaire which was used to gather the general impression on the system and its features.

This questionnaire comprised 27 questions, which were classified in four distinct parts:

- Personal information regarding the evaluator;
- Results on the use of Translib;
- Personal opinion of Translib.;
- Comments.

In some cases, the questionnaire reply boxes ranged from 1 to 5 by degree of satisfaction. Finally, a total of 42 library users filled the questionnaires.

They were selected on the basis of the following criteria:

- To be familiar with OPACs;
- To possess a good knowledge of English and/or Spanish;
- To have different sex and age;
- To be willing to participate in the evaluation process.

The results of the evaluation are encouraging and pinpoint the strength as well as the potential weaknesses of this system. Some of the most important results are listed below:

Multilingual Search:

- 95 per cent of the users performed multilingual searches in the library database rather than monolingual ones.
- Approximately 45 per cent of the users felt rather satisfied or completely satisfied about the results of their search, while 9 per cent of them were dissatisfied.
- Less than 25 per cent of the dissatisfied users considered multilingual aspects not supported in Translib responsible for their dissatisfaction.
- Approximately 85 per cent of the users considered the search via the multilingual thesaurus more accurate and complete.

Translation of Titles:

- Approximately 80 per cent of the users considered the translation of titles rather useful or very useful.
- Over 55 per cent of the users considered the translations of titles comprehensible. Note that users with high familiarity with OPACs tended to be slightly more satisfied with the quality of the translation.
- Over 90 per cent of the users found the functionality of the translation component very easy.

Multilingual Presentation:

- Over 70 per cent of the users considered the system easy to use by anyone, not just experts.
- Over 60 per cent of the users considered Translib more friendly, useful, and easier to understand than other OPACs they had used in

the past. It is noteworthy that users with a high familiarity in OPACs were considerably more satisfied.

- Finally, over 65 per cent of the users found the help and error messages of Translib clear, useful, and adequate.

As noted earlier, the selection of an interlingua affects the quality as well as the comprehension of the translation of titles. Hence, translations to and from English are more comprehensible than from Greek to Spanish and *vice versa*. Nevertheless, approximately 95 per cent of the performed translations are translations to and from English, since, the vast majority of the book/journal titles contained in a library consists of titles in the local language and English.

The satisfaction of the users with the multilingual thesaurus and the overall search results they obtained from the system in contrast to other OPACs was remarkable. The localisation of the user interface was one of the main reasons why the users favoured this system.

In conclusion, the reaction of the users to the Translib system appears to be closely dependent on their previous experience:

- Users find multilingual search very useful.
- Users with a higher familiarity with OPACs find Translib a simple, friendly, and easy to learn system. Users with a lower familiarity with OPACs find it more difficult to use Translib. This is a satisfactory conclusion, as Translib neither intends to replace OPAC nor makes its baseline operation simpler. It is simply intended to overcome the linguistic barriers posed by multilingual library holdings.
- Users appear to search for titles in languages in which they are familiar. For this reason they tend to show limited appreciation of the usefulness of the translation of titles, while they expect a better translation.
- Although the user reaction is positive, there appears to be room for improvement with respect to the terminology used, the help and error messages, and the way that the system keeps the user informed of what is being done at any time.
- The satisfaction of the users depends highly on both the Translib system as well as on the bibliographic database and the library holdings. As a result it is difficult to assess the impact of Translib on the quality of the search results. More extensive experiments would be needed for this purpose, preferably in a distributed, transnational bibliographic database.

TRANSLIB

The user interacts with the Translib module by choosing the languages to be used as well as the search fields, the search key topics, and the type of searching to be initiated. Translib combines all this information to support multilingual access to the library system, by sending it a query for each key topic and receiving from it the records that match the users' query. Finally, Translib presents the query results to the user in the preferred language as well as the predefined search field labels, information windows, and all messages. If the query results are empty, Translib allows the user to repeat the search using synonyms, super categories, or subcategories of the search keywords. Translib is an OPAC that provides the users with a capability for multilingual access to library catalogues.

Translib is fully implemented, runs under Windows 95, and currently supports three languages, that is English, Greek, and Spanish. These three languages are considered to be sufficient to both demonstrate the feasibility of this type of multilingual access and to highlight potential problems in the future adoption of additional European or non-European languages.

Translib offers bibliographic information retrieval, whether from a local library database or from remote databases, through servers that support the Z39.50 standard, that is, a standard specifying a client/server- based protocol for information retrieval that was originally proposed for use with bibliographic information. One of the main characteristics of Translib is its ability to be easily integrated into the majority of library automated tools. *In order to achieve this objective, we have had to consider seriously the following problems*:

- All library automated systems do not use the same type of database;
- There will be libraries that will not give access to their databases to developers' groups so that they can be connected with the Translib system.

Our solution has been to integrate a Z39.50 client tool into Translib. Thus, the Translib interface can now connect with any library automated system that supports the Z39.50 protocol. All other processes, such as retrieving bibliographic information in any language and translating the titles and keywords into English are also supported by the new Translib with the Z39.50 client module.

Translib comprises two basic tools:

- The multilingual search tool that supports the retrieval of multilingual bibliographic information; and
- The multilingual presentation tool that allows multilingual presentation of the retrieved information.

The following subsections illustrate the features of these tools.

By taking advantage of them, Translib offers the following facilities in contrast to up-to-date library systems:

- Localisation of user-interface is supported.
- The user is able to enter a query in his/her native language and search for entries that match this query in all the possible languages for which there is at least one entry in the current database.

- The retrieval of all the entries for a given query as well as for its synonyms in any language is possible. Furthermore, the user is able to indicate the type of search, which can be based on narrower and/ or broader terms of the query.
- Finally, translation of the retrieved books/journals titles and keywords in any language is provided in order to give the user an idea of the content of these books/journals.

MULTILINGUAL SEARCH TOOL

This tool enables the user to enter the query in the language (s)he prefers and select the languages in which the matching entries have to be found. Essentially, this tool performs a conversion from monolingual to multilingual queries.

The user can select the input language and the search languages (s)he prefers:

- *Input language*: The language used to introduce the search criteria, that is, the title, author, publication year, etc.
- *Search language(s)*: One or more languages in which the user wishes to find some documents matching his queries.

Furthermore, the user is able to determine the search depth by selecting to search with synonyms, and/or narrower terms, and/or broader terms of the search criteria.

The multilingual search tool utilises:

- A multilingual terminology lexicon, allowing the search of keywords in several languages, and
- A multilingual thesaurus, enabling sophisticated bibliographic information retrieval by means of synonyms, narrower and broader terms.

An example of broader and narrower terms of some keywords is shown in table.

Table Example for Broader/Narrower Terms

Keyword	Broader Terms	Narrower Terms
Academic	Journal	—
Book	Publication	Manual, Introduction
Brochure	Publication	—
Industrial	Journal	—
Introduction	Book	—
Journal	Publication	Academic, Industrial
Manual	Book	Tutorial, Reference
Publication	—	Book, Brochure, Journal
Reference	Manual	—
Tutorial	Manual	—

The search criteria can be specified in a search screen. A search can be started for publications that match the search criteria. For instance, if the user types part of a keyword in the field Keyword and selects the button Keyword Search, the application searches the multilingual terminology lexicon for keywords to match.

The results can be shown in a drop down list. Then a keyword from this list can be selected. The multilingual terminology lexicon contains a list of key topics in three languages, that is, Greek, English, and Spanish.

A search for publications that match the search criteria is executed when the button Search is selected from the Search Screen. The number of publications found appears in the field Records Found.

The search fields are as follows:

- *Title*: The title or part of the title of a publications.
- *Author*: The name or part of the name of an author.
- *Publishing year*: The issuing year of a publication.
- *Keyword*: A Keyword or part of a keyword.
- *Series*: The series or part of the series of a publication.
- *All fields*: All the fields associated with a publication.

When a search starts, all the fields associated with a publication are searched for a string that matches the string typed in this field. The application searches for matching publications by using the 'OR' operator between data entered in the search fields. For example, if the search criteria contain the title 'Democracy', the author 'Cat Stevens,' and the keyword 'Ancient Greece,' a search is performed for publications with the title 'Democracy' or publications written by "Cat Stevens" or publications that contain the keyword "Ancient Greece." Finally, fields that are left blank are not included in the search criteria. For example, if the user leaves the fields Publishing Year, Keyword, Series, and All Fields blank, the search criteria include only the fields Title and Author.

MULTILINGUAL PRESENTATION TOOL

This tool allows localisation of the user interface as well as presentation of the library database entries matching the user query in any of the sup- ported languages. This can be achieved by translating publication titles and keywords, if needed. Particularly, the user has the capability of selecting the Message Language and the Output Languages (s)he prefers.

More specifically, these languages stand for:

- *Message language*: The language used for presenting labels and messages to the user as well as help screens.
- *Output language(s)*: One or more languages used for presenting the query results. The multilingual presentation tool utilises.
- A multilingual conversion table, converting labels and messages into the Message Language.
- A simplified translation tool, supporting the translation of book and journal titles and/or keywords into the specified Output Language(s).

A CLARIFYING EXAMPLE

The following clarifying example aims at further illustrating the definitions. Let us assume that the user selects English as the Input Language, English and Greek as the Search Language(s), English, Greek, and Spanish as the Output Language(s), and the search criteria contain the keyword democracy. The multilingual search tool searches the library data- base for entries containing the keywords democracy and the multilingual presentation tool lists the publications that match these keywords and translates their titles and keywords into Spanish as is shown in table.

Table A Clarifying Example

Input Language	**Search Language(s)**	**Output Language(s)**	
English	English, Greek	English, Greek, Spanish	
Search Criteria (keyword)	**Search for**	**Results** (Title)	(Keywords)
Democracy	*Democracy* *Δημοκρατία*	*Democracy in Ancient Greece* (English translation) *La Democracia en Grecia Antigua* (Spanish translation) *Η Δημοκρατία στην Αρχαία Ελλάδα* (original language)	*Democracy, Ancient Greece* *Democracia, Grecia Antigua* *Δημοκρατία, Αρχαία Ελλάδα*

The system can also present the query results by using a short description of the retrieved book entry. At times a query can retrieve multiple records. In this case, the records are presented to the user ranked in alphabetical order. The original language of these records is also clearly labelled.

MULTILINGUAL RESOURCES

Translib is a system built through the integration of both new and existing information tools. Since, the advantages of the use of reusable resources are well known, we tried to utilise general purpose and state-of-the-art resources where possible, in order to avoid the excessive cost of building a resource from scratch, as well as to ensure the quality and the adequacy of the resources.

MULTILINGUAL THESAURUS

After an extensive market survey and taking into account the advantages and disadvantages of using an existing multilingual thesaurus, we decided that EUROVOC suits the needs of the Translib system. EUROVOC is based on ISO-5964/85, which is an international standard for the development of multilingual thesauri. EUROVOC is a multilingual thesaurus, which was originally built specifically for processing documentation of the European commission. It is implemented in the official languages of the European community.

The edition we used was compiled in 1994 in nine languages:

- Danish
- Dutch
- English
- French
- German
- Greek
- Italian
- Portuguese
- Spanish

Our version of EUROVOC contains only the following languages, which cover the needs of the current Translib system: English, Greek, and Spanish. All these languages have equal status—each descriptor in one language necessarily matches a descriptor in each of the other languages.

At the specific level of descriptors and non-descriptors, the internal structure of EUROVOC depends on semantic relations:

- Scope note (SN)
- Microthesaurus relationship (MT)
- Equivalence relationship (UF, USE)
- Hierarchical relationship (BT, NT)
- Associative relationship (RT)

The EUROVOC thesaurus covers all the subjects that are of importance to the activities of the European community institutions:

- Politics, international relations, European communities, law, economics, trade;
- Finance, social questions, education and communications, science, environment;
- Business and competition, employment and working conditions, transport, energy;
- Agriculture, forestry and fisheries, agri-food stuffs, production;
- Technology and research, industry, geography, international organisations.

We mainly focused on the use of the following subjects: economics, trade, finance, education and communications, science, business and competition, production, technology and research, energy, industry, without excluding the others. Technically speaking, EUROVOC is a single file that contains a significant number of terms relevant to the subjects. EUROVOC's architecture consists of a number of micro- thesauri. Each one of them consists of a set of terms for a given topic.

Each record in a micro thesaurus has several fields indicating the relation between the records and the terms themselves in the nine languages of the European community. Each term is given in two forms for each language. Two terms can have a hierarchical relation, that is, one can be narrower or broader than the other. Each record in the EUROVOC file fits on a single line. The fields occupy fixed positions on the line and have concrete names. Our goal was to transfer the data from EUROVOC to a commercial database.

A set of routines was thus developed for the compilation of the EUROVOC thesaurus into files with a special format that can be easily read by database procedures. Several files constitute the Translib multilingual thesaurus derived from EUROVOC. There are separate files for the terms of each language. The terms are stored in the same order in each of the three files, so that the files are matching. If a term has no equivalents in one or more languages, there is a blank line in the corresponding position. The line number of each term in the files is used as a unique code during the building of the tree, which is stored in another file and does not include the terms themselves.

Thus, the multilingual thesaurus of TRANSLIB has been designed as a simple ASCII table file which contains all the material that is included in the EUROVOC thesaurus. Software was written in order to be able to extract the terms and relevant terms from this huge data store quickly. B+ trees algorithms have been used to make the extraction process as quick as possible.

In conclusion, the multilingual thesaurus helps the user retrieve bibliography related to the relevant keywords (s)he has entered, as its sophisticated search mechanism automatically builds the tree structure of the keywords in all the preferred search languages and sends a complex query to the data-base. In the case where the user does not use the thesaurus, he may not retrieve all the available bibliographic records, since, the keyword he uses to describe his query may not be the same as that used by the librarian for the record classification.

Even when the user enters a query which has no keywords in the multilingual thesaurus, it is possible to update it by means of an editing tool that caters for a number of data entry fields, such as New Keyword, Related Keyword, Keyword Language, Kind of Relationship, etc.

MULTILINGUAL TERMINOLOGY LEXICON

The result of another extensive market survey encouraged us to adopt EURODICAUTOM as a terminology tool. However, after we had completed the decoding of EURODICAUTOM, a problem emerged. The terms of the multilingual thesaurus were entirely incompatible with those of the multilingual terminology lexicon. This meant that the library database could not be searched using keywords from the multilingual terminology lexicon, nor by using synonyms, broader or narrower terms of it. The solution decided on was to create a multilingual terminology lexicon from the terms of EUROVOC.

This was analysed into two sections:

- The informative part; and
- The data retrieval part.

The former mainly consists of a file containing all the terms that are used as keywords in all the Translib supported languages. This file is a three- column file, which contains the same term in each line for all the supported languages. The latter uses a binary search algorithm to achieve maximum efficiency. In this case, it was necessary to create a sequence of files, which contain an upper case description of terms and a numeric label used to locate the term and its description in all languages.

The multilingual terminology lexicon helps the user choose one term in the preferred Input Language, and search the database for this term as well as for all the equivalent terms in all the preferred Search Languages. Again the user can check the new keywords to be included in the multilingual terminology lexicon by means of an editing tool that caters for a number of data entry fields, such as New Keyword, English Keyword, Spanish Keyword, Greek Keyword, etc.

MULTILINGUAL CONVERSION TABLE

The multilingual conversion table is responsible for the interaction between the user and the system in the user's preferred language. It contains all the label fields, messages, and help screens of the user interface in all the supported languages and provides the user with the ability to both choose the language of the user interface and effectively change it at runtime according to his/her preferences. It is independent of any actual data store that is used as the base of the information storage. Finally, the information kept in the Multilingual Conversion Table is logically grouped into three files, one for each language.

A new file can be used for a new supported language, so that maximum source independence and management can be achieved. The Multilingual Conversion Table is stored at the client's site in relational database tables. One table in the database includes the label fields, messages and on- line help information in the three languages supported by the project. Its internal structure is compatible with a future addition of equivalent terms in other European languages.

The table has the following attributes:

- *Code*: A unique number that acts as the tuple's identifier.
- *Kind*: Reflects the type of the user interface item that is contained in the tuple.
- *EngContent*: Content in English.
- *SpaContent*: Content in Spanish.
- *GreContent*: Content in Greek.

When the user wants to customise any label fields, messages, or help screens, this can be accomplished through an editing tool that caters for a number of data entry fields, such as code label, Greek message, Spanish message, etc.

LIBRARY DATABASE

The Translib system follows the UNIMARC standard so as to be easily portable to all library automated systems following the same standard. Regarding the library database, two medium- sized bibliographic data- bases have been utilised. The Greek one possesses about 10,000 titles concerning mainly engineering and computer science sectors, while the Spanish one possesses about 20,000 titles regarding political and financial topics. More specifically, the Greek library database contains 5,500 Greek titles, 3,500 English titles, and 1,000 titles in other European languages. On the contrary, the Spanish library database contains 12,000 Spanish titles, 6,300 English titles, and 1,700 titles in other European languages. Both data- bases were considered appropriate and representative to test the performance of the TRANSLIB system.

SIMPLIFIED TRANSLATION TOOL

The translation of the titles carried out by this tool should give the user an idea of the content of a retrieved book/journal. Even when the translation is not completely correct, it should help the user understand the subject of the document. Translating titles is, in general, easier than translating a whole sentence or even entire texts. The simplest title is a single noun while the most complex one may be a whole phrase. Few titles, however, are composed of a long phrase, *i.e.*, the combination of both noun and prepositional phrases. Furthermore, a title is selected carefully by the author to represent the content of a book.

This fact means that a title must not be ambiguous in order to be comprehensible immediately by the reader. In most cases, syntactic or referential ambiguities can easily be solved. Additionally, titles are usually typed carefully by the editors of a book, so that no grammatical or syntactic errors occur. Needless to say, the titles of books and journals are totally different from those found in a newspaper. Looking at the translation of the titles from a computational point-of-view, the translation process can be facilitated further by making a set of assumptions.

These can be described as follows:

- Translation from one language into another is realised via English which is used as an interlingua.
- For each title only one translation is provided. In addition, a set of titles may have the same translation.
- Only the main title of a bibliographic entry is translated. Subtitles, version numbers, etc., are ignored.
- The titles are considered to be linguistically correct. Hence, syntactically incorrect interpretations are ignored.
- No semantic and/or pragmatic information is used. All the titles are referred to the scientific domain of engineering and computer science. Moreover, for every word in the dictionary there is only one

translation.

- Finally, the input as well as the output files of the translators are ASCII files containing one title per line. If a title cannot be translated, the output file contains an empty line for it.

The selection of an interlingua was adopted to achieve system robustness and reduce the translation costs. Translation between a pair of languages implies translation to and from interlingua. Additionally, the upgrade of the system with a new supported language would only require the implementation of a ling ware for the new language, able to provide translation to and from interlingua. We selected English as the interlingua, since, it was found that it is the most widespread foreign language among the OPAC users. In fact, our interlingua is not plain English but an artificial language, that is, an abstract form that represents the structure of the title based on the English translations of its consisting words. Thus, the interlingua is composed of a list of structures that correspond to the words of the title.

These structures have the following form in PROLOG language for a given word of the line: where English-Lemma is the English translation of the Greek or Spanish word of the title, and Part-of-Speech, Number, and Case are the corresponding morphological information of this word in the source language. Taking all the points into account and in order to strengthen our claim that an AI-based translation tool is needed in the translation process, we tried two translation scenarios. We first implemented a simple word-by-word translation, in order to simplify the translation process and consequently minimize the computational cost.

The evaluation of this approach• has shown that only a small percentage of the translated titles were comprehensible, particularly in translations from Greek to English, Spanish to English, and *vice versa*. We decided, then, to implement a more sophisticated approach that would improve the quality of the translations by taking advantage of AI- based methods.

For instance, the following tools for the implementation of the Greek and English ling-ware were used:

- An existing two-level morphological analyser for morphological recognition and synthesis of Modern Greek words. This is a PC KIMMO-based analyser that was designed for general purpose morphological analysis of Modern Greek and uses a 30,000-word lexicon. According to the two-level morphological model, the surface form of a word is derived by applying a set of rules to the lexical form of that word and *vice versa*. The main advantage of such a model is that these rules are applied in parallel and in both directions, that is, surface to lexical form and lexical to surface form. In linguistic terms, the two- level rules are not processing rules, but more like the realisation rules of stratification linguistics.

- A public domain two-level morphological analyser for morphological recognition and synthesis of English words. This is a PC KIMMO-based analyser that was designed for general purpose morphological analysis of English and uses a 10,000-word lexicon.
- Two syntactic parsers built from scratch and able to recognise the basic phrase structures of the title. These parsers are based on a context-free grammar model consisting of 28 rewriting rules for each one of them. As an example, the four first rules of the modern Greek grammar are given below:
  — Title ⇐ Phrase.
  — Title ⇐ Phrase, Conjunction, Phrase.
  — Phrase ⇐ NounPhrases, Prepositional Phrases.
  — Phrase ⇐ Prepositional Phrases.
- Two medium-sized bilingual morphological dictionaries containing words from the scientific domains of engineering and computer science found in the Central Library of the University of Patras. In particular, these dictionaries stemmed from the PC KIMMO-based dictionaries and translation information as well as new words from the previous scientific domains were added.

Similar tools for the implementation of the Spanish ling ware were utilised.

Just to illustrate the translation process from a Greek title into a corresponding English one, we give below the sequence of transitions among the different tools:

- Greek Title→Greek Morphological Analyser→ Morphologically Analyser Greek Title
- Morphologically Analysed Greek Title→Greek Syntactic Parser→ Abstract Syntactical Form
- Abstract Syntactical Form→Greek-English Translator, Greek-English Bilingual Dictionary→Translated Abstract Form
- Translated Abstract Form→English Morphological Analyser→Morphologically Correct English Title
- Morphologically Correct English Title→English Syntactic Parser→Well-Formed English Title

In contrast to the word- by- word translation, approximately 86 per cent of the translated titles are comprehensible.• It has to be noted here that the quality and comprehension of the provided translations depend on the scientific domain of the library database.

For instance, the Greek word has two meanings:

- Series; and
- Line.

Hence, if the library database comprises books/journals concerning the scientific domain of mathematics, then the former translation should be included in the bilingual dictionaries. Finally, an editing tool is used for updating entries in the English-Greek and Greek-English dictionaries. The user is able to update the nouns and adjectives that are included in the selected bilingual dictionary.

A new entry may be inserted or an existing one may be changed or deleted. When inserting a new entry, the user must insert the new lemma as well as its translation. Additionally, (s)he should also select an inflectional category in order to determine the various word forms of the new entry.

CONCLUSION

Today's libraries have automated their everyday transactions such as acquisition, cataloguing, and circulation. An automated library appears to users as an online public access catalogue (OPAC) through which they can quickly search and obtain the desired information. Such systems support bibliographic search according to author name, title, publication year, etc., and provide free text and keyword facilities. Hence, computer systems have replaced the librarian's role as intermediary between user and library, and expert systems that simulate this role providing general information to the user have been developed. Moreover, the application of AI to information retrieval has recently attracted the attention of information scientists. Advanced applications of natural language processing (NLP), such as machine translation, have already improved the capabilities of several systems in this area. Translation-based methods for translingual information retrieval require the query be translated into the target language.

In this case, full-fledged machine translation is not applicable. Experience shows that of three well-known translation approaches, which is dictionary-based term translation (DICT), example-based term translation (EBT), and example- based term-to-sentence (EBS), DICT presents the best solution for queries consisting of isolated words, or at best, short phrases. Other approaches in information retrieval are concerned with systems with cross-language functionality. A few of them, especially in trade trans-actions and Web-based information services, make use of a controlled language in order to improve the recall and precision rates. The majority of these systems utilise free text retrieval.

The corpus-based approach, MIRTH, supports within- language retrieval in English and Chinese and in specific areas, such as computing, linguistics and litreature. The limitations of this system lie in the lack of a complete linguistic tool to guide translation, as well as in the absence of any maintenance system to deal with tasks such as add, insert, delete, update, replace, and sort links with their keywords. Knowledge- based information retrieval is used in Gilarranz where the features of the EuroWordNet multilingual lexical knowledge base are described.

However, although both approaches tackle the cross- language functionality of the retrieval, they do not consider as yet the localizability of their system by adopting, for instance, an internationalised methodology in their design. In addition, libraries have not paid special attention to multilingual features of OPACs, despite the fact that it is a serious problem. The National Library of Canada was one of the first libraries to offer multilingual access to its users, in the form of controlled bilingual that is English and French, authority files. It is also worthwhile mentioning the ETHICS project that produced an OPAC with multilingual user interface and help screens and a subject index in three languages.

So far, multilinguality in OPACs has been dictated by the needs of a specific multilingual community and restricted to the provision of bilingual or multilingual lists of controlled terms such as controlled authority files, subject headings, and thesauri. Multilinguality as a potential problem for the common user of the library was only explicitly investigated in the NORDINFO survey. According to the results of this survey, multilingual access to online catalogues can improve remarkably the quality of the provided services. Similar user surveys were undertaken by the Central Library of the University of Patras, the Library of the Spanish Agency of International Co-operation, and the Municipal Library of Patras.

The main outcomes of the surveys have been as follows: in a conventional OPAC by using controlled:

- Searching or uncontrolled terms is time consuming, requiring repeated effort from the user who in a lot of cases remains unsatisfied.
- The libraries express their interest in a multilingual access tool, because they understand that multilinguality poses problems to their users as well as to the interconnection with libraries from other countries.
- The translation tool, if any, should be able to retrieve information from the title, subject, and author fields.
- An important indication is that the specific national conditions should be taken very seriously into account, especially with respect to dialects and unofficial languages. A very good example is the relatively high interest of the Spanish library in the Catalan language.

These surveys were aimed at an analysis of the attitude of the users towards the OPAC they used and investigation about their eventual need for a multilingual tool. The results of these surveys are essentially independent of the sex, educational status, familiarity of computer use, and frequency of the use of the OPAC by sample users.

The analysis of the results was very illuminating:

- Approximately 75 per cent of the users were either moderately satisfied or dissatisfied with the results of their searches in the OPAC.
- Over 80 per cent of the dissatisfied users noted that the hits were not in the user's native language or that the search was based only on a single language;

- Approximately 70 per cent of the users were interested in bibliographies written in foreign languages.
- 65 per cent of those who used books in only one language considered being able to search in multiple languages either useful or very useful.

In this chapter, we present Translib, a multilingual interface system to library automated systems. It takes full advantage of tools such as bilingual dictionaries, conversion tables, terminology lexica, intelligent thesauri, and simplified translation tools in order to support multilingual access to library catalogues. This system stemmed from the integration of new and existing multilingual information tools and has been tested in existing medium- sized bibliographic databases in Greece and Spain. The tools are characterised by a high degree of modularity and user- friendliness that allow easy and low-cost maintenance. The following section contains an overview of the Translib system, describes briefly its architecture and gives its basic features.

9

Reference Services and Serials

INTRODUCTION

There are a number of issues that are still of concern in offering reference GIS services. In addition to establishing standards for GIS centers and services to reduce variance in user needs and expectations across academic libraries, reference librarians have several other key opportunities in collection development, instruction on accessing spatial information and software tools, and facilitating user knowledge of GIS concepts and applications. GIS is an example of an interdisciplinary tool that is used across colleges, departments, and academic administration. Regardless of the size of the college or university, libraries may be the point-of-access for students, faculty, and community users.

Further, since GIS is data centered and makes use of many secondary and tertiary products, the library is a natural choice to establish a GIS service point. More importantly, GIS offers libraries a new venue to create, market, and distribute specialised content. Finally, as the level of reference services using GIS data increases, so does the level of complexity and base knowledge the librarian must have to interact effectively with advanced users or participate on research teams. This has implications for continuing professional development and library education. However, the rewards of working in a more dimensional manner with students and faculty, as well as highlighting the library's support of research at the university level, are well worth the time and effort involved.

ACHIEVING INFORMATION COMPETENCIES

Whether one calls it information skills or information literacy competencies, these skills are essential to the learning process. Using geospatial data requires the user to have a range of skills, from determining the nature and extent of the information needed to using information effectively to accomplish specific purpose. Solving problem scenarios and answering geospatially based questions requires proficiency in a number of competency standards that must be completed successfully.

Compounding requisite skills sets is the evaluative component of technology and its use. Users must develop skills to judge the reliability and validity of information as well as emerging technologies and methodologies. Adding to the discussion of literacy is the American Library Association's requirements for information literacy, which has four components. These components focus on the user's ability to recognise when information is needed; the ability to locate the needed information; the ability to evaluate the suitability of retrieved information; and the ability to use effectively and appropriately the needed information.

However, information professionals must also consider new models of reasoning, new systems or applications, or work processes from the perspectives of both naïve and experienced users. Shapiro and Hughes suggest seven dimensions when designing a curriculum that promotes comprehensive information literacy. These dimensions begin with tool and resource literacy, that is, the ability to use print and electronic resources and software and to understand their form, format, and access issues.

These are followed by literacies in the context of information in academia, such as the import of discipline and scholarly publications Social-structural literacy, research literacy, and publishing literacy address how information is socially situated and produced, how tools are used to conduct research, and publication and production of research results.

The literacies end with emerging technology literacy and critical literacy, which address the adaptation, adoption, and evaluation of information technology in terms of their intellectual and social capital, as well as their benefits and costs. Considering the intensive computational and technology skills sets necessary to work with geospatial data, additional approaches to literacy may be necessary. Vitolo and Coulston suggest that analytical and model-based reasoning consider the understanding of relationships among objects, the application of ordering principles to the objects, and the use of basic computational tasks/relevant operations relevant to the relationships and ordering, critical skills for working with geospatial data.

Therefore, information literacy, analytical reasoning, and model-based reasoning all begin with the ability to gather data about an environment, to understand cause and effect relationships, and to do deductive reasoning within an environment.

They suggest that a new information literacy competency taxonomy can be created by mapping the six levels of the educational objectives of Bloom's Taxonomy to the five fundamental units of information systems. This provides an expanded way of thinking about not only the skills, but also how one may assist a user to acquire and hone those skills. Devised to express educational objectives, "intended behaviours which the student shall display at the end of some period of education", Bloom's Taxonomy ties these educational objectives to larger information literacy competencies, "*e.g.*, intended behaviours *in the context of information literacy* which the student shall display at the end of some period of education.".

This taxonomy allows the librarian to identify those areas in which he or she needs to augment his or her skills, while honing current skills to perform more effectively in the delivery of reference services using GIS. This new way of looking at skills and competencies makes sense in a statistically intensive, computing-intensive, and quickly evolving field such as GIS. The evolution of the National Spatial Digital Infrastructure has required librarians to deal with multi-institutional standards and the dynamic nature of the geospatial knowledge. It has also required that GIS librarians not only learn, but also understand the theoretical and methodological choices used in geospatial and geoscience research.

The end products of GIS research efforts are "large, interdependent databases of specific statistics, high-resolution images, textual data sets, and complicated algorithms that must be sustained in a dynamic computer environment that supports their easy migration from one research application to another".

Librarians are natural partners in research collaborations. They are the individuals who seek out datasets, help define information queries, assist and instruct users in resource discovery, and create collaborative arrangements with other academic and research libraries. Shuler suggests the new geospatial literacy "demands that librarians work in partnership with their community among a new set of knowledge choices, and then preserving a credible record of how well those choices were made".

SPATIAL THINKING

Any discussion on reference services must begin with a definition of what it mcans to work with geospatial data. To work effectively with geospatial data requires the librarian and the user to understand spatial concepts, tools used to create representations of geospatial data, and the cognitive processes used to frame questions in a geospatial manner. The Geographical Committee of the National Research Council suggests, "It depends on understanding the meaning of space and using the properties of space as a vehicle for structuring problems, for finding answers, and for expressing solutions. By visualising relationships within spatial structures, we can perceive, remember, and analyse the static and, via transformations, the dynamic properties of objects and the relationships between objects.

We can use representations in a variety of modes and media to describe, explain, and communicate about the structure, operation, and function of those objects and their relationships". Many of the elements identified in this passage are currently activities done by reference librarians, such as "structuring problems" are a function of the reference interview.

However, for many librarians, providing reference services using geospatial data is a new, sometimes overwhelming experience. There are different levels of GIS services libraries can offer. These range from high-level, which require a full GIS set-up, to mid-level, which utilise Web-based GIS applications and require user input, to low-level, which uses online static maps. In 1997, the Association of Research Libraries (ARL) surveyed their research library members who participated in the GIS literacy project. Of the 72 respondents, 64 reported that they provide GIS services, either at the library or at academic departments offering GIS. Among libraries that offer GIS services but do not administer them, the most common activity is offering guidance in finding appropriate data sets. For those libraries that do not have a GIS unit, GIS services are offered at the general reference desk. Librarians use a variety of hardware; platforms.

The training offered by the Literacy Project was aimed primarily at documents and map librarians. Most of the respondents also had training by GIS software providers or GIS coursework. Technical support for GIS hardware or software was provided by library staff at 51 institutions. GIS patrons were primarily students and faculty/staff, although there were a number of users from community, business, and government. A 2005 survey examined the use of GIS implementation within 168 academic libraries in institutions classed as Master's Colleges and Universities I and II. Almost a third of the respondents either currently support or plan to implement GIS services in the future. Only half of the libraries surveyed have staff devoted to GIS part time. Librarians had to have knowledge of a range of hardware, platforms, software.

Further, training is variable, from no training, to training outside of the library, to on-site training that itself ranged from one-on-one instruction to the use of group or individual tutorial programmes. Further, the collection resources ranged from Internet resources, software package data, reference databases with spatial data, archives, and institutional research. Staffing levels were widely divergent, ranging from full-time employees who assist with GIS in addition to other duties to student workers who were knowledgeable about GIS. Finally, academic patrons' interests, specialties, and areas of interest included geography, geology, natural resources, business, engineering, sociology, political science, environmental science, biology, landscape architecture, planning, history, and nursing.

The findings of these, and other surveys, touch on four of the five challenges mentioned in the introduction to the chapter:

- Interpreting the socioeconomic milieu, which characterises the attribute data and the environment in which it describes and making it accessible for the user community,
- Reinterpreting the reference interview,
- Reconfiguring instruction and instructional support, and

- Instructing patrons to achieve appropriate levels of information competencies.

RECONFIGURING INSTRUCTION, TRAINING, AND INSTRUCTIONAL SUPPORT

In 1966, four skills were considered critical for understanding GIS:

1. Literacy,
2. Articulacy,
3. Numeracy, and
4. Graphicacy.

All four skills enhance one's ability to communicate effectively and understand those relationships that cannot be expressed solely with text, spoken words, mathematical notation, or visually. Text, mathematics, graphics, and discourse complement one another, and all are necessary in various contexts for the successful comprehension and exchange of ideas. Balchin and Coleman argue "neither words nor numbers nor diagrams are simpler or more complex, superior or inferior.

They are only more suitable or less suitable for particular purposes". For example, users may have difficulties in conveying their information needs to learn content-based image retrieval systems or to deconstruct a map. Compounding communication is recent research that suggests only a very small percentage of the general population prefer to learn by reading. Clearly, understanding when a particular communication mode is more appropriate than another is and how to use each mode effectively become essential knowledge-sets and skill-sets for librarians.

CREATING PATTERNS: INFORMATION-SEEKING MODELS

Digital geospatial data archives and repositories are directly related to specific question- answering research, which "reflect[s] the information needs of their creators" and "tend[s] to be tailored to the specific cultures of research communities, rather than adhering to existing blueprints for access resources". Since disciplines play an important role, especially in the influence of context and search task on information seeking, the impact of the different types of conceptual models for information seeking and retrieval will impact how librarians themselves learn and instruct others in the use of geospatial information.

Such models serve different research purposes. What kind of models are there and in what ways may they help librarians to better instruct, train, and support GIS research and reference activities? Are different types of models needed for various purposes? Differences in discipline affect faculty and student information seeking skills.

Individuals in the hard sciences, such as engineering and math, use a search strategy based on a specific problem-solving process while individuals in the humanities are more likely to be based on a topical interest that is extensively researched. Understanding diverse analytical models of task-based information seeking can contribute to the development of a research area, that is, "Conceptual models may and should map reality, guide research and systematise knowledge, for example, by integration and by proposing systems of hypotheses". One such critical model on information-seeking behaviours was developed by Ellis based on Glaser and Strauss's grounded theory for data analysis.

He determined six generic information behaviours: *starting*, *chaining*, *browsing*, *differentiating*, *monitoring*, and *extracting*. Each of these activities can involve a librarian. For example, *starting* is comprised of the initial steps to finding information, such as a review of indexing and abstracting sources or consultation with a librarian in starting a literature review. *Chaining* is following "chains of citations" between sources identified, such as following references from an initial source or following other sources that refer to an original source.

Browsing includes scanning of published journals and tables of contents, as well as references and abstracts of other literature reviews or bibliographies. *Differentiating* is qualifying sources of information to ensure relevance in one's information search. *Monitoring* is a current awareness activity in which one regularly examines core journals, conferences, new books, and catalogs of resources via hand searching or by using current awareness services. *Extracting* selectively identifies and acquires relevant material from resources.

Ellis notes:

- The detailed interrelation or interaction of the features in any individual information seeking pattern will depend on the unique circumstances of the information seeking activities of the person concerned at that particular point in time".

Similar to Kuhlthau's model in terms of the various types of activities or tasks carried out within the overall information-seeking process, Ellis's empirically based model is considered authoritative in its classification of types of information seeking behaviours. Building on Ellis' work, four new areas have been added to his model: *accessing*, *verifying*, *networking*, and *information managing*. With the increasing dependence on online resources, Meho and Tibbo suggest that, "Although not all of these new features are information searching or gathering activities, they are tasks that have significant roles in enhancing information retrieval and facilitating research". *Accessing* is a critical component of information seeking because without access, one may miss essential pieces of data to answer one's question.

In addition, given the importance of archival materials and other forms of primary sources in geospatial data, librarians may need to investigate why access to information is denied and to intervene to obtain the items. *Verifying* are those activities that establish the accuracy and authority of the data or information.

Librarians and researchers should consider bias and lack of reliability and accuracy in materials produced by governmental agencies as well as private sector organisations.

Detailed metadata on lineage of data can alert users to discrepancies in data and in use of such information. Data comparison with other sources can also point out errors in data. *Networking* is those activities associated with communicating or maintaining relationships with fellow researchers or governmental and non-governmental organisations, or individuals who could provide access to or verify information or data.

The final information-seeking activity is *information managing*, which emphasises the importance of filing, archiving, and organising the information used to facilitate one's research. Ellis, Meho, and Tibbo conclude that the activities identified in their studies may not be entirely or always sequential. However, Meho and Tibbo suggest that the information-seeking behaviours of social scientists are divided into four interrelated stages, *searching*, *accessing*, *processing*, and *ending*, that then contain a number of activities. For example, during the *searching* stage, all of Ellis' activities and Meho and Tibbo's networking activity begin. During the *accessing* stage, decision-making to continue on to *processing* or to return to *searching* is based on acquisition of requested materials.

It is the author's belief that *information managing* also begins in this stage to document acquired items. During the *processing stage*, chaining, extracting, differentiating, verifying, and information-managing activities begin or continue as do syntheses and analyses.

There will be constant motion between the searching, accessing, and/or the processing stages until the *ending* stage, when the project is completed. Ellis' existing and extended models, which examined primarily social scientists, are expanded upon by Palmer, who suggests that scientists and humanists use primarily four research activities: confirmation searching, discovery searching, collecting, and consultation. Further, there are important distinctions in source selection, decision making, and how materials are used, which can impact reference services and support to research faculty.

To act as a consultant, reference staff need to increase significantly their own understanding of the different research processes and information-seeking behaviours. In addition to activity models, reference librarians also need to be familiar with various cognitive models for information seeking. Ingwersen's cognitive model examines how the search process itself affects information retrieval. He suggests that the all facets of the information-seeking system, from the user's questions, documents, or objects retrieved, interaction with intermediaries, such as search engines, and, by extension, librarians, are the result of explicit or implicit cognitive models of the domain of interest at that particular point.

Ingwersen also suggests that the user experiences various cognitive transformations from where he or she begins the information-seeking process to the point where a search is successful in identifying objects to answer the user's questions. Therefore, users usually have implicit models of their information need or work task that they can tell individuals or query systems. These cognitive structures and their transformations need to be effectively communicated throughout the information system as identified previously, again which includes the reference librarian. What is even more crucial is the cognitive framework of the reference librarian, since his or her knowledge structures "are determined by the individual and its social/collective experiences, education, etc.".

The librarian and, ultimately, the user, are influenced by his or her environment "which may possess social conventions, preferences, and collective cognitive structures adhering to domains".

This extends to the transformative aspect of knowledge and the importance of effective communication, since "elements of a communicated message must be perceived or recognised, in order to allow the message to transform into a new state of knowledge. This transformation does not necessarily produce a simple accumulation of categories or concepts, but can be seen as a reconfiguration, a restructuring or a compression in part of the recipient's knowledge structures". Järvelin and Wilson expand on a cognitive model and address how user-perceived tasks must be considered. They suggest that individuals interpret the same objective task differently, particularly for what is perceived to be a complex task.

Task complexity entails a number of variables: "repetition, analysability, *a priori* determinability, the number of alternative paths of task performance, outcome novelty, number of goals and conflicting dependencies among them, uncertainties between performance and goals, number of inputs, cognitive and skill requirements, as well as the time-varying conditions of task performance". How the user perceives the task is the basis for the actual performance of the task, the interpretation of his or her information needs, and the decision making to ensure satisfaction, or successful completion of the task. Järvelin and Wilson consider five classes of tasks.

These are automatic information processing tasks; normal information processing tasks; normal decision tasks; known, genuine decision tasks; and genuine decision tasks. These range from simple computational tasks that are *a priori* completely determinable and structured to decision-making tasks, where information, result, or process is unknown, and the first task must be to create the information-seeking structure.

Byström and Järvelin examined what types of information are sought through which types of channels, from what kinds of sources, in which kinds of tasks. They determined that as task complexity increases the needs for domain information and problem-solving information increases. Complexity also increases the proportion of general-purpose sources and decreases that of problem- and fact-oriented sources. Finally, complexity decreases the success of information seeking, decreases the internality of channels, and increases the number of sources.

There are a number of studies that show clear differences in student and faculty information-seeking behaviour across disciplines and in how faculty and students teach and learn. Cole *et.al.* found that domain novice users in the beginning stages of researching a topic find themselves searching for information before they have clearly identified their information need.

Data also supported their hypothesis that the user's information need is identified through transformation of his or her knowledge structure. Heinström investigated whether information-seeking patterns relate to discipline differences, study approaches, or personality traits. Her quantitative study of master's thesis students found that both the level and scope of information students wished to retrieve and the way they searched for it determined if searches were exploratory or precise. The most common patterns seen in users' information seeking can be described along a continuum of broadness vs. specificity. Users with a broad divergent learning style typically start their learning process through an overall understanding of a topic, addressing several aspects of the information need at the same time, relating new information, much like a "big picture" approach. This style is often used to become acquainted with a new area, to build basic knowledge, or to understand causal relations.

There can be redundancy in these types of searches, which may not be strictly relevant to the user's information needs. This type of information-seeking behaviour generally uses a broad search pattern throughout project stages. Users with a convergent rational, problem- focused style use a different learning approach, concentrating on one item at a time. They often generate precise searches, mastering one component of a topic before moving on to the next. For these users, the broad, or big, conceptual picture emerges late in the search. Users with this type of "serialist" learning style also generate controlled and systematic seeking with precise goals. Both types of users may perform "effortful information search and processing," believing that the investment of additional cognitive effort in an information processing task is the best way to achieve accuracy.

For most geospatial-based queries, a problem-based learning model would also be appropriate. Similar to students using a problem-based learning model, GIS users also tend to be frequent library users, use a wider variety of resources, and ask more complex reference questions. Both types of students also show more independence in information gathering and generally acquire information skills sooner than their peers. Learning styles have implications in the development of instructional materials for users as well as for librarians. Using instructional materials structured to suit individualistic learning styles is significantly superior for both types of learners, and serialist instructional materials resulted in overall better learning performance and efficiency than did holist materials. Adaptive training methodologies have the potential to accommodate individual differences within required time limits to avoid instructional failures, ensure minimal proficiency outcome, and maximize individual proficiencies. Creating instructional models that capitalise on student strengths and match content and structure of training events to the student's conceptual structure provides librarians more insight into the information-seeking and resource-discovery process.

Further, the development of adaptive instructional systems, an emerging trend in education, addresses learner styles with personalised training schemes, with a focus on lifelong learning, just-in-time training delivery, and integrated training across campus settings.

With personalisation, the learners' objectives, current status of skills/ knowledge, and learning style preferences are targeted to better deliver content as well as to monitor progress in skills sets. Another advantage of personalisation is the repurposing and scaffolding of materials to create reusable learning objects. This is a critical component in a complex knowledge area such as GIS. Tancheva suggests that tutorials be problem-based, teach concepts, and be anchored to class-based instruction support or discipline. This is essential since students often lack sound mental models of databases or datasets. Conceptual models ensure the transferability of competencies across systems, and improve synthesis and evaluative thinking.

Interactivity is an attribute highly valued by generation Xs and Ys. It provides active and situated learning through simulations as well as opportunity for online collaboration with other learners and instructors. Interactive mapping and direct manipulation of data to create graphic display mirrors many simulation and real-time activities with which users have grown up. Geospatial data is also very media rich, with multiple formats and output styles and indexing or descriptive metadata.

Adaptive learning systems permit a variety of presentation styles, and also allow users to index and organise data for their own use. Users will wait to the last possible moment to learn a new system for a class project or paper. Just-in-time, or point-of-need, delivery provides training at the exact time and place that it is needed for the user to complete a specific task. Adaptive instructional methods emphasise user-centric environments.

In this type of environment, the learner takes responsibility for his or her own learning and the librarian is seen more as an expert guide and facilitator. However, tutorials are best seen as complementary or as supplementary instruction rather than as an effective stand-alone teaching tool. Gutierrez and

Wang found that "students who regularly used the library benefited the most" from literacy instruction. Their study reinforces the argument that research skills require practice, that is, a single, traditionally conducted library research class will not significantly improve the ability of the user to perform research. In addition to user education, librarians have important roles in curriculum development. Serving on a curriculum committee provides reference librarians a stronger voice in the planning and implementation of a curriculum's information management component and information resources by students. Librarians also become more involved as a resource person for faculty, instructional support staff, and students, ranging from basic assistance or instruction at the reference desk to resource management and utilisation to consultation with faculty and students.

How librarians conceptualise government information should be changed. Cheney suggests that librarians "teach faculty and student researchers why, not just how, to use government information rather than agency organisation and its function". This concept reduces the emphasis on government information as "a separate specialisation, based on its provenance, rather than its subject content". This approach clearly favours the range and breadth of GIS as both a subject within a discipline as well as a discipline in its own right. Understanding the user's information-seeking need, based on identification of the user's discipline and question, can create better use of government information as well as better users of that information. Users generally do not care how the information is organised as to agency, division, or department, just "does it answer my question?" This applies not just to search skills, but also to our "how to use the library on X" lectures, instructions, workshops, and tutorials.

Both broad exploration and specific searching have their particular benefits dependent on the stage of the research process, or a preferred way of learning, which also affect instruction. Järvelin and Wilšon emphasise the use of conceptual models to "map reality, guide research and systematise knowledge, for example, by integration and by proposing systems of hypotheses". Teaching and research models developed by reference staff should focus on developing problem solving skills, critical thinking skills, and effective information-seeking behaviours. By focusing on how "... information contributes to their critical thinking within the context of a discipline", librarians will be able to create effective instructional and training materials for their users.

REINTERPRETING TRADITIONAL PATRON INTERACTIONS

If most questions asked are based on "what" and "how" in reference to a particular location and time, a GIS has two characteristics that allow it to answer these types of questions:

1. The ability to apply spatial operators to the data and
2. The ability to link data sets together.

As librarians provide more resources, services, and technologies to patrons, the increase on more specialised, targeted reference questions and consultations also increase. Further, the range and depth of each reference interaction may differ significantly based upon patron, services offered, training provided, staffing, and the question asked. Kowal suggests that the type of patron experience and knowledge will require the reference librarian to gauge and match service to user need.

For example, a high-level service user has a holistic understanding of his or her information needs, is computer and GIS-application literate, and is able to analyse and identify information from primary and raw data. A mid-level service user uses dynamic, Web-based GIS resources to answer specific questions. A low-level service user uses static maps generated off Web-, CD-ROM-, or DVD-based resources. Morris describes the importance of content issues in the performance of a reference interview.

The data extent, or coverage of the study area, is often the first question, followed by thematic content. Currency of the information and its relationship to other data/information used in the project is an important factor in selecting content. The availability of the attributes of the data, such as percent of street addresses available for a specific project, or if the data can be easily geocoded, is also key. The format of the data determines if it can be used "as is." It also determines if conversion is necessary or if there will be unacceptable data loss when converted. Coordinate systems may need to be reprojected while data may need conversion. Is there information accompanying the dataset that describes if these activities need to be performed or how best to perform them? Ease of access is also a basic question, from one large download to numerous extractions of data that are then recompiled. Licensing and pricing concerns may also require examination of redistribution rights for faculty and/or researchers.

Additional questions may concern types of service, such as image, feature, or geocoding, access protocols, and reliability and uptime. Also, for all beta or demonstration content/services, *caveat emptor*. Kinikin and Hench's survey of smaller academic libraries reported significantly different results from that of larger academic libraries. Of the 11 smaller academic libraries surveyed, 8 of the libraries indicated fewer than two users per week with only one library reporting more than five users per week. Houser describes the joint Library and GIS/Data Lab services at the University of Kansas Libraries. After the integration of the Map Library and GIS lab services, the number of data consultations with library staff increased from 82 to almost 160 interactions during 2003-2004, with the 2005 monthly averages showing an increase of 16 per cent over the previous year.

As with the Kinikin and Hench study, more granular statistics were not available. However, longitudinal study from the Yale Map Collection GIS Service indicated that the average amount of time spent per consultation with a GIS librarian is about 4 hours. The Yale statistics also indicate that faculty and doctoral students typically average about twice as much time per consultation than undergraduate or master's level students. The Yale Map Collection GIS Service staff average approximately 155 consultations a year, with faculty and students generally making four visits each, most face-to-face. However, it is not uncommon during complex, long-term projects for the librarians to have multiple consults with a single patron.

The Yale statistics show that 30 consults between one patron and a GIS librarian. Abbott and Argentati saw the provision "of access to spatial information and software tools and facilitating intellectual access to GIS concepts and applications" as a "natural evolution and extension of existing library services and expertise".

However, researchers and librarians have also warned about the complexity and technical difficulty of GIS reference. For example, a staff person may need a minimum of at least 20 hours to complete a GIS tutorial that will allow him or her to begin working on complicated research problems.

One also must be practical. Finding or processing spatial data usually takes twice as long as initially expected. Basic cartographic elements and their placements require a knowledge of map display and rudimentary statistics to insure that appropriate statistical measures are used to calculate and display information. Reference librarians also need to be aware that paper maps may themselves be essential in determining preliminary data patterns or trends, for collecting additional data, or may themselves be repurposed to digital formats.

Visualisation and analysis of digital spatial data is in itself a complex process, involving the understanding and use of legacy materials in other formats, and requiring the reference librarian to delve into new, uncharted areas or to think in new ways about content and context of information. Questions may be asked at all stages of a research process or arise serendipitously.

In addition to the traditional interview, reference librarians will need to know other service parameters for their GIS users. These include basic access questions, such as whether they have access to the necessary data or what are the rules regarding access to a GIS laboratory.

Other issues include knowing the appropriate software and hardware for that researcher, if there is enough data storage capacity, and how data may be distributed. Reference librarians may have to determine if there is a need to obtain GIS assistance from campus staff or other expert users and the types and levels of training and related resources required for the project. Librarians may be asked about purchasing and licensing of GIS software, if there are campus GIS listservs, and what commonly used datasets are housed and maintained by the library. The availability of grant sources to support GIS development and use in research projects, collection development, staff training, and new services will be a frequently asked question by doctoral students and research and teaching faculty.

Traditional maps and statistical publications are static resources, with no capability for the researcher or librarian to merge, create, or modify data spontaneously. GIS adds an opportunity for librarians to become producers of information as well as enter into collegial, scholarly relationships with fellow academic researchers.

However, entering into new publishing or scholarly relationships require reference librarians to understand not just the traditional reference question but also the acquisition and use of geospatial resources. A clear understanding of intellectual property, data redistribution rights, and derivative rights are critical in the reuse or manipulation of geospatial data, whether public domain, public sector, or leased proprietary data. Opportunities and challenges presented by new information technologies redefine intellectual property issues around the world, almost on a daily basis. Since researchers have responsibilities to promulgate their research, retaining rights over how their results are used is essential, especially for long-term or multiyear studies.

Intellectual property issues can influence their ability to distribute their products. Reference librarians who work with researchers need to be current to be effective.

For example, national and international projects may be affected by confidentiality clauses that may exist in software licences, use and access agreements for geospatial data, project documents, or funding arrangements. For librarians who are acquiring, supporting, or providing access to researchers, contract terms and/or license language will need to accommodate different countries or different legal jurisdictions. Longhorn suggest that "[b]oth staff and institutions should recognise their rights and responsibilities in such cases, and stated policies should be in place, including appropriate non-disclosure and confidentiality agreements and forms, both in contracts of employment and perhaps even on a project basis".

Since university policies vary, the reader is asked to consult the General Counsel's Office of their university as well as to review the policies of the corporate entity owning rights to the original datasets.

Ethics also come into play. Researchers conducting research with groups of people must go under an institutional review board (IRB). Any study involving observation of or interaction with human subjects that originates at an academic or research setting, including course projects, reports, or research papers, must be reviewed and approved by the IRB for the protection of human subjects in research and researchrelated activities. The IRB ensures that data about study participants are kept confidential, secure, and, if health related, that the data complies with the parameters of the federal Health Information Portability and

Accountability Act. Further, in academic libraries that host human subjects datasets, researchers are responsible for obtaining approval of their research projects from the appropriate local or private IRB responsible for assuring protection of human research subjects.

For example, if a library hosts research data from a local or national study, and students need to access it as part of a class project, IRB approval may be needed before access to the system is provided. Librarians should be familiar with what requirements must be formally filed and approved, as in the IRB, for access to certain datasets or even the GIS, if bought for that project. Understanding how to operate within current intellectual property and copyright concerns is also crucial in developing resource management policies and procedures as part of a research team when working with multiple private and public sector vendors.

If the reference librarian has part of his or her time assigned to a research project, he or she may be considered a research collaborator. Either as an official or unofficial member of a research project, or as a reference guide, the librarian may be held accountable should liability issues arise. As a result, librarians seek to adapt their behaviour, resources, and services to better serve their clientele and define their own roles.

EVALUATING AND ASSESSING SERVICES

Library measurement has been defined as "the collection and analysis of objective data describing library performance on which evaluation judgements can be based". It has been suggested that librarians use effectiveness, cost effectiveness, cost benefit, and performance measurement as measures for evaluation which can be related to inputs, outputs and outcomes. Inputs are system resources, such as library budgets and finances, staffing, and print and digital resources. Outputs are the activities the system provides, such as transactions, hours of access, the availability, use, and usability of resources. Although there have been numerous reinventions of the role of librarians, the quantitative and qualitative measures by which they determine how well they are performing have not changed. Input measures, such as volumes held, serial subscriptions, expenditures, and staffing are not correlated to output measures, typically transactions.

This is compounded by counting data downloads that can only measure what the library does have, not what it does not. More rigourous market analysis may be required to adequately assess use, identify shortcomings, and predict demand. When creating a new service area or services, quantitative and qualitative measures allow library management to determine the implications of a major change in order to deal with all of the elements that must be addressed. Using quantitative indicators, such as frequencies of interactions, and qualitative indicators, such as effectiveness, libraries can "increase their visibility, restructure to meet the needs of their users, achieving their objective of remaining the pre-eminent source of information within the academy".

In addition, statistics and measures are powerful planning tools that show emerging trends that require additional resources, workflow processes, training needs, staffing changes, and entrepreneurial opportunities. They also allow comparison with peer institutions and aid areas planning a new service to project staff, instructional, and technology demands. Problems with library measures are legion.

Traditional counts of productivity may underestimate the actual volume of work performed, as the actual volume of business is becoming more complex to gauge. Ways of counting are problematic. Few libraries use their reference counts to determine frequently asked questions or monitoring changes in the types and complexity of questions asked. In the interest of accumulating higher numbers, these qualitative aspects are often lost. Even if the question comes through an "Ask-A" service, there is no systematic coding or review of the questions, recording the length of time spent on answering it, or the number of and types of resources consulted to answer a particularly exotic question. Repurposing and measuring existing operations may provide more effective library measures. For example, Steinhart's description of the benefits of sharing data provides additional measures that could address institutional and academic support as well as outreach and partnerships.

The number of interorganisational activities and reuse of geographic data by external organisations certainly count as outreach or academic-community partnership activity. Data error correction can be counted as response to user feedback and the use of geospatial data may be counted as part of public distribution requirements. Training and education also measure professional development as well as meeting institutional or organisational competencies in the use of geospatial data. Definition of quality of services also varies and, in the library literature, the concepts of quality and satisfaction are used interchangeably, even though the two are not necessarily the same. Further, instruments meant to measure service quality are often better measures of satisfaction.

However, service quality is seen as the antecedent of satisfaction, that is, without service quality, satisfaction cannot be measured. Assessing customer satisfaction may be more critical if there are other service providers or competing resources for users than just the library's GIS services and resources. Sometimes, the difference is never clarified on the questionnaire or survey. Take the example of the service quality measure, LibQual+™, created in 1999 as a standardised measure of library service quality by the Association of Research Libraries (ARL) in collaboration with Texas AandM University. LibQual+™, measures library users' evaluations of service quality on four dimensions: "Affect of Service," "Library as Place," "Personal Control," and

"Access to Information." The structure of LibQual+ ™ mirrors that of SERVQUAL™, an industry- based service performance measure. Although LibQual+ ™ is described as a measure of service quality rather than satisfaction, users of the questionnaire frequently consider it a measure of the latter.

In addition, many library measures have a problem with validity and reliability. For example, performance-only assessment is the most valid framework for gauging customer satisfaction when using LibQual+ ™ or SERVQUAL™.

By eliminating the difference scores in these instruments, the problems with reliability and validity are eliminated and respondents will need less time to complete them. Another suggestion is to use a shorter version of the LibQual+ ™ with just performance-only ratings, as in the case of the SERVPERF, the performance- only variant of SERVQUAL.

Libraries may also choose to use assessment guidelines in higher education as a model for library or service assessment. Dow describes how the University of Rochester, a Carnegie 1 research university, used the American Association of Higher Education's (AAHE) *Principles of Good Practice for Assessing Student Learning*, as part of its strategic assessment. The principles identified included effective ongoing assessment, asking questions that people cared about, attentiveness to outcomes, and gathering evidence as to how and to what degree its programmes influenced the quality of effort that students and faculty invested in learning experiences. This was a departure from traditional resource-based input and output measures to define quality and impact.

The ARL New Measures agenda examines learning outcomes, research outcomes, institutional outcomes, and personal control or electronic service quality issues. Smith examined how accreditation agencies were identifying student outcomes while tying them back into institutional objectives. He suggests that a library should understand its students, not just what their knowledge and skills are when they arrive, but also what challenges they face in the future as to learning. He also suggests that a library should understand what learning outcomes are required for student success and on which dimensions of learning it should focus its efforts on. He further suggests that a library effectively measure the extent to which outcomes are achieved as well as those that are not achieved.

After all, without understanding where problems lie, there is no opportunity to correct or change them. Finally, after correcting the problems or making identified changes, is the library meeting its defined outcome? Franklin examines the relationship between a library and sponsored research activities within university settings through a review of 20 years of KPMG reports.

Using three indicators, total research and development funding at a university; total library expenditures, and library expenditures in support of sponsored research as a percentage of total library expenditures, there was a high correlation between total R&D funding and total library expenditures. Little or no correlation was found between total library expenditures and percent of library expenditures in support of sponsored research. Little or no correlation was also found between an institution's R&D funding and percent of library expenditures in support of sponsored research. This may be due to the fact that few libraries track expenditures other than by departmental/college codes and do not track by contract or grant codes.

INTERPRETING THE MILIEU OF SPATIAL DATA

Traditional reference is "a mediated, one-on-one service that intervenes, and stands ready to intervene, at the information seeker's point of need. That need ... is every information seeker's universal predicament of wanting to move forward but being unable to progress until some missing information is found". Today's information seekers want and need that gap filled with as little interruption as possible, so they can continue where they left off.

Further, users want support in *their use of information* instead of *their seeking of information*. Today's users of geospatial data also require simple yet stable means of data distribution, innovative data discovery and interpretation mechanisms, and enhanced spatial content publishing, including the means to create and propagate spatial data beyond the academy while retaining local control of the data content.

Multilingual support is becoming a necessity with geospatial content crossing boundaries and users forging new, global partnerships. For this new patron group, librarians need to be well versed in geospatial and geographic data discovery tools and support. A quick review of job opportunities illustrate minimum requirements for libraria

ns working with geospatial data: develop and manage spatial and numeric data resources and services; support teaching, research, and engagement; provide consultation to faculty and students; develop instructional modules; handle and create data documentation and research resources; and establish configurations for GIS workstations. This has implications for the traditional roles of librarians in collection development, which now has an intensive data focus; cataloging and creating metadata; current awareness and selective dissemination of information; scholarly activity, and university service via committees, task forces, and teams.

Reference services now range from finding and selecting data to providing technical support, from troubleshooting application- and network-based questions to facilitating licenses and software installations. Instruction is also increasing, from comprehensive group workshops and trainings to individual, intensive instructional events. The content of these workshops range from highlighting new resources to targeting the reference/technical support continuum. Outreach services are also in demand, as libraries market their resources and services to very diverse clientele across colleges and disciplines. Outreach also creates new partnership opportunities, as data-intensive labs merge with libraries to form joint-use facilities. New functionality in geospatial data use, through new protocols, such as simple object access protocol (SOAP) and application programme interfaces (API), continue to create new opportunities for librarians in the provision of reference services.

Expanding reference services to research services is an emerging area, as librarians become essential members of research collaborations and multiuniversity partnerships. What is new for reference librarians is the emphasis on product development, a focus on intensive and in-depth consultation, and the transition to being a member of a research project. Traditional libraries provided reference service for paper-based information resources, such as maps, statistical data, books, journals, and archival collections.

Although maps are frequently housed in government documents or a map library, other materials that have a connection to geographic or geospatial data are dispersed throughout the library's collections (physical locations, such as reference, documents, general, special, and virtual locations on servers, desktops, laptops, and phones).

Since today's researchers often have a geographic or geospatial component to their reference/research questions, reference and research consultation assistance with queries involves GIS, spatial, and numeric data, and traditional cartographic materials as well as "fugitive" print materials in books, documents, and journals. A question on assessing a neighbourhood, for example, may involve demographic and outcomes data, service data, geographic data, infrastructure data, and resource data1, which may be in numeric datasets, reports, maps, or even in photographs.

CONCLUSION

Geographers often define the spatial parameters of different environments by integrating diverse data sets with locational coordinates to create an attribute-rich digital geospatial dataset. From these datasets, researchers can observe and record phenomena and create new geographic metaphors in describing the geographic spaces of places, physical or virtual. One challenge for librarians is to be cognizant of not only the spatial extent of geospatial data, but to have the ability to interpret the socioeconomic milieu, which characterises the attribute data and the environment in which it describes and to make it accessible for the user community.

A second challenge is how to reinterpret traditional patron interactions in an increasingly online service environment and the best use of applications that must be used to "push" information to the patron. A third is how to market the library's GIS services and resources to our patrons, both old and new. A fourth challenge is how instruction and instructional support must be reconfigured to meet the needs of a variety of users, including librarians, with a range of skills and knowledge levels.

The final challenge is instructing patrons to achieve appropriate levels of information competencies. This chapter will examine the "new world" that reference librarians find themselves in today, how they may approach the challenges of geospatial reference, and inculcate information competencies and lifelong learning skills in their patrons.

10

Participatory Networks

AN OVERVIEW

Knowledge is created through conversation. Conversations can take place between friends and colleagues in the 'here and now.' But, they can also take place over centuries, with the participants changing but the theme remaining the same, and the conversation being recorded in thousands of artifacts, like books, pictures, and digital files. In many conversations users need sophisticated processes to facilitate the conversation. Facilitation not only enriches conversations with diverse and deep information, it also serves as a memory keeper, documenting agreements and outcomes to facilitate future conversations.

The library serves this vital role for many communities. The implication of this rather abstract concept is that libraries are in the conversation business. This theoretical argument can be seen in traditional brick-and-mortar libraries as library speaker series, book groups, and even the collection development processes. Yet online, the library has fallen far short of this ideal of conversation facilitator. Key library systems, such as the catalogue for example, are at best one-way conversations.

Libraries have a great opportunity to provide invaluable conversational, participatory infrastructure to their communities online. By adopting concepts and technologies from Web 2.0 and tightly integrating them into their services, libraries can advance not just their communities but also their positions within them. The opportunities inherent in participatory networks have not emerged because of current Internet developments such as Web 2.0, but, rather, these technologies make it easier to meet an identified and long-standing role of libraries. Wikis, blogs, and recommender systems replace dial-up bulletin boards and local databases as a means to empower our communities.

What's more, these technologies can bring the ideal of the participatory model to our most fundamental library systems. Libraries should adopt participatory network concepts and software not because they are new or sexy, but because they match our most fundamental mission: knowledge creation and dissemination. This document describes the participatory model of libraries and provides an overview of current Web 2.0 technologies and a brief discussion of how current Library 2.0 efforts point the way to an even greater change in library as a facilitator of conversations. Specific challenges and opportunities of participatory networking are reviewed. Finally, the authors recommend the creation of a shared participatory test bed for libraries.

This network would not only experiment with new collaborative Web technologies, but also work with library organisations and vendors to speed innovation in traditional library systems. Finally, the network test bed would create a shared infrastructure to provide participatory technologies – such as Wikis, blogs, and RSS feeds—to libraries for inclusion in their day-to-day services.

THE GOAL

Knowledge is created through conversation. Libraries are in the knowledge business. Therefore, libraries are in the conversation business. Some of those conversations span millennia, while others only span a few seconds. Some of these conversations happen in real time. In some conversations, there is a broadcast of ideas from one author to multiple audiences. Some conversations are sparked by a book or a video or a Web page. Some of these conversations are as trivial as directing someone to the bathroom. Other conversations centre on the foundations of ourselves and our humanity. It may be odd to start a technology brief with such seemingly abstract comments. Yet, without this firm, if theoretical, footing the advent of Web 2.0, social networking, Library 2.0, and participatory networks seems like a clutter of new terminology, tools, and acronyms.

In fact, as will be discussed, without this conceptual footing, many library functions can seem disconnected, and the field that serves lawyers, doctors, single mothers, and 8 year olds fragmented. The scale of this technology brief is limited; it is to present library decision makers with the opportunities and challenges of participatory networks. It is only a single piece of a much larger puzzle that seeks to present a cohesive framework for libraries. This framework will not only fit tools such as blogs and Wikis into their offerings, but also will show how a more participatory, conversational approach to libraries in general can help libraries better integrate current and future functions.

Think of this document as an overview or introduction to participatory librarianship. Readers will find plenty of examples and definitions of Web 2.0 and social networking later in this chapter. However, to jump right into the technology without a larger framework invites the rightful skepticism of a library organisation that feels constantly buffeted by new technological advances. In any environment with no larger conceptual founding to measure the importance of an advance in technology or practice selection of any one technology or practice is nearly arbitrary. Without a framework the field becomes open to the influence of personalities and trendy technology.

Therefore, it is vital to ground any technological, social, or policy conversation into a larger, rooted concept. As Susser said, "...to practice without theory is to sail an uncharted sea; theory without practice is not to set sail at all." For this chapter, the chart will be conversation theory.

The core of this brief is in four sections that follow:

- A conceptual framework for understanding and evaluating participatory networks;
- A discussion of key concepts and technologies in participatory networks drawn primarily from Web 2.0 and Library 2.0;
- A merging of the conceptual framework with the technological discussion to present a sort of roadmap for library systems development; and
- A set of recommendations to foster greater discussion and action on the topic of participatory networks and, more broadly, participatory librarianship.

LIBRARY AS A FACILITATOR OF CONVERSATION

So let us return to the concept that knowledge is created through conversation. This notion stretches back to Socrates and the Socratic Method. However, the specific foundation for this statement comes from 'Conversation Theory,' a means of explaining cognition and how people learn. It is not the purpose of this chapter to provide a detailed description of Conversation Theory, a task already admirably accomplished by Pask. Rather, let us use the theory as a structure upon which to hang an exploration of participatory networking and, more broadly, participatory librarianship.

The core of conversation theory is simple: people learn through conversation. Different communities have different standards for conversations, from the scientific community's rigourous formalisms to the religious community's embedded meaning in scripture to the sometimes impenetrable dialect of teens. The point remains, however, that different actors establish meaning through determining common definitions and building upon shared concepts. The library has been a place where we facilitate conversations, though often implicitly.

The concept of learning through conversations is evidenced in libraries in large initiatives like information litreacy and teaching critical thinking skills and in the smaller events of book groups, reference interviews, and speaker series. Library activities such as building collections of artifacts inform scholars' research through a formal conversation process where ideas are supported with evidence and methods. Similarly, preservation efforts, perhaps of wax cylinders with spoken word content or of ancient maps that embody an ongoing dialogue about the shape and nature of the physical world, seek to save, or at least document, important conversations. Common use of the word 'conversation' is completely in accordance with the use of the term in Conversation Theory.

The term is, however, more specifically defined as an act of communication and agreement between a set of agents. So, a conversation can be between two people, two organisations, two countries, or even within an individual. How can a conversation take place within an individual? Educators and school librarians may be familiar with the term 'metacognition,' or the act of reflecting on one's learning. Yet, even the most casual reader will be familiar with the concept of debating oneself.

The point is that a conversation is with at least two agents trying to come to an understanding. Also note that those two agents can change over time. So, while Socrates and Plato are dead the conversation they started about the nature of knowledge and the world is carried forward by new generations of thinkers...same conversation, different agents. People converse, organisations converse, states converse, societies converse.

The requirements, in the terms of Conversation Theory, are two cognitive systems seeking agreement. The results of these conversations, what Pask would call 'cognitive entanglements,' are books, videos, and artifacts that either document, expand, or result from conversations. So, while one cannot converse with a book that book certainly can be a starting point for many conversations within the reader and within a larger community.

If the theory is that conversation creates knowledge, the library community has added a corollary: the best knowledge comes from an 'optimal information environment,' one in which the most diverse and complete information is available to the conversant. Library ethics show an implicit understanding of this corollary in the advocacy of intellectual freedom and unfettered access. Libraries seek to create rich environments for knowledge and have taken the stance that they are not in the job of arbitrating the conversations that occur or the 'appropriateness' of the information used to inform those conversations. As will be discussed later, this belief in openness of conversations will have some far-reaching implications for the library collection and is an ideal that can never truly be met.

For now, the reader may take away that conversation theory is very much in line with current and past library practice, and it also shows a clear trajectory for the future. The value to this viewpoint is not just theoretical; it has real consequences and uses. For example, much of library evaluation has been based in numeric counts of tangible outputs: books circulated, collection size, reference transactions, and so on. Yet this quantitative approach has been frustrating to many who feel they are counting outcomes but not getting at true impact of library service. Librarians may ask themselves, "Which numbers are important...and why?" If libraries focused on conversations there might be some clarity and cohesion between statistics and other outcomes. Suddenly, the number of reference questions can be linked to items cataloged or to circulation numbers...they are all markers of the scope and scale of conversations within the library context.

This approach might enable the library community to better identify 'important' conversations and demonstrate direct contributions to these conversations across functions. For example, a school district identifies early litreacy as important. There is a discussion about public policy options, new programmes, and school goals to achieve greater litreacy in the K-5 grades. The library should be able to track two streams in this conversation.

The first is the one libraries are used to counting; that is, the library's contribution to K-5 litreacy. But the library can also document and demonstrate how it furthered the conversation about children's litreacy in general. It could show the resources provided to community officials. It could show the litreacy pathfinders that were created. The point of this example is that the library is both participant in the conversation and facilitator of conversation. The theoretical discussion leads us to a discussion about the second topic of this technology brief: pragmatic aspects of the knowledge as conversation approach, or a participatory approach as it will be called.

As new technologies are developed and deployed in the current environment of limited resources, there must be some means of evaluating their utility. The utility of a technology is appropriately measured against a given library's mission, which is in turn developed to respond to the needs of the community that library serves. First, however, let us identify some of the new technologies and describe them briefly.

PARTICIPATORY NETWORKING, SOCIAL NETWORKS, AND WEB 2.0

Let us now move from the theoretical to the operational. The impetus behind this chapter is the relatively recent emergence of a new group of Internet services and capabilities. Suddenly, terms like Wiki, blog, mashup, Web 2.0, and biblioblogosphere have become commonplace. As with any new wave of technological creation, these terms can seem ambiguous and they also come wrapped in varying amounts of hype.

They may all, however, be grouped under the phenomenon of participatory networking. While we now have a conceptual framework to evaluate these technologies that support participatory networking, we still need to know the basics of the terminology and technologies. This section outlines key concepts in the pragmatics of participatory networking. The section after this one will join the theoretical and operational to outline key challenges and opportunities for the library world. We begin with Web 2.0

WEB 2.0

Much of what we call participatory networking, at least the technological foundation of it, stems from developments in 'Web 2.0.' As with many buzzwords, the exact definition of Web 2.0 is not clear. It is more an aggregation of concepts that range from software development to abstractions. What pervades the Web 2.0 approach is the notion that Internet services are increasingly facilitators of conversations.

Web 2.0 Characteristic: Social Networks

A core concept of Web 2.0 is that people are the content of sites; that is, a site is not populated with information for users to consume. Instead, services are provided to individual users for them to build networks of friends and other groups. The content of a site, then, comprises user-provided information that attracts new members of an ever-expanding network.

Examples:

- *Flickr*: Flickr provides users with free Web space to upload images and create photo albums. Users can then share these photos with friends or with the public at large. Flickr facilitates the creation of shared photo galleries around themes and places.
- *The Cheshire Public Library*: The Teen Book Blog at the Cheshire Public Library offers book reviews created only by the students who use the library.
- *Memorial Hall Library*: The Memorial Hall Library in Andover Massachusetts offers podcasts of poetry contests in which the content is created by students.
- *Libraries in MySpace*: MySpace searches show that there are MySpace sites for hundreds of individual libraries and scores of library groups. Alexandrian Public Library. This practice is growing among public libraries and is an attempt to reach out to users in their preferred online environments. In this venue, the more friends a library MySpace site has the more successful it may be considered. The Alexandrian Public Library has 75 friends and 15 comments. The Brooklyn College Library has 2195 friends and 270 comments.

Web 2.0 Characteristic: Wisdom of Crowds

There has been some research into the quality of mass decision-making. That research shows how remarkably accurate groups are in their judgements. Web 2.0 pools large groups of users to comment on decisions. This aggregation of input is facilitated by the ready availability of social networking sites. Certainly, this approach of community organisation and verification of knowledge also has its detractors. Many, for example, question the wisdom seen in some entries of Wikipedia. Yet, recent articles have compared this mass editing process favourably to traditional sources of information such as the Encyclopaedia Britannica.

Examples

eBay

eBay has perhaps the most studied and copied community policing and reputation systems. All buyers and sellers can be rated. The aggregation of many users' experiences create a 'Feedback Score' that is equivalent to a group credibility rating. These kinds of group feedback systems can now be seen in most major Internet retailers.

LibraryThing

LibraryThing.com makes book recommendations based on the collective intelligence of all users of the site. The greater the pool of collective intelligence the more information is available to the user for decision-making.

The Diary Project

The Diary Project Library is a non-profit organisation that encourages teens to write about their day-to-day experiences growing up. The goal of this site is to encourage communication among teens of all cultures and backgrounds, provide peer-to-peer support, stimulate discussion, and generate feedback that can help ease some of the concerns encountered along the way and let them know that they are not alone. To that end, the site comprises thousands of entries in 24 categories. Because of the great number of entries, most youth can find helpful materials.

Web 2.0 Characteristic: Loosely Coupled APIs

API is short hand for 'Application Programming Interface.' It provides a set of instructions that a programmer can use to communicate between applications.

APIs allow programmers to incorporate one piece of software they may not be able to directly manipulate into another. For example, Google Maps has made a public API that allows Web page designers to include satellite images into their Web pages with little more than a latitude and longitude. APIs vary in their ease of integration. Loosely coupled APIs allow for very easy integration using high-level scripting languages.

Examples

Google Maps

Google Maps displays street or satellite map showing markers on specific locations provided by an external source with simple sets of longitudes and latitudes. So, it becomes extremely easy to create Geographic Information Systems with little knowledge of GIS principles.

Flickr

Flickr provides easy means to integrate these hosted images into other Web pages or applications.

YouTube

YouTube provides users with the capability to upload and comment upon video on the Internet.

It also allows for easy integration of the videos into other Web pages and blogs. With a simple line of HTML code anyone can access streaming video for their content.

Web 2.0 Characteristic: Mashups

Mashups are combinations of APIs and data that result in new information resources and services. This ease of incorporation has led to an assumption of a 'right to remix.'

In the world of open source software and the creative commons, the right to remix refers to a growing expectation among Internet users that they are not limited by the interfaces and uses presented to them by a single organisation.

Examples

ChicagoCrime.org

An often-cited example of a mashup is ChicagoCrime.org, which uses Google Maps to plot crime data for the city of Chicago. Users can now see exactly which street corner had the most murders.

Book Burro

Book Burro "is a Web 2.0 extension for Firefox and Flock. When it senses you are looking at a page that contains a book, it will overlay a small panel which when opened lists prices at online bookstores such as Amazon, Buy, Half and whether the book is available at your library."

Web 2.0 Characteristic: Permanent Betas

The concept of a permanent beta is, in part, a realisation that no software is ever truly complete so long as the user community is still commenting upon it. For example, Google does not release services from beta until it has achieved a sufficient user base no matter how fixed the underlying source code is. Permanent beta is also a design strategy.

Large applications are broken into smaller constituent parts that can be manipulated separately. This allows large applications to be continually developed by a more diverse and distributed community.

Examples

MIT Libraries

The MIT Libraries are experimenting with new technologies to help make access to information easier.

The tools are offered to the public with an appeal for feedback and additional tools, and the there is a permanent address designed just to collect feedback from the beta-phase tools, which include:

- The New Humanities Virtual Browsery, which highlights new books and incorporates an RSS feed, the ability to comment on books, links to book reviews, availability information, and links to other books by the same author.
- The LibXMIT Edition, which is a Firefox toolbar that allows users to search the Barton catalogue, Vera, Google Scholar, the SFX FullText Finder, and other search tools; it embeds links to MIT-only resources in Amazon, Barnes and Noble, Google Scholar, and NYT Book Reviews.
- The Dewey Research Advisor Business and Economics: Q&A, which provides starting points for specific research questions in the fields of business, management, and economics.

Google Labs

Google has a site named 'Google Labs' that puts out company-generated tools and services. In fact, part of a Google employee's work time is dedicated to creating the resources and tools through personal projects and exploration. These tools and services remain a part of the 'Lab' until they are finished and have sufficient user bases. Projects range from the simple to the extensive.

Web 2.0 Characteristic: Software Gets Better the More People Use It

An increasing number of Web 2.0 sites emphasise social networks, where these services gain value only as they gain users.

Malcolm Gladwell recounts this principle and the work of Kevin Kelly with an earlier telecommunications network, the network of fax machines connected to the phone system: "The first fax machine ever made...cost about $2,000 at retail. But it was worth nothing because there was no other fax machine for it to communicate with.

The second fax machine made the first fax machine more valuable, and the third fax made the first two more valuable, and so on...When you buy a fax machine, then, what you are really buying is access to the entire fax network—which is infinitely more valuable than the machine itself."

With social networking sites, and all sites that seek to capitalise on user input, the true value of each site is defined by the number of people it can bring together.

Examples

Amazon

A classic example of this characteristic is Amazon.com. Amazon sells books and other merchandise, but, in reality, Amazon is very much about the marketing of information. Amazon gains tremendous value by allowing its users to review and rate items. The more people use Amazon and the more they comment, the more visibility these active users gain and the more credibility markers they take on.

Web 2.0 Characteristic: Folksonomies

A folksonomy is a classification system created in a bottom-up fashion and with no central coordination. This differs from the deductive approach of classifications systems like the Dewey Decimal System, where the world of ideas is broken into ten nominal classes. It also differs from other means of developing classifications where some central authority determines if a term should be included. In a folksonomy, the members of a group simply attach terms to items and the aggregate of these terms is seen as the classification. What emerges is a classification scheme that prioritises common usage over semantic clarity.

Examples

PennTags

PennTags is a social bookmarking tool for locating, organising, and sharing one's favourite online resources. Members of the Penn Community can collect and maintain URLs, links to journal articles, and records in Franklin, the online catalogue, and VCat, the online video catalogue. Once resources are compiled, users can organise them by assigning tags and/or by grouping them into projects, according to specific preferences.

PennTags can also be used collaboratively, because it acts as a repository of the varied interests and academic pursuits of the Penn community, and a user can find topics and other users related to his or her own favourite online resources.

Hillsdale Teen Library

The Hillsdale Teen Library uses Flickr to post pictures of events at the Hillsdale Teen Library.

These tags allow users to easily retrieve the images in which they are interested.

There are more characteristics of Web 2.0, but these give some overall concepts.

CORE NEW TECHNOLOGIES: AJAX AND WEB SERVICES

As we have jut discussed, Web 2.0 is little more than set of related concepts, albeit with a lot of value being currently attached to these concepts. These concepts are supported by two underlying technologies that have facilitated Web 2.0 development and brought a substantially new user experience to the Web. The first is AJAX, which allows a more desktop-like experience for users. The second is the advent of Web services. These technologies are not necessary for Web 2.0 concepts, but they have made Web 2.0 sites much more compelling.

AJAX

AJAX stands for Asynchronous JavaScript and XML. It is a set of existing Web technologies brought together. At the most basic, AJAX allows a browser and a server to send data back and forth without needing to refresh the entire Web page being worked on. Think about the Web sites you work with. You click on a link, the browser freezes and waits for the data, then draws it on the screen. Early versions of sites like MapQuest would show a map. If you wanted to zoom into the map, you would press a zoom icon and wait while the new map, and the rest of the Web page was redrawn. Compare this to Google Maps, where you click in the middle of a map and drag left or right and the map moves dynamically.

This kind of interaction we are used to in desktop applications. Click and drag has become second nature on the desktop and AJAX is making it second nature on the Web, too. Another advantage of AJAX is that it is open and requires only light programming skills. Javascript on the client and almost any server side scripting language are easily accessible languages. This fact allows for both fast development and easier integration with existing systems. As an example, it should now be easier to bring more interactive Web interfaces to existing online catalogues.

Web Services

Web services allow for software-to-software interactions on the Web. Using Web protocols and XML, applications exchange queries and information in order to facilitate the larger functioning of a system. One example would be a system that uses an ISBN number to query multiple online catalogues and commercial vendors for availability of a book. This simple process might be part of a much larger library catalogue that shows users a book and its availability. The point is that unlike federated search systems such as Z39.50, Web services are small. They also tend to be lightweight, and are aggregated for greater functionality.

LIBRARY 2.0

Library 2.0 is a somewhat diffuse concept. Walt Crawford, in his extended essay Library 2.0 and 'Library 2.0' found 62 different views and seven distinct definitions of Library 2.0. It is no wonder that people are confused. However, it is natural for emerging ideas and groups to function in an environment of high ambiguity. For use in this technology brief the authors see Library 2.0 as an attempt to apply Web 2.0 concepts to the purpose of the library. In the words of Ormsby, "The purpose of a library is not to ... showcase new gadgetry ...; rather, it is to make possible that instant of insight when all the facts come together in the shape of new knowledge."

How the applications are used will determine whether they support Ormsby's "instant of insight." Many libraries and librarians are already pursuing this goal. Some, for instance, are using blogs to reach other librarians, their own users, and potential users.

They are using Wikis to deliver reports, teach information litreacy, and serve as repositories. One has developed an API that allows WordPress posts to be directly integrated into a library catalogue. Clearly, the Internet and newer tools that empower users seem to be aligned with the library mission. After all, librarians blogging and allowing the catalogue to be 'mashed up' can be seen as an extension of current information services. But this abundance of new applications poses a challenge.

Given the speed with which new tools are invented, librarians may find it difficult to create strategies that include all the desired services that they make possible. For every new application that becomes available, library administrators must decide whether it can serve the library, how to use it, and how to find additional resources to manage it. This problem stems from focussing excessively on the technology. Librarians should, instead, focus on the phenomena made possible by the technology. Most important of these phenomena, the library invites participation.

As Chad and Miller state:

- Library 2.0 facilitates and encourages a culture of participation, drawing upon the perspectives and contributions of library staff, technology partners and the wider community. Library 2.0 means harnessing this type of participation so that libraries can benefit from increasingly rich collaborative cataloguing efforts, such as including contributions from partner libraries as well as adding rich enhancements, such as book jackets or movie files, to records from publishers and others.
- Library 2.0 is about encouraging and enabling a library's community of users to participate, contributing their own views on resources they have used and new ones to which they might wish access.
- With Library 2.0, a library will continue to develop and deploy the rich descriptive standards of the domain, whilst embracing more participative approaches that encourage interaction with and the formation of communities of interest.

The carte blanche statement that users participating in the library is 'good,' however, is insufficient. Library administers must ask, 'What is the ultimate goal?' In summary, current initiatives in the library world to bring the tools of Web 2.0 to the service of Library 2.0 are exciting and innovative, and more to the point, they are supportive of the library's purpose.

They may, however, incur costs, such as monitoring blogs and Wikis and creating content and corresponding with users that stretch already inadequate resources even further.

Ultimately, the value of Library 2.0 concepts requires us to answer some important questions: will they be used to further knowledge, or will they simply create more work for librarians? What does the 'next version' of Library 2.0 look like? Is its mission the same and just the tools different? What makes the library different from MySpace... simply a legacy? Should we incorporate new services into the current library offerings? How do we, as facilitators of conversations, point the way to the next generation of library? It is hoped that some of the concepts in participatory librarianship may answer these questions and help further the innovations of the Library 2.0 community.

PARTICIPATORY NETWORKS

The authors use the phrase participatory networking to encompass the concept of using Web 2.0 principles and technologies to implement a conversational model within a community.

Why not simply adopt social networking, Web 2.0, or Library 2.0 for that matter? Let us examine each term's limitations:

- *Social networking*: Social network sites such as MySpace and Facebook have certainly captured public attention. They have also proven very popular. In their short life spans these sites have garnered an immense audience and drawn much attention from the press. Some of that attention, however, has been very negative. MySpace, for example, has been typified as a refuge for pedophiles and online predators. Even the television show Saturday Night Live has parodied the site for the ease with which users can create false personas and engage in risky online behaviours. To say you are starting a social networking site in your library may draw either enthusiastic support, vehement opposition or simply confused looks. Add to the potential negative connotations the ambiguity of the term. Is a blog a social networking site? Is Flickr? To compound this confusion, the academic domain of Social Network Theory predates MySpace by about a decade.
- *Web 2.0*: Ambiguity also dogs the Web 2.0 world. For some, it is technology. For others, it is simply a buzzword for the current crop of Internet sites that survived the burst of the.com bubble. In any

case, Web 2.0 certainly implies more than just the inclusion of users in systems.

- *Library 2.0*: As stated before, the term Library 2.0 is a vague term used by some as a goad to the library community. Further, this term limits the discussion of user-inclusive Web services to the library world. While this brief focuses on the library community, it also sees the library community as a potential leader in a much broader field.

So, ultimately, the authors propose 'participatory networking' as a positive term and concept that libraries can use and promote without the confusion and limitations of previous language.

The phrase 'participatory network' also has a history of prior use that can be built upon. The phrase 'participatory networks' represents systems of exchange and integration and has long been used in discussions of policy, art, and government. The phrase has also been used to describe online communities that exchange and integrate information.

LIBRARIES AS PARTICIPATORY CONVERSATIONS

So where are we? We started with the abstract statement that knowledge is created through conversation. We then looked at the current landscape of technologies that can facilitate these conversations and showed examples of how libraries, other industries, and individuals are using these technologies. In this section we combine the larger framework with the technologies to see how libraries can incorporate participatory networks to further their knowledge mission.

PARTICIPATORY LIBRARIANSHIP IN ACTION

Let us look specifically at how participatory networks can be used in the library's role as facilitator of knowledge through conversation. An obvious example is libraries hosting blogs and Wikis for their communities creating virtual meeting spaces for individuals and groups, just as libraries do in the physical world. Indeed, these are increasingly useful functions for libraries. They meet a perceived need in the community, and can generate excitement both within the library and in the community.

The idea of creating online sites for individuals and organisations makes sense for a library, although it is not without difficulties. Libraries could also use freely available open source software to create library versions of Wikipedia. Another way for libraries to offer these services would be through a cooperative or other third-party vendor.

Such a service can easily be seen as a knowledge management activity capturing and providing local expertise while linking this expertise to that produced at other libraries. Another reason for libraries to engage in participatory networking is that one library can more easily collaborate with other libraries in richer dialogues. We currently have systems that connect our online catalogues and share resources through interlibrary loan. These conduits exist and can be used for the transferal of richer data, as has been proved through collaborative virtual reference systems.

In our current systems, as in traditional library practice, when users are referred to other libraries, they are sent out and not brought back. In a participatory library setting, libraries would facilitate a conversation between the user, the community of the local library, and then through the developed conduits, other libraries and their communities.

The end result would be a seamless web of libraries where the user can ignore the intricacies of the library's organisation structure and boundaries, and in which the libraries are using the best local resources to meet local needs. Bringing libraries seamlessly together to participate in conversations with a single user has another significant advantage: the Library would make it easy for users to join the conversation regardless of where they are, through the presentation of a single façade.

There is, for example, only one Google, one Amazon, and one Wikipedia. Why should users have to search from among thousands of libraries to find the conversations they want? Participatory networking will be most effective when libraries work together, when the whole is greater than its parts. We currently see elements of The Participatory Library in the OCLC Open Worldcat project. For example, users searching Google may come across a listing provided by OCLC.

After selecting the entry for the book, the user can then jump to his or her own local library's information about the book. Users do not have to know which library to visit to find a book near them. Extending this concept to conversations, one goal of these participatory networks is to make it easier for the user to enter a conversation with The Library without having to work to discover their own specific entry points. However, ensuring this effective seamless access to the Library will require more than simply adding elements of participatory networking around the edges of the library. Adding services like blogs and Wikis may be seen merely as adjunct to current library offerings. As with any technological advance, scarce resources must be weighed against a desire to incorporate new services. Do we expand the collection, improve the Web site, or offer blogs to students? A better approach for making these kinds of decisions is to look at the needs of the community served in context with the commonly accepted, core tasks of a library, and see how they can be recast as conversational, or participatory tools.

In point of fact, every service, patron, and access point is a starting point for a conversation. Let's start with the catalogue. If the catalogue is a conversation, it is decidedly formal and, more importantly, one way. Think of today's catalogue as the educational equivalent of a college lecture. A formal system is used to serve up a series of presentations on a given topic. The presentations are rigid in their construction. They follow an abstract model and provide minimal opportunities to the receiver of the information to provide feedback or input.

They provide no constructive means for the user to improve or shape the conversation. Even recent advances in catalogue functions do little more than make the presentation of information more varied. They are still not truly interactive because they do not allow user participation; they do not allow for conversation. To highlight the one-way nature of the catalogue, ask a simple question: what happens when the user doesn't find something?

Do we assume that the information is there, but that the user is simply incapable of finding it? Do we assume that the information does not exist? Do we assume that the catalogue itself is limited? What if we assume that the catalogue is just the current place a user is involving in an ongoing conversation…what would that look like? How can such a traditionally rigid system be made more participatory? What if the user, finding no relevant information in the catalogue, adds either the information or a placeholder for someone else to fill in the missing information? Possibly the user adds information from his or her expertise.

However, assuming that most people go to a catalogue because they don't have the information, perhaps the user instead begins a process for adding the information. The user might ask a question using a virtual reference service; at the end of the transaction, the user then has the option to add the question, along with the answer and associated materials, to the catalogue. Or perhaps, the user simply leaves the query in the catalogue for other patrons to answer, requesting to be notified when an answer is posted. In that case, when a new user does a catalogue search and runs across the question, he or she can provide an answer.

That answer might be a textual entry, or simply a new query that directs the original questioner or new patrons to existing information in the catalogue. The catalogue can also associate conversations with any data point. For example, a user pulls up the record for a book s/he feels might be relevant to an information need s/he is having. This process starts a conversation between that user and the library, its users and authors of associated works. The user can see comments and ratings associated with this book from not only users of this library but users of other libraries. Also associated is a list of related works and the full audio of a lecture by the author. The user might also be directed to an in-person or online book group that is reading that book.

The point is that the catalogue facilitates a conversation as opposed to simply presenting what it 'knows' about a topic and then stepping out of the process. The catalogue, then, does not simply present information, but instead helps users construct knowledge by allowing the user to participate in a conversation. There are other means of improving systems in a conversational library. Take the implicit link between the catalogue and circulation. Of course these systems have always been linked in that items found in the catalogue can be checked out and checked out items have their status reflected in the catalogue. But this kind of 'state' information is a pretty meagre offering.

Imagine using circulation data to improve the actual functionality of the catalogue. Take the example of a user who is searching the catalogue for fictional books on magic. Currently, a relevance score between an item's metadata and the query is computed and then all the items are ranked in a retrieval set. This relevance score can be computed in many ways, but is usually based on the number of times a keyword appears in the record and the placement of that keyword in the metadata record. What is missing is the actual, real-world circulation of an item. Wouldn't it make sense, given such an abstract query, to present the user with Harry Potter first? What if we added circulation data to our relevance rankings: how many times this item has been checked out? It turns out that using a simple statistic is amasingly powerful.

It is akin to Google's page rank algorithm that presents sites most linked to higher in the results. Also, for those worried that users would be flooded with only popular materials, studies show that while these algorithms do change the very top ranked material, the effect quickly fades so that the user can still easily find other materials. Another consideration for adjusting a search is to allow the user to tweak the algorithms used to retrieve works. In the example, a user could turn off the 'popularity' feature. The user could also toggle switches for currency, authority, and other facets of relevancy rankings.

The conversational model requires us to rethink the catalogue as a dynamic system, with data of varying levels of currency and, frankly, quality, coming into and out of the system. In a conversational catalogue there is no reason that some data can't exist in the catalogue for limited durations. Records of well-groomed physical collections may be a core and durable collection in the catalogue, but that is only one of many types of information that could exist in the catalogue space. Furthermore, even this core data can be annotated and linked to more transient media.

So, the user might see a review from a blog as part of a catalogue record on one day, but when s/he pulls the record up again in a few days, that review might be absent, the blog writer having withdrawn the comment. This is akin to weeding the collection; however, it would happen in a more dynamic fashion than occurs with the content on library shelves. The conversational model can also be used in other areas of the library. What do we digitise? What do we select? What programmes do we offer? What do we preserve? The empowered user can participate in answering all of these questions but does not replace the expert librarian; rather, the user contributes additional and diverse information and commentary. In fact, the catalogue scenario just proposed already assumes that the library catalogue does more than store metadata. In order for the scenario to work the 'catalogue' must store questions, answers, video, audio…in essence the catalogue must be expanded and integrated with other library systems so that a final Participatory Library System can present a coherent view of The Library to patrons.

FRAMEWORK FOR INTEGRATION OF PARTICIPATORY LIBRARIANSHIP

As has been noted, participatory networks and libraries as conversations are not brand new concepts sprung from the head of Zeus. Instead they are means to integrate past and current innovations, and create a viable plan forward. The sort of road map of how the library might make the transition from current systems to a truly participatory system. It includes current systems, systems under development, and new concepts. It seeks to capture current momentum and push the field forward to a larger view instead of getting bogged down in the intricacies of any one development activity. Along the left hand of the graph are current library systems. While the terminology may differ from library to library, nearly every system can be found on today's library web sites. By showing the systems together, the problems of user confusion and library management burden become obvious. Users must often navigate these systems based on their needs, and often with little help. Should they search the catalogues first or the databases? Isn't the catalogue really just another database? Which database do they choose? In our attempts to better serve the users by creating a rich set of resources and services, we have instead complicated their information seeking lives.

As one librarian puts it, "don't give me one more system I, or my patrons, have to deal with." From the array of systems on the left hand, we can see that libraries have not been doing themselves any favours either. We are maintaining many systems, therefore making the calls for yet more systems not only impractical but unwise. The answer is to integrate systems, combining the best of each while discarding the complexity of the whole. The library world is in the midst of doing just that. This section seeks to highlight promising developments in integrating library systems well beyond the library catalogue and to highlight not only an ideal endpoint, but also how this ideal system is truly participatory.

Merging Reference and Community Involvement

The functional area furthest along in the integration of participatory librarianship is reference; since, reference is most readily recognisable as a conversation, this comes as no surprise. Over the last decade, reference services have gone online, and have led to shared reference services. More importantly, reference done online creates artifacts of reference conversations: electronic files than can be cleaned of personal information and placed in a knowledge base, and used as a resource for other users.

A new development in reference is the reference blog, in which multiple librarians and other users can be part of a question answering community with conversations that can live on beyond a single transaction. Another functional area of libraries that is already involved with participatory librarianship is community involvement. For decades, public libraries have supported local community groups through meeting spaces. Some libraries are now hosting Web spaces for local groups.

As libraries incorporate participatory technologies into their offerings, they can create virtual places such as discussion forums, Wikis, and blogs for these community groups to use.

If there are standards for these discussion areas, then groups from different communities could also easily participate in shared boards; this makes sense for groups such as Weight Watchers or Alcoholics Anonymous that have local branches and national involvement. In an academic setting, these groups can be student, faculty, or staff organisations or courses. In addition to reference and hosted community conversations, the library has been actively creating digital collections of materials. Parallel to the digital collection building of library materials is an active attempt to create institutional repositories of faculty papers, teacher lesson plans, organisational documentation, and the like.

These services are participatory systems in which collections come from users' contributions, and they may evolve into digital repositories that include both user-created and librarian-created artifacts.

These different conversations can be archived into a single repository, and if properly planned, the reference conversations can live alongside, and eventually be intermingled with, the community conversations, and the digital repository into a community repository. Community repositories allow librarians to be more easily involved in the conversations of the community and capture important artifacts of these conversations for later use.

Merging Library Metadata into an Enhanced Catalogue

Participatory librarianship can be supported by another functional area of the library: collections. Traditionally, the collection comprises books, magazines, and other information resources paid for by the library. Electronic resources such as databases that are leased instead of purchased make up a large portion of library expenditures. More recently, Web-based resources have been selected and added to the virtual collection. Several kinds of finding aids are used to locate these information resources.

The catalogue and databases both contain descriptions of resources and searching interfaces. In order to improve access, libraries include records for databases within the catalogue. Conversely, federated searching tools combine the records from different databases and could allow the retrieval of both books and articles by combining records from both the traditional catalogue and databases into one tool. If community-created resources are part of the catalogue, then these resources would also be findable alongside other traditional library resources.

The tools for describing information resources can also be participatory. In traditional librarianship, the librarians provide metadata that patrons then use to make selections. By examining this use data, recommender systems can be created to help users locate new materials. In participatory networking, patrons will be encouraged to add comments about items. If standards are used for these comments, then they can be shared among libraries to create larger pools of recommendations. As these comments are analysed, they can be combined with usage databases to create stronger recommender systems to present patrons with additional choices based upon what is being explored.

The end result is an enhanced catalogue that allows users and libraries to find information regardless of which system the information resides in. However, the enhanced catalogue is still just that, a catalogue. It contains surrogates of digital information and is managed separately from the artifacts themselves. In the case of physical items, this may be all the library systems can manage, but in the case of digital content, there is one more step that needs to be taken. Namely, the artificial barrier between catalogue and content must come down.

Building the Participatory Library

At this point in the evolution of distributed systems into a truly integrated library system, the Participatory Library, we have two large collections: one of resources and one of information about the resources. The first collection of digital content, the community repository, is built by the library and its users collaboratively. The second collection, the enhanced catalogue, includes metadata, both formal and user-created. Both the community repository and the enriched catalogue are participatory. Yet to realise the dream of a seamless system of functionality, these two systems must be merged allowing users to find resources and, much more importantly, conversations.

Furthermore the users must be able to add to both metadata and content. The result may be conceived of as a single integrated information resource, which, for the purposes of this conversation, is called the Participatory Library. Users may access the Participatory Library directly through the library, or they may access it as a series of services in Google, MySpace, or their own homepages. The point is that the access to the library takes place at the point of conversation, not at the point the user realises he or she needs information from the library.

CONVERSATIONS AND PRESERVATION

The conversation model highlights the need for preservation. Aside from simply providing systems that facilitate conversation, libraries serve as the vital community memory. Conversations construct knowledge, but someone must remember what has already been said, and know how to access that dialog. Scientific conversations, for example, are built on previous conversations. Capturing conversations and 'playing them back' at the right time is essential.

This might mean the preservation of artifacts but it also means the increasingly important tasks of capturing the digital dialogs. This highlights the need for institutional repositories. Specifically, Web sites, lectures, courseware, articles must be kept. Further, they must be kept in true conversational repositories that capture the artifacts the methods and the process. They must be kept in information structures that make them readily available as conversations: in other words, users must be able to search for materials, and be able to reconstruct a conversation in its entirety from one fragment.

BEING WHERE THE CONVERSATION IS

Imagine the conversations that are going on in your local library as you read this. Imagine the physicist chatting with the gardener, and the trustee talking with the volunteer who is reading the latest best seller. What knowledge can be gleaned from these novel interactions? Can you measure it? Can you enhance it? Can you capture it? Can you recall it when it would be precisely what a user needs to meet an information need? Note also that these conversations do not belong solely to the library. The library is only part of the conversation. Faced with the daunting variety of resources available on the Web, many organisations try to become the single point of entry into it. Remember that conversations are varied in their mode, places and players, and, more importantly, that they are intensely personal.

This means that participants need to have ownership in them, and often in their locations as well. This also means that the library, as facilitator, needs to be varied in its modes and access points. In many cases, it is better to either create a personal space in which users may converse, or, increasingly, to be part of someone else's space. What we can learn from Web 2.0's Mashups is that smaller sets of limited functionalities lead to greater incorporation of tools into people's lives.

In the ChicagoCrime Google Maps Mashup, combining maps from Google and Chicago crime statistics, it was important for the host of the site to brand the space and shape the interface for his conversation on crime. Can your library functions be as easily incorporated into these types of conversations? Can a user search your catalogue and present the results on his or her Web site? The point is that libraries need to be proactive in a new way. Instead of the mantra, 'Be where the user is', we need to, 'Be where the conversation is. 'It is not enough to be at the users' desktops; you need to be in their e-mail programme, in their MySpace pages, in their IM lists, and in their RSS feed readers. All of these examples point to a significant mental shift that librarians will need to make in moving from delivering information from a centralised location to delivering information in a decentralised manner where the conversations of users are taking place.

The catalogue example presented earlier is an example of a centralised place for conversations. What if, Instead of only being in a catalogue, the same data were split into smaller components and embedded in the user's browser and e-mail programmes? Just as Google's mail system embeds advertising based upon the content of a message, The Library could also provide links to its resources based upon what a user is working on.

By disaggregating the information within its system, The Library can deliver just what is needed to a user, provide connections into Mashups, and can live in the space of the user instead of forcing the user to come to the space of the library.

CHALLENGES AND OPPORTUNITIES

There is clearly a host of challenges in incorporating participatory networks and a participatory model into the library. This is to be expected when we are dealing with something as fundamental as knowledge and as personal as conversations. We consider four major challenges that must be met by libraries before they can truly get into the business of participatory librarianship.

Technical

There is a rich suite of participatory networking software that libraries can incorporate into their daily operations. Implementing a blog, a Wiki, or RSS feeds these days is not a hard task, and they can easily be used to deliver information about library services and conversations to the user's space. Furthermore, these systems are often tested in very large-scale environments and are, in some cases, the same tools used in large participatory networking sites such as Wikipedia and Blogger. Some of these packages are commercial, but others are open source software. Open source software is cheaper, easier to adapt, and, in some cases, more advanced.

The downside to open source is that it requires a considerable amount of technical knowledge by the library and does not come with a technical support hotline. The largest technological impediment, however, may be the currently installed base of software within libraries. Integrated library systems have a long history, and include a broad range of library functions. Legacy code and near monolithic systems have restricted the easy exchange of a diverse set of information. Were these systems written today they would use modular code and loosely coupled APIs and allow customers much more customizability of interface.

These changes may come to integrated library systems but it may take years. Several libraries are currently attempting to pick apart these integrated systems themselves. Often, libraries go to the underlying databases that hold the library metadata or create their own data structures, such as the University of Pennsylvania Data Farm project. Once components of this system are exposed, the catalogue simply becomes another database that can be federated into new and unified interfaces. However, such integration requires a great deal of technological expertise.

There is an opportunity for ILS vendors or large consortial groups such as OCLC to move quickly into this space. In the meantime, there is an opportunity for the larger library community. This technology brief was created in response to a perceived need. Whether evidenced in the Library 2.0 community or in conversations at LITA, libraries are now interested in incorporating new Web technologies into their offerings and operations.

The technologies under consideration here present platforms for experimentation. Rather than setting up thousands of separated experiments, however, the library community should create a participatory network of its own. The technology certainly exists to create a test bed for libraries to set up various combinations of communication technologies to test new Web services against pooled data and even to incorporate new services into the current library offerings. By combining resources in a single, large-scale test bed, libraries cannot only get greater impact for the their investments, but can also directly experience life as a connected conversation. These connections, if built at the ground level, will then make it easier for The Library to come into existence. Terminology can be clarified, claims tested, and best practices collaboratively developed, greatly accelerating innovation and dissemination.

Operational

In addition to being in the conversation business, libraries are in the infrastructure business. One of the most powerful aspects of a library is its ability not only to develop a collection of some type of information but to maintain it over time. Sometimes infrastructure can be problematic but more often than not, it provides a stable foundation from which to operate. There are many conversations going on that need infrastructure but have none. Think of the opportunities in your community for using the Web to facilitate a conversation. It might be a researcher wanting to disseminate the results of his or her latest study. It might be a community organisation seeking funding. It might be a business trying to manage its basic operational knowledge.

The point is that such individuals and community organisations are not in the infrastructure business and could use a partner who is. Imagine a local organisation coming to the library, and within a few minutes setting up a Web site with an RSS feed, a blog and bulletin boards. The library facilitates, but does not own, that individual's or organisation's conversation. It does form a strong partnership, however, that can be leveraged into resources and support.

The true power of participatory networking in libraries is not to give every librarian a blog; it is in giving every community member a blog. In addition, the library can play the role of connecting these conversations to other users when appropriate. Participatory libraries allow the concept of community centre to be extended to the Web. Many public libraries have no problem providing meeting space to local non-profits. Why not provide Web meeting space in the form of a Web site or Web conferencing? Many academic libraries attempt to capture the scholarly output of their faculties, why not help generate the output with research data stores? The answers to these questions inevitably come back to time and money.

However, there is nothing in this brief that says such services have to be free. In fact, the best partnerships are formed when all partners are invested in the process. The true problem is that libraries have no idea of how to charge for such services. Faculty would be glad to write library support into grants, but need a dollar figure to include and how long each task will take. Many libraries aren't used to positioning their services on a per item basis, and this makes it difficult to build partnerships. Sometimes it is not a lack of money, but a lack of structure to take in money that is the problem.

Policy

As always, it is policy that presents the greatest challenges. The idea of opening the library functions to a greater set of inputs is rife with potential pitfalls. How can libraries use the technologies and concepts of Facebook and MySpace without being plagued by their problems? How can users truly be made part of the collection without the library being liable for all of their actions? The answers may lie in a seemingly obscure concept: identity management. Conversations can range in their mode, topic, and duration. They can also vary in the conversants.

The library needs to know a conversant's status to determine policy; and requires a unique identifier like a library card, to uphold it. In traditional libraries, that is the extent of identity management. In a participatory model, distinctions among identities become complex and graduated, and require us to consider a new approach.

This new model, of patrons adding information directly to library systems, is not as radical as it may first appear. We have become very used to the idea of roles and tiered levels of authority in many other settings. Most modern computer systems allow for some gradation in user abilities. Online communities have even introduced merit systems, by which continual high-quality contributions to a site equals greater power in the site.

Think about Amazon, Wikipedia, even eBay; as users contribute more to the community they gain status and recognition. From participants to editors, from readers to writers, these organisations have seen membership as a sliding scale of trust, and libraries need to adopt this approach in all of their basic systems.

We currently do, to a degree, in the form of librarians, paraprofessionals, and other staff. Yet even these distinctions tend to be rigid and often class based, with high walls between the strata. Some of this is imposed by outside organisations but a great deal is there by inertia of the field. Skillful use of identity management will help libraries avoid the baggage of MySpace and Facebook.

As users grain greater access, greater responsibility, and greater autonomy, libraries need to be more certain of their identities. That is, for a user to do more requires the library to know more. Knowing about a user may involve traditional identity verification, or tracking an activity trail whereby intentions can be judged in relation to actions. These concepts may be expressed as, 'The more we know you, the more control you can have in valuable services such as blogging, or the catalogue."

The concepts are illustrated in Blogger and LiveJournal, both of which require some level of identity information. In another example: to join LiveJournal you must be invited, thus the community confers identity. The common theme is that verifying identity is community based. The difference between the library and MySpace is that the library works in an established community with traditional norms of identity, whereas MySpace is seeking to create a community. Both the library and the services, however, base their functions and services on identity.

Ethical

As knowledge is developed through conversation, and libraries facilitate this process, libraries have a powerful impact on the knowledge generated. Can librarians interfere with and shape conversations? Absolutely. Should we? We can't help it. Our collections, our reference work, our mere presence will influence conversations. The question is, in what ways? By dedicating a library mission to directly align with the needs of a finite community, we are accepting the biases, norms and priorities of the community. While a library may seek to expand or change the community, it does so from within. When Internet filtering became a requirement for federal Internet funding, public and school libraries could not simply quit, or ignore the fact, because they are agents of their communities. School libraries had to accept filtering with federal funding because their parent organisations, the schools, accepted filtering.

We see, from this example, that libraries may shift from facilitating conversations to becoming active conversant, but they are always doing both.

Thus, the question is not whether the library shapes conversations, but which ones, and how actively? These questions are hardly new to the underlying principles of librarianship. And nothing in the participatory model seeks to change those underlying principles. The participatory model does, however, highlight the fact that those principles shape conversations and have an impact on the community.

WIRELESS NETWORKS IN MEDIUM-SIZED ACADEMIC LIBRARIES

Wireless networking offers a way to meet the needs of an increasingly mobile, tech-savvy student population. While many research libraries offer wireless access to their patrons, academic libraries serving smaller populations must heavily weigh both the potential benefits and disadvantages of this new technology. Will wireless networks become essential components of the modern academic library, or is this new technology just a passing fad? Prompted by plans to implement a wireless network at the Houston Cole Library (HCL), which serves a student enrollment close to ten thousand, this study was conducted to gather information about whether libraries similar in size and mission to HCL have adopted wireless technology. The study also sought to find out what, if any, problems other libraries have encountered with wireless networks and how successful they have perceived those networks to be. Other questions addressed include level of technical support offered, planning, type of equipment used to access the network, and patron-use levels.

REVIEW OF LITERATURE

A review of the literature on wireless networks revealed a number of articles on wireless networks and checkout programmes for laptop computers at large research institutions. Seventy percent of major research libraries surveyed by Kwon and Soules in 2003 offered some degree of wireless access to their networks. No articles, however, specifically addressed the use of wireless networks in medium-sized academic libraries.

Many articles can also be found on wireless-network use in medical libraries and other institutions. Library instruction using wireless classrooms and laptops has been another subject of enquiry as well. Breeding wrote that there are a number of successful uses for wireless technology in libraries, and a wireless Local Area Network (WLAN) can be a natural extension of existing networks.

He added that since, it is sometimes difficult to install wiring in library buildings, wireless is more cost effective. A yearly survey conducted by the Campus Computing Project found that the number of schools planning for and deploying wireless networks rose dramatically from 2002 to 2003. “For example, the portion of campuses reporting strategic plans for wireless networks rose to 45.5 per cent in fall 2003, up from 34.7 per cent in 2002 and 24.3 per cent in 2001.”

The use of wireless access in academia is expected to keep growing. According to a summary of a study conducted by the EDUCAUSE Centre for Applied Research (ECAR), the higher-education community will keep investing in the technology infrastructure, and institutions will continue to refine and update networks.

The move towards wireless access "represents a user-centred shift, providing students and faculty with greater access than ever before." In an article on ubiquitous computing, Drew provides a straightforward look at how WLANs work, security issues, planning, and the uses and ramifications of wireless technology in libraries.

He suggests, "Perhaps one of the most important reasons for implementing wireless networking across an entire campus or in a library is the highly mobile lifestyle of students and faculty." The use of wireless will only increase with the advent of new portable devices, he added. Wireless networking is the best and least expensive way for students, faculty, and staff to take their office with them wherever they go. The circulation of laptop computers is a frequent topic in the available literature.

The 2003 study by Kwon and Soules primarily focussed on laptop-lending services in academic-research libraries. Fifty per cent of the institutions that responded to their survey provided laptops for checkout. The majority indicated moderate-to-high use of laptop services. Positive user response and improved 'public reputation, image, and relations" were the greatest advantages reported with laptop circulation. The major disadvantages associated with these services were related to labour and cost. A study of laptop checkout service at the Mildred F. Sawyer Library at Suffolk University in Boston revealed that laptop usage was popular during the fall semester of 1999. Students checked out the computers to work on group projects.

A laptop area was set aside on one library floor to provide wired Internet access for eight users. However, students wanted to use the laptops anywhere, not one designated place. The wired laptop areas were not popular, Dugan wrote, adding that "Few students used the wired area and the wires were repeatedly stolen or intentionally broken." An interim phase involved providing wireless network cards for checkout to encourage patrons to use their own laptops, and, when a wireless network was put into place in the fall of 2000, demand exceeded the number of available laptops for checkout.

METHOD

A survey was designed to find out how many libraries similar in size and mission to HCL have adopted wireless networks, the experiences they have encountered in offering wireless access, and, most importantly, whether they felt the investment in wireless technology has been worth the effort. The National Centre for Education Statistic's Academic Library Peer Comparison

Tool, a database composed of statistical information on libraries throughout the United States, was used to select institutions for this study.

A search on this database retrieved eighty-eight academic libraries that met two criteria: full-time enrollments of between five thousand and ten thousand, and classification by the Carnegie Classification of Higher Education as Master's Colleges and Universities I. The survey was administered to those thought most likely to be responsible for systems in the library; they were selected from staff listings on library Web sites. If such a person could not be identified, the survey was sent to the head of library systems or to the library director.

The survey was divided into the following sections:

- Implementation of wireless network
- Planning and installation stages
- User services
- Technical problems
- Benefits specific to use of network

Surveys were mailed out in March 2004. An Internet address was provided in the cover letter if participants wished to take the survey online rather than return it by mail. An e-mail reminder with a link to the online survey was sent out three weeks after the initial survey was mailed. All letters and e-mails were personalised, and a self-addressed stamped envelope and a ballpoint pen with the JSU logo were included with the mail surveys. In the e-mail reminder, the authors offered to share the results of the project with anyone who was interested, and received several enthusiastic responses.

RESULTS

A total of fifty-three completed surveys were returned, resulting in a response rate of 60 per cent. The overwhelming majority responded that their library offered wireless-network access. Even if the thirty-five surveys that were not returned had reported that wireless networks were not available, more than 50 per cent would still have offered wireless networks. Survey results also pointed to the newness of the technology. Only four of the fifty-three institutions have had wireless networks for more than three years. The majority has implemented wireless networks just within the last two years.

When asked to identify the major reasons for offering wireless networks to their patrons, the three responses most chosen were:

- To provide greater access to users;
- The flexibility of a network unfettered by the limitations of tedious wiring; and
- To keep up with technological innovation.

Least significant factors in the decision to implement wireless networks were cost; use by library faculty and staff; to aid in bibliographic instruction;

and use for carrying out technical services. Somewhat to the authors' surprise, wireless use in bibliographic instruction was not high on the list of reasons for installing a wireless network, identified by only 9 percent of respondents. The benefits of wireless for library instruction was stressed in the litreature by Mathias and Heser and Patton. In addition to obtaining an instrument for gauging how many libraries similar in scope and size to HCL have implemented wireless networks and why they chose to do so, questions on the survey were also designed to gather information on planning and implementation, user services, technical problems, and perceived benefits.

PLANNING AND IMPLEMENTATION

Although Tolson mentions that some schools have used committees composed of faculty, staff, and students to look into the adoption of wireless technology, responses from this survey indicated that the majority of the libraries did not form committees specifically for the planning of their wireless networks.

In addition, 49 per cent of the libraries took fewer than six months to plan for implementation of a network, 37 per cent required six months to one year, and 15 per cent reported more than one to two years. Actual time spent on installation and configuration of wireless networks was relatively short, 98 per cent indicating less than one year. One of the most important issues to consider when planning to implement a wireless network is extent of coverage—where wireless access will be available. Survey responses revealed varying degrees of wireless coverage among institutions. 20 per cent had campus-wide access, 55 per cent had some level of coverage throughout the entire library, 37 per cent provided a limited range of coverage outside the building, and 20 per cent offered access only in certain areas within the library.

Institutions vary in their approaches to networking depending on enrollment. Smaller colleges and universities with fewer than ten thousand students are "more likely to implement campuswide wireless networks from the start. Larger institutions are more likely to implement wireless technology in specific buildings, consistent with a desire to move forward at a modest pace, as resources and comfort with the technology grow." Questions on the survey also queried respondents about the popularity of spaces in the library where users access the library's wireless network. Answers revealed that the most popular areas for wireless access are study carrels, tables, and study rooms. 19 per cent indicated that accessing wireless networks in the stacks is popular. Of particular concern to HCL, a thirteen-story building, was how the environment of the library would accommodate a wireless network.

A thorough site survey is important to locate the best spots within the library to install access points and to determine whether there are architectural barriers in the building that might interfere with access. The majority of survey respondents indicated that the site survey conducted in their library for a wireless network was carried out by their academic institution's IT staff. While library staff conducted 35 percent of site surveys, only 17 per cent were conducted by outside companies.

USER SERVICES

An issue to be addressed by libraries deciding to go wireless is whether laptop computers should also be provided for checkout in the library. After all, it might be hard to justify the usefulness of a wireless network if users do not have access to laptops or other hardware with wireless capabilities. While one individual reported working at a 'laptop university' in which campuswide wireless networking exists and all students are required to own laptops, not all college students will have that luxury.

In order to provide more equal access to students, checking out laptops has become an increasingly common service in academic libraries. Seventy percent of this survey's respondents whose institutions offered wireless access also made laptops available for checkout. Comments made throughout the survey seemed to imply that while checking out laptops to patrons is an invaluable complement to offering wireless access, librarians should be prepared for a myriad of hassles that accompany laptop checkout. Wear and tear of laptops, massive battery use, cost of laptops, and maintenance were some of the biggest problems reported. One participant, whose institution decided to stop offering laptops for checkout to patrons in the library, wrote, "It required too much staff time to maintain and we decided the money was better spent elsewhere.

The college now encourages students to purchase a laptop [instead of] a full-sized PC." One participant worried that the rising use of laptops in his library would lead to the obsolescence of its more than one hundred wired desktops, writing, "Our desktops are very popular and we think having them is one of the reasons our gate count has increased in recent years. What happens when everyone has a laptop?" The number of laptops checked out in the libraries varied. The majority of libraries had purchased between one and thirty laptops available for checkout.

Three institutions had more than forty-one laptops available for checkout. One library could boast that it had sixty laptops available for checkout with twelve pagers to notify students waiting in line to use laptops. When asked about the use of laptops in libraries, 46 percent observed moderate use, while 32 per cent reported heavy use of laptops. Only 3 percent indicated that they hardly ever noticed use of laptops in the library. For those students who chose to bring their own laptop to access the library's wireless network, half of the institutions surveyed required students to purchase their own network-interface cards for their laptops, while 19 per cent allowed students to check them out from the library.

In addition to laptops, personal digital assistants, (PDAs) were listed by 37 per cent of respondents as devices that may access wireless networks. One librarian indicated that cell phones could access the wireless network in his library. 56 per cent of respondents indicated that users are able to print to a central printer in the library from their wireless device. An important consideration for implementing a wireless network is how users will authenticate. Authentication protocol is defined by the Microsoft Encyclopaedia of Networking as "any protocol used for validating the identity of a user to determine whether to grant the user access to resources over a network." Authentication methods listed by the institutions surveyed varied greatly and the authors could not identify all of them.

Methods mentioned were Lightweight Directory Access Protocol (LDAP), virtual private network (VPN), and Media Access Control (MAC) addresses, Bluesocket, Remote Authentication Dial in User Service (RADIUS), pluggable Graphical Identification and Authentication (pGINA), Protected Extensive Authentication Protocol (PEAP), and e-mail logins. Out of the thirty-nine responses to this question, seven individuals indicated that they do not require any type of authentication at the present. Although some individuals noted that they are planning to enable some type of authentication in the future, one participant suggested that there were ethical issues involved in requiring users to authenticate. This person argued that "anonymous access to information is valued" and praised his institution's current policy of allowing "anyone who can find the network" to use it.

A concern about offering wireless network access in the library is how library staff will be prepared to handle the flood of technical questions that are likely to ensue. The level of technical support offered to users varied among the institutions surveyed. More than half of the respondents indicated that users receive help specifically from IT staff or from the campus computer centre. 39 per cent of users received help from the reference desk, while 19 per cent received help from circulation staff. 33 per cent of the responding institutions offered technical help from a Web site, while 7 per cent indicated that they did not offer any type of technical support to users.

Technical Problems

The technical problems most often encountered with wireless networks centered on architectural barriers that cause black-outs or slow-spots where wireless access fails. This confirms the importance of carrying out thorough site surveys and testing prior to installation of access points. Site surveys may be carried out by companies specially equipped and trained to determine where access points should be installed, the most appropriate type of antennae and how many access points are needed to provide the greatest amount of coverage. Configuration of the network was the second most highly reported problem associated with installing wireless networks, seeming to suggest the need for librarians to coordinate their efforts and rely on the knowledge provided by the IT coordinator within their institution.

Lack of technical support available to users, slow speed, and authentication were also indicated as technical problems most encountered. Integrating the wireless network with the existing wired network was the least-mentioned problem associated with wireless networks. Although security problems, particularly concerning Wired Equivalency Protocol (WEP) vulnerabilities, have been pointed out as one of the major drawbacks of a wireless network, the majority of users had not as yet experienced security problems. Although one participant wrote, "Don't be too casual about the security risks," another individual wrote, "Talk to your networking department," as many of them are overly worried about security.

Perceived Benefits

Respondents reported that the number-one benefit of offering wireless access was user satisfaction. Giving patrons the ability to use their laptops anywhere in the library and do multiple tasks from one machine is simply becoming what more and more users expect. The second largest benefit revolved around flexibility and ease of use due to the lack of wires. 35 per cent indicated that allowing students to roam the stacks while accessing the network was a significant benefit. Although a few studies have suggested the promise of wireless networks for aiding bibliographic instruction, only 9 per cent of respondents indicated this as a benefit of wireless technology. Use of wireless technology for instruction, it might be recalled, was not a significant factor noted by respondents in the decision to implement a wireless network.

Likewise, use of this type of network to carry out technical services was also low on the scale of benefits. 73 per cent of users claimed that wireless networks have thus far been worth the cost-benefit ratio. While 70 per cent indicated moderate to heavy use of the wireless network, 27 per cent reported low usage. When asked what advice they would give to others considering adopting wireless networks in their libraries, the overwhelming majority of responses were positive, recommending that HCL take the plunge.

As one individual wrote, "Offer it and they will come. It has really increased the usage of our library." Other individuals noted that it is simply necessary to offer wireless access to keep up with technological innovation, and that students expect it. The most significant warning, however, revolved around checkout and maintenance of laptops, which, from the results of this survey, seems be both a big advantage and a headache. Several individuals echoed the importance of doing site surveys to test bandwidth limitations and access.

One particularly energised participant, using multiple exclamations for emphasis, shared a plethora of advice. "Throttle connection speeds! Allow only http access! Block ports and unnecessary protocols! Secure your network and disallow unauthenticated users! Use access control lists! Establish policies that describe [wireless fidelity] Wi-Fi risks and liabilities on your part!".

Useful advice on wireless-access implementation gleaned from this survey fell under the following categories:

- Be aware of slower speed.
- Create a policy and guide for users.
- Do it because more users are going wireless, it is necessary to keep up with technological innovation, and because students love it.
- Provide plenty of access points.
- Install access points in appropriate places.
- Ensure continuous connectivity by allowing overlap between access points.
- Purchase battery chargers and heavy-duty laptops with extended warranties.
- Get support from IT staff for planning and maintenance.
- Offering wireless will increase library usage.
- Perform or have an expert perform a careful site survey and do lots of testing to locate dead or slow spots in the library due to architectural barriers.
- Enable some type of authorisation.
- Be aware of security concerns.
- Although the majority of participants' networks support 802.11b, a few participants suggest using the 802.11g standard because it is 'the fastest' and 'backwards compatible to 802.11b'.

11

Accessibility

INTRODUCTION

Clearly, accessibility has many parameters that must be determined to achieve syntactical and semantic operability. There appears to be a merging of concepts, at least with respect to the geometries involved, which shows an evolution from "mere data exchange at the interface level to systems integration with common semantics". There are areas in GIS knowledge management, such as ontology design principles, quality issues surrounding the creation of subject metadata, limitations of subject analysis, or the concerns of decentralised versus centralised provision of resource description, discovery, retrieval, that require librarians to learn how better to handle these issues from the research in library and information science.

One of the future areas of research is the role that service discovery plays within the larger task of service composition, and what other subtasks play a role in ensuring semantic interoperability in service composition. For network and standards developers, as well as libraries, the task of service composition is an area worth exploring.

THE LIBRARY'S ROLE

The role of librarians as custodians and disseminators of information is not new. It has been suggested their role in the use of spatial data is increasingly challenging, "navigat[ing] emerging geospatial data standards, disparate data, and shifting technologies" not to mention organisational and collaborative issues. Libraries prefer to provide their users transparent and integrated access to digital spatial information, and distributed, autonomous, and heterogeneous information services.

How best to handle issues of interoperability and provide access to their users? Dataset format, semantics, scale, resolution, and geographic area can compound the delivery of geospatial information. Hunt and Joselyn offer several possible solutions: data conversion, data organisation, intelligent retrieval software, and physical upgrade.

Converting data to a software-dependent form may be feasible but will be labour intensive for library staff. However, the trade-off for end-user ease of access may be worth the additional training and product development. Data organisation may involve physically partitioning or consolidating data by appropriate geographic units. It may also involve logically identifying, coding, or cataloging data to make their retrieval more intuitive to the user. Intelligent retrieval requires the patron to identify, access, and retrieve a specific subset of a given dataset at an appropriate scale or resolution in a timely fashion, again which may require more back-end coding of data or more front-end training of the patron on available applications. As addressed in the chapter on collection development, the application software necessary to bring functionality to a dataset may determine if it will be accessible to the user as preformatted data or for use in an analytic GIS environment.

Another solution is the use of topic navigation maps, an international standard project. Much like library pathfinders, topic maps can assist in improved retrieval of online information, allowing users to define their own navigation strategies in electronic resources. Further, topic maps can also assist in the creation and navigation of living documents and dataset repositories. Whether the resource is a structured information environment or an unstructured information environment, topic maps provide "outside views," or a user-structured model, for navigating the resource. Again, this could become an extended skills set for catalogers as well as a revised skills set for subject bibliographers.

Sigel building a topic map from a structured information resource is almost 100 per cent automatic, easing burden on staff time and project completion. If there is no previous information structure, building a useful topic map will take more staff and user time. However, both results enhance resource discovery and create new metadata relationships between controlled and user vocabulary. Stoimenov and Djordjevic-Kajan recommend using a hybrid ontology approach to resolve semantic heterogeneity of data sources. Not only is the meaning of the terminology of each community specified in the local ontology, they have created a methodology and software support for resolving semantic mismatches between terminologies.

Although their methodology is computationally intense, work defining and mapping terminology is standard practice for librarians in establishing authority control. Their formal ontology, which consists of "definitions of terms, ... includes concepts with associated attributes, relationships and constraints defined between the concepts and entities that are instances of concepts" could take the intellectual aspects of authority control to a higher level in the analysis and description of resources.

As with any data-based resource, formal ontologies are "best for sharing, merging, and querying data, but not for reading and efficient processing".

However, perhaps the new model for library catalogs should consider the incorporation of data dictionaries, thesauri, and semantic rules, ontologies that are stored together as a knowledge base, and metadata that specify a common model. Semantic Web technologies such as these can bridge formal ontologies and natural language. In academia, personalisation of services and resources in the support of learning activities is an emergent area in library services.

As geospatial learning continues to become more interactive and collaborative, personal project spaces allow individuals to work in their personalised environment with a mix of private and public data and simultaneously share data with team members. Portability of resources, interoperability assurances, and enhanced resource discovery through multiple perspectives is critical. Librarians are particularly suited to work with users on a one-to-one and small group basis to establish a common knowledge base and navigation/discovery skills. In another example, scholars play the role of both consumer and contributor of intellectual works in the digital environment. How they seek, use, and create implicit and explicit implicit assemblages of resources provide a useful framework for the collection and organisation of access resources in research libraries. As the roles of libraries continue to shift and mutate into new organisational constructs and services, the same should apply to how librarians see their roles in managing data-intensive information. Green suggests that four questions need to be addressed in information or knowledge management:

1. "Is there a universal set of relationship types applicable across all contexts?
2. "How can we build integrated knowledge organisation schemes that reflect a multiplicity of relational views?
3. "Is the incorporation of a relational approach to retrieval feasible, given the volume and diversity of material online?
4. "How could we evaluate the impact of incorporating a relational approach to online retrieval?"

All four questions have relevance to the everyday work of librarians. Librarians determine the basic concepts and relations used in the description of an item. The current emphasis on catalogue design reflects the importance of providing a multiplicity of views, based on user perspective, from the naïve user to the more sophisticated researcher, as well as the conceptual view of the librarian. The field also reflects the concerns over the feasibility and evaluation of indexing resources with many semantic relations and the effect on retrieval and resource discovery.

How librarians integrate their knowledge and skills with other information specialists and database designers in the management of GIS data and resources is yet to be determined. The integration is a necessary and critical juncture in the field of librarianship.

THE EMERGENCE OF CRITICAL GIS

Semantics are enmeshed in philosophy and perception. Maps or geospatial data are sites of critical enquiry. If "[m]aps are a technology of power, ... the key to this internal power is cartographic process ... the way maps are compiled and the categories of information selected; the way they are generalised, a set of rules for the abstraction of the landscape". Therefore, "[m]aps and GIS are important sources for the production of geographic knowledge. What are the power-knowledge relations of mapping as they occur against the historical horizon of possibilities and how can that horizon be enlarged?".

Two definitions seem to cover the continuum of thought on what is critical GIS. It is a "part of a contemporary network of knowledge, ideology, and practice that defines, inscribes, and represents environmental and social patterns within a broader economy of signification that calls forth new ways of thinking, acting, and writing". It is also "concerned with limitations in the ways that populations, locational conflict and natural resources are represented within current GISs, and the extent to which these limits can be overcome by extending the possibilities of geographic information technologies". With the sophistication of present-day GIS applications and the emergence of critical geographic information science, GIS researchers and academic practitioners are more reflexive, that is, reflecting upon the relationships between events, actions, and observers.

Kwan addresses the social-theory/spatial analysis split in geography. She suggests social-cultural and spatial-analytical geographies can "enrich each other in meaningful ways and to consider various possibilities to reconnect them". This is echoed by others, who believe that the science can positively affect society. Schuurman describes three waves of philosophical and epistemological debate between GIS practitioners and their critics in human geography. The first wave focused on the uses of GIS, with an emphasis on positivism. The second wave focused more on the social effects of GIS. In the third wave, debates about the technology shifted to the subtlety and granularity available with GIS technology. As noted, the cartographic epistemology of maps is influenced by positivism and social constructionism. Positivists tend to focus their critiques on the value-neutral aspect of GIS technology, or, "retreating from knowledge to information". Taylor suggests that "[k]nowledge is about ideas, about putting ideas together into integrated systems of thought we call disciplines" and information is about facts, about separating out a particular feature of a situation and recording it as an autonomous observation.

Therefore, "disciplines are defined by the knowledge they produce and not by facts: a 'geographical fact' that is not linked to geographical knowledge". Social constructionists see maps as "practices of power-knowledge" and geographic visualisation as providing "multiple, contingent and exploratory perspectives of data". They posit that GIS practices shape and are shaped by institutional contexts.

How a discipline conceptualises itself plays a large role in how it then perceives, defines, and extends its reach vis-à-vis ontological and epistemological research. With a new discipline, such as GIScience, the current emphasis of its ontology and spatial reasoning are "primarily concerned with implementation of complex philosophical and cognitive concepts in a computational environment". Or, simply, "To catalogue the world is to appropriate it, so that all these technical processes represent acts of control over its image which extend beyond the professed uses of cartography".

INDIVIDUAL AND ORGANISATIONAL END USERS: ISSUES IN ACCESSIBILITY

Data sharing is defined as the "transfer of spatial data/information between two or more organisational units where there is independence between the holder of the data and the prospective user". Nine factors or conditions create a conducive environment for sharing:

1. Sharing classes;
2. Project environment;
3. The need for shared data;
4. Opportunities to share data;
5. Willingness to share data;
6. Incentive(s) to share data;
7. Barriers to sharing;
8. The technical capability to share; and
9. Resources for sharing.

Users and the organisational constructs can create obstacles in the use of GIS data. These include variation in priorities among participants, differences in capacity to exploit GIS resources and services, dissimilarity in the level of awareness and spatial data handling skills; and inability to achieve agreements over access to information, leadership, data standards, equipment and training. Others have seen obstacles to sharing as primarily behavioural factors as well as organisational dynamics. For individuals to be willing to engage in spatial data sharing, constructs, such as "attitude towards the behaviour," "social norm," and "perceived control over the behaviour," become important. The literature suggests that these constructs influence the structures, processes, and policies used in interorganisational relationships that facilitate building and sharing spatial databases.

By examining the contextual factors that affect geographic information relationships, one can learn what mechanisms are effective in accomplishing database development and sharing. Nedovi□-Budi□ suggest that "appropriate organisational motivation, attitudes, and structure are required for geographic data sharing to happen". For example, attitude towards data can significantly affect cooperative or sharing relationships. Limits on open access are contraindicated in facilitating sharing, but user expectations may not match with data restrictions/access. Economic, political, professional, or regulatory factors may also hinder incentives to share data. Structural and functional characteristics of organisations also affect user access, such as "new coordination mechanisms, communication channels, overarching bodies, responsibilities, and authority". Power equations between organisations regarding access will continue to change as the online environment becomes more pervasive.

Initiatives, such as the NSDI and open standards development, encourage data sharing, infrastructure development, institutional arrangements, clearinghouse tools, enhanced metadata, and data transfer standards. However, to accommodate end-user needs and expectations, there must be clearly defined policies on access, cost recovery, data documentation, liability, interorganisational agreements, legal authority, and participant roles that accommodate the end user as well as the organisational structure. Policies should address the data itself; responsibility/ownership; cost; incentives; and formalisation of the interorganisational relationship. Although there has been increased acceptance and use of GIS and other digital data sets in private and public sector organisations, successful interorganisational GIS use is still problematic. Characteristics that determine successful interorganisational GIS range from the intensity, quality, and interdependence of interorganisational relationships to resources and structure.

Stability, culture, politics, and leadership affect success of GIS partnerships and collaborations. Nedovi□-Budi□ and Pinto address the importance of coordination mechanisms that manifest through established structures, processes, and policies. Structure is couched in a communication perspective, viewing the flow of information via channels, direction, and methods as well as level of shared components, which range from hardware and software to personnel and space. They firmly believe that coordination process is best undertaken through standardisation, joint planning, or mutual adjustment, as formal or informal policies are established to address data-related issues, responsibilities, ownership, contributions, and incentives. As with all initiatives, outcomes must be evaluated on a number of criteria, including efficiency, effectiveness, decision-making impact, and equity. A combination of functionality, usability, and accessibility evaluation strategies applied iteratively to assess libraries from the perspective of patron needs also seems appropriate.

Harvey emphasises the function of metadata in supporting trust in the collaborative process. He suggests that collective intentionality and status functions comprise an individual's trust in the institution's operating processes, or institutional reality. He posits that there are two types of trust, the type based on personal relations and the type based on the exchange of impersonal objective data. There is an interdependence and causality between the two, "[t]he reliance on objective data can undermine personal trust relationships in some cases". Since technical solutions to data sharing can hinder the understanding of shared data, "data sharing must move one rung higher and become information sharing, which requires the collective recognition of status functions and the creation of collective intentionality". Therefore, an environment of trust, at both the personal and data levels, is integral to successful information sharing.

One way to assist the trust relationship is through the of rich, descriptive metadata that can create a collective understanding of the uses of GIS data. Other important qualities include equity in the use of the data or other common resources; a fair decision-making process; ensuring users have an adequate control of common activities, organisational persistence to make the interorganisational arrangements succeed despite differing agendas and management styles, and coalition building, bargaining, and willingness to compromise. Users may also be impacted by the lack of strategic information management, to institutionalise information and decision support tools, and to transfer the technology to planning settings. Problems in these areas also affect users in the workflow process and in the creation of effective infrastructure needed for teaching, research, and technology transfer.

Nedovic-Budic suggests further research and policy development in education and technology transfer, database creation, data maintenance and access, standards development, and legislation and policy. In summary, the use of GIS needs to mitigate organisational and political factors that "apparently offset, in many instances, the theoretical benefits to be obtained from structures which seek to promote information sharing", which may have serious implications for end users in their use of geospatial information.

ONTOLOGIES AND SEMANTICS

As the focus in GIS changes from format integration to semantic interoperability, new descriptive classifications identify functionalities, creating new ontologies for GIS. An ontology is a specification of a conceptualisation of a knowledge domain. It can also be described as a controlled vocabulary or a faceted taxonomy with richer semantic relationships among terms and attributes that formally describes objects and the relations between objects. This vocabulary has its own grammar so the user can create meaningful expressions within the specified domain of interest. The vocabulary and grammar are used to make queries and assertions.

Individuals or groups make ontological commitments, or agreements, to use the vocabulary in a consistent way for knowledge or data sharing. Often thought of as knowledge representation, ontologies play an important role in "supporting query disambiguation and query term expansion of the required query, relevance ranking of the retrieved search results, the creation of the spatial indexes to support the search and the annotation of Web resources, Web documents and geographic data sets". Further, ontologies play a key role in enabling semantic interoperability. Since an ontology describes a specific reality with a specific vocabulary, using a set of assumptions regarding the intended meaning of the vocabulary words, it can be seen as an explicit specification of a conceptualisation, which is a formal structure of reality as perceived and organised by an agent, independent of the vocabulary used or the actual occurrence of a specific situation. Defining geographic space requires the definition and study of geographic objects, their attributes, and relationships.

FROM THE PHYSICAL UNIVERSE TO ONTOLOGIES

A properly constructed ontology can integrate different ontological approaches in a unified system. The result is a formal framework that explains a mapping between a spatial ontology and a geographic conceptual schema. Three different levels of abstraction are used in the mapping of ontologies to conceptual schemas: the formal level, which uses highly abstract concepts to express schema and ontologies; the domain level, where the schema is one instance of a generic data model; and the application level, which addresses the particular case of necessary geographic applications. Building on Frank's five tiers, Fonseca *et. al.* introduce the five-universes paradigm that attempts to provide the perspective from the geographic world.

Each of the five levels in the model, the physical universe, the cognitive universe, the logical universe, the representation universe, and the implementation universe, deals with conceptual characteristics of the geographic phenomena of the real world. A geographic phenomenon in the physical world is first perceived by an individual. He or she then classes the phenomena according to his or her cognitive framework, providing explicit and formal structures based on the vocabulary of his or her logical universe. GIS reference systems, such as fields and objects, are part of the representation universe. The implementation universe occurs when components of the representation universe are translated into data structures and computer language constructs. To be used effectively, the computer must know a number of things, such as what application is being used, what language the "text" is in, encryption and encoding protocols, transmission protocols, and platforms. When one moves out of the monolingual state to a multilingual world, the computer's basic knowledge extends to meta-languages, mark-up languages and applications, and software operating systems.

Both language and script become important information for the computer to know. Imagine, if you will, the sheer amount of information that must be considered for "intelligent" processing by a word processing programme: spell-check, grammar-check, word wrapping, hyphenation, automated word correction, use of symbols for non- Latinate languages, use of accented characters for non-English words, *inter.alia*. If numeric data, there is a similar host of commands that ensue in the creation and checking of data. Then, move to transmission over a network, across platforms, and receipt by the end user's computer. To effectively handle just the linguistic properties of text, standardised language codes must support document longevity and interoperability of computing and network solutions.

The same applies to the creation of network and platform protocols. Standards, whether data, semantic, or syntactic, apply equally to querying, searching, and accessing information from both vendor and the end-user perspectives. Since the 1990s, geospatial data interoperability has been the target of standardisation bodies, developers, and the research community: "interoperability has been seen as a solution for sharing and integrating geospatial data, more specifically to solve the syntactic, schematic, and semantic as well as the spatial and temporal heterogeneities between various real world phenomena". The transition to a distributed, online environment has eased some of the issues based on previous monolithic architectures for GISs. These new architectures, the Internet, and data mining technologies have led to a renewed emphasis on discovery, dissemination, and exploitation of geospatial data. Encoding and decoding functions are crucial components. They respectively generate and recognise geospatial conceptual representations.

DIGITAL LIBRARIES: SOLUTIONS AND POSSIBILITIES

Dealing flexibly with differences among systems, ontologies, and data formats while respecting information sources' autonomy requires considerable thought. Adapting object-oriented digital libraries involves a number of solutions, such as mediation middleware, use and integration of Internet harvesting techniques, and new architectures based on object-oriented ontologies that affect the development of search modules and metadata description. Much of the research focuses on text-deciphering or linguistic equivalency algorithms or consensual activities on meanings of categories for resource description, interoperability of simple schemas with complex schemas, or designing frameworks for managing equivalencies between metadata models in different fields and languages. Questions, such as best problem-solving practices or balance between human and machine for resource discovery, emerge.

Since the transparent and integrated access to distributed and heterogeneous data sources is key to leveraging research, how would it be best to integrate data suitable for knowledge or information domains? Controlled annotation of semantic rich metadata with diverse types of data allows the use of sophisticated query schemes. Information systems can address these questions by applying and extending metadata harvesting, and by building upon existing componentised frameworks. Two very important issues are:

- how to reconcile the diversity found within the harvested data to create a single, integrated collection view for the end-user and
- how to create an integrated framework that addresses data quality, flexible and efficient search, and scalability.

To provide technologies that improve the access to heterogeneous and distributed resources, several layers of metadata, related to users, communities, devices, and data sources, must be handled and efficiently used. Further, in order to understand class and property hierarchies, support for inference should be available.

The quality of the information available to the information specialist to adequately address the semantics of requirements and resources is critical. The explicitness, structuring, and formality of this information can differ considerably leading to different types of matchmaking. Lutz *et al.* describes one sample framework for the analysis of practical problems. First, the information required for the matchmaking process is identified.

Once identified, the required information is classified according to the qualities of explicitness, structuring, and formality. The information is assessed to determine the quality level of the required information that is appropriate for the task-at-hand. Finally, the different levels of explicitness, structuring, and formality can easily be associated to predefined scenarios that indicate possible implementation methods. The research also has found that multiword terms provide the most effective snapshot of user searching behaviour for query categorisation. Using both approaches, researchers to classify their approach and judge whether the applied methods are appropriate for the task-at-hand. This is particularly important for the naïve user, since research shows that an information seeker's information need is identified through transformation of his/her knowledge structure.

QUALITY ASSURANCE

The W3C has published several formalised quality assurance (QA) resources for various languages and protocols developed by them. Although some of the features of the QA specification are unique to W3C's technical process and tools, other features have broad applicability to formal specification development by other standards organisations. For example, there are guidelines on how to write unambiguous and clear specifications, how to define and specify conformance, and how a specification might allow variation among conforming implementations. W3C suggests that developers consider conformance models, normative language usage, test suites, extensibility, profiles, levels, validation services, and conformance claims during the development and documentation process. Design decisions of a specification's conformance model may affect its implementation and the interoperability of its implementations.

VARIABILITY

Specifications allow some sort of variation between conforming implementations. The concept of variability addresses how much these implementations may vary among themselves. There are seven dimensions of variability. These range from the most independence to the least independence from other design factors with a variety of possible associations, dependencies, and interrelationships among the dimensions. The dimensions are classes of product, profiles, levels, modules, discretionary items, deprecation, and extensibility.

A product is a generic name for any group of items that would implement a specification for the same purpose. In technology subsets, a profile is tailored to meet specific functional requirements of a particular application community and defines how a set of technologies are required to operate together, while a level is one of a hierarchy of nested subsets, ranging from minimal functionality to full functionally.

A module is a collection of semantically related features that represents a unit of functionality, such as an image module. While modules can be implemented independently of one another, a module's definition and implementation may be explicitly dependent upon another or multiple modules.

Discretionary items are those items in an implementation that have options in behaviour, functionality, parameter values, error handling, and so forth. Deprecation and extensibility are self-explanatory. Deprecated features are marked as outdated and being phased out.

Extensibility allows any developer to create extensions beyond what is defined in the specification. Since the seven dimensions of variability are at the core of the definition of a specification's conformance model, there is "significant potential for negative interoperability impacts if they are handled carelessly or without careful deliberation".

Generally, implementation variability complicates interoperability; identical implementations are better. However, there are cases when the net effect of conformance variability is not necessarily negative. Consider the use of profiles. Profiles are developed for specific applications communities. Two different community profiles may not communicate well between themselves. However, if the two profiles are subsets of a large monolithic specification, each targeted at a specific application sector, then subdivision by profiles may actually enhance interoperability. Two areas where variability is dangerous are excessive variability in a specification or the multiplicative effect on variability when several dimensions are combined.

Augmenting test documentation, metadata plays an important role in helping users to understand and execute the tests: "...Well-defined metadata can help in:

- Tracking tests during the development and review process;
- Filtering tests according to a variety of criteria — for example,

whether or not they are applicable for a particular profile or optional feature;

- Identifying the area of the specification that is tested by the tests;
- Constructing a test harness to automatically execute the tests;
- Formatting test results so that they are easily understood".

By defining and using a minimal set of metadata elements, standardised tools are more likely to be developed since ambiguity is lessened.

TAXONOMIES

The emergence in recent years of digital libraries and of Internet-based communication applications have led some researchers to propose that the emerging data infrastructure of the Internet and digital libraries can be used to ease mining digital geospatial data across the Internet. Descriptive cataloging and metadata standards describe attributes of items to enhance the user's ability to restrict their research to appropriate content. As the amount of networked digital information continues to grow, the demand for "seamless" access also increases. However, for a single theory-neutral taxonomy to support granularity, language groupings, data classification, categorisation, and linguistic annotation is asking a lot.

For written and spoken language materials in minority languages, depending upon the person providing the description, for example, librarians, archivists, linguists, and so forth, existing ISO standards may not be granular enough to distinguish regional, social, or dialectical variations, or the standards may be too complex for the intended audience or describer.

For example, ANSI/NISO Z39.53-200X.provides "a standardised 3-character code to indicate language in the exchange of information is defined. Codes are given for languages, contemporary and historical. The purpose of this standard is to provide libraries, information services, and publishers a standardised code to indicate language in the exchange of information. This standard for language codes is not a prescriptive device for the definition of language and dialects but rather a list reflecting the need to distinguish recorded information by language".

Although there are no standards for prescriptive or descriptive information for data elements or metatags, it is this type of work, common in librarianship, that may provide a necessary bridge to establish a common language/framework across standards, among users, and increase interoperability. Geospatial data may incorporate numeric datasets of socioeconomic information, epidemiologic datasets, textual datasets, or use vector, raster, or tabular data. These data become digital objects when they are geocoded, or linked to a Cartesian coordinate system. These digital objects, whether tabular or thematic data, require description of their attributes, the geographic features of the extent of the area, and linkage to a unique identifier. Taxonomies for thematic data may use technical, specialised vocabulary, unfamiliar to the librarian, the person describing the data, or the end-user who is trying to acquire the data. Brodeur *et al.* suggest that field of the interpersonal communication may provide a better framework with which to understand the issues in geospatial data interoperability.

This communication process examines the interaction "between two agents, including the underlying internal representation of concepts along with encoding and decoding operations" in both human- to-computer communication and computer-to-computer communication. Harvey *et al.* also examine how to navigate differences in meaning. Their research takes a communications perspective since a central question in their research is "how people and social groups with different perspectives identify and possibly resolve their semantic differences".

They suggest using a multidisciplinary approach using cognitive, computer science, and linguistic bases to examine semantic interoperability. Their cognitive approach, based on Fauconnier's general mappings among conceptual domains and Lakoff's metaphorical mappings, follows how partial mappings from multiple sources structure a target concept. This model also uses mathematically rigourous formalisation and implementations. Their computer science approach, based on the work of Sheth's interoperable computer system semantics, assesses context in semantic proximity. Sheth's approach looks at vocabulary, content, and structure, not just database ontologies and declarative descriptions.

Briefly, domains between two objects are mapped, and the contextual descriptions of the two objects are compared and described in a descriptive logic language that links the semantic and schematic level.

The third framework is a linguistic framework that considers the processes social groups engage in to assure collaborative action or participatory design. It emphasises the importance of involving relevant groups in articulating their differences in order to find common and viable solutions. Harvey *et al.* suggest, "If semantics are cultural agreements between independent agents observing the real world, then we expect that illuminating insights will come from the examination of the group processes that lead to 'accepted' understandings, and the role of language as the most fundamental way of finding and assuring agreement". They further suggest that information communities should conceptualise and articulate technical, organisational, and political semantic differences to resolve differences in consensual terminology and procedures.

BUILDING INTEROPERABLE, SEMANTIC SYSTEMS

In order to achieve semantic interoperability in heterogeneous information systems, systems must understand the meaning of the exchanged information, that is, the precise meaning of the data must be readily accessible and the system able to translate the data into an understandable form. Metadata is not just a description of the schema definition in a data set, but also a description of the conceptualisation of the geospatial "reality."

If semantics refers to user's interpretation of the computer representation of the world, then metadata should contain a representation of the semantics of the data. Clearly, the dynamic data exchanges possible in GIS communities provide substantial advantages for sharing geographic information. However, to fully realise the advantages in heterogeneous, operational, and organisational environments requires developers and users to understand and resolve semantic differences.

While there has been substantial progress on technical interoperability, semantic interoperability remains a significant hurdle. Identifying and resolving semantic interoperability issues is especially pertinent for data sharing and considering future developments of standards. Solutions to semantic interoperability involve three major frameworks: cognitive, computer science, and sociotechnical. Brodeur *et al.* suggest that a broader view of geospatial data interoperability is also in order. Using an ontology of geospatial data interoperability to refine the description of the conceptual framework, they identify the notions of concept, proximity, and ontology as fundamental to creating a new approach to geosemantic proximity. Providing integrated access to data from a diverse, heterogeneous network requires a breadth of knowledge, not only about the structure of the data represented at each server, but also about the commonly occurring differences in the intended semantics of this data.

The semantics of data are often couched in local schemas that may meet the needs of that user group, but lack the ability to be interoperable when searched by users in another setting. These semantically weak local schemas are a consequence of the limited expressiveness of traditional data models. Stoimenov and Djordjevic-Kajan suggest the creation of architectures that can address semantic interoperability of distributed and heterogeneous GIS. A local community environment informs the perspective; mediation and ontologies define the architecture. First, they formally specify the meaning of the terminology of each community using local ontology.

Then they define a translation between each community's terminologies, with an intermediate terminology represented by top-level ontology and common data model. If a *concept.* consists of "the set of knowledge with the accompanying processes that an agent maintains about a phenomenon, which generate and recognise different representations of the concept", then domain-specific metadata is one possibility to upgrade the semantic level of local information systems. By considering an integrated framework, users receive better access and enhanced, semantically rich schema models. There are a number of frameworks, in development or currently available, that enrich the data definition language of resident servers. The schema's semantic knowledge is organised by levels of schematic granularity: database, schema, attribute, and instance. Another possibility is geosemantic proximity, a framework that concurrently assesses the components of a geosemantic space between a geospatial concept and a geospatial conceptual representation. Visually, these concepts and conceptual representations are segments on an axis made of an interior and a boundary. Geosemantic proximity is the intersection of their respective contexts.

The interior of a concept "consists of its intrinsic properties that are components providing literal meaning" while the boundary of a concept "consists of its extrinsic properties that are components providing meaning through relationships with other concepts". Consequently, intersection between intrinsic and extrinsic properties illustrate attributes that can be assessed qualitatively taking into account the contexts of the respective representations.

CONCLUSION

With the creation of the Internet and the continued evolution of technologies in GIS, networking, and knowledge management, access to geospatial information is a critical component of research and practice. Interoperability is the "new paradigm for joining heterogeneous computer systems into synergistic units that facilitate a more efficient use of geographic information resources". As geographers reassess the description of geographic methodologies and techniques across different platforms in the online environment, so have researchers in other disciplines assessed the use of applied geographic techniques for a wide variety of analysis. Such efforts have led some researchers to use new descriptive classifications to identify functionalities in the new scholarship, such as in creating new ontologies for GIS. This chapter examines the impact of these new ontologies, reviews the impact standards have on access and issues for end-users in accessing geospatial information.

Bibliography

Aaron, E.: *Abstracts Produced Using Computer Assistance,* Washington: National Academy Press, 2000.

Aghatise, E.: *Automation and Academic Library Structure*, Maharashtra: Pune Publication, 2004.

Anderson, B.: *Library Management Styles and Structures: A Need to Rethink*, Toronto: Thomson Nelson, 2008.

Arora Kanu : *University Library System : Centralization and Decentralization*, Regal, Delhi, 2008.

Balkus, R.: *Writing Abstracts for Free-text Searching*, Washington: Social Security Administration, 2009.

Ballabh, Anand : *New Approaches to Library Administration,* Rajat, Delhi, 2002.

Bandyopadhyay, N.: *Library Automation as a Source of Management Information*, Hyderabad: Economic and Political Weekly Press, 2005.

Bertozzi, S.: *Management Information: The Academic Library,* Maharashtra: Pune Publications, 2006.

Buckland Michael : *Book Availability and the Library Users,* New York: Perga-mon Press, 1975.

Burnette, D.: *Library Patrons and the Law*, Alexandria: Council on Library Science Education, 2003.

Chattopadhyay, A.: *Principles of Information Systems for Management*, Hyderabad: Economic and Political Weekly Press, 2005.

Cockburn, A.: *Management Information Systems can Help Senior Library Managers,* New Delhi: Long Life Publication, 2006.

Cohen, M.: *Maintaining the Privacy of Library Records*, London: Waverly Book Company, 2003.

Doezema, J.: *Measuring Academic Library Performance: A Practical Approach*, Maharashtra: Pune Publication, 2000.

Glaser, B.: *Confidentiality in the Use of Library Materials*, Mill Valley: Sociology Press, 2001.

Guba, E.: *RSS for Non-Techie Librarians*, San Francisco: Jossey Bass Press, 2003.

Jackson, Sideny L. : *Libraries and Librarianship in the West: A Brief History,* New Yokr: McGraw-Hill Book Company, 1974.

Jana, S.: *A Model of a Management Information System for Library and Information Service Managers,* New Delhi: Long Life Publication, 2003.

Jeffreys, S.: *Effective Library and Information Centre Management,* Toronto: Thomson Nelson, 2006.

LeCompte, M.: *Computers in Libraries*, San Diego: Academic Press, 2004.

Mackenzie, A.G.: *Academic Libraries in Contraction: Facts, Theories and Fancies*, USA: Aslib Proceedings, 1996.

Madhusudana, B.: *Management Information and Decision Support Systems in Libraries*, London: Weekly Press, 2002.

Meyers, William P.: *Indexing Books: Lessons in Language Computations*, UK: British Library, 2005.

Mishler, E.: *Accessibility in the Virtual Library*: London: Harvard University Press, 2002.

Payne, P. and Willers, J.M.: *Using Management Information in a Polytechnic Library.* NJ: Journal of Librarianship, 1999.

Sparrow, E.: *Management Information in the British Library Humanities and Social Sciences Division*, UK: Journal of Librarianship, 2002.

Strauss, A.: *Assistive Technology in Special Libraries*, San Francisco: Harper Bowling Green State University, 2000.

Van Maanen, J.: *Library Assistive Technology: Predictions and Trends*, Chicago: The Hotel Monthly Press, 2006.

Vygotsky, L.: *Adaptive Technology Equipment for the Library,* New York: Columbia Press, 2001.

Index

I

L

M

N

O

P

Q

R

S

T

U

V